OTHER BOOKS BY SHANA ALEXANDER

The Pizza Connection

Nutcracker

Very Much a Lady

Anyone's Daughter

Talking Woman

Shana Alexander's State-by-State
Guide to Women's Legal Rights

The Feminine Eye

WHEN SHE WAS BAD

WHEN SHE WAS BAD

The Story of Bess, Hortense, Sukhreet & Nancy

BAD

SHANA ALEXANDER

RANDOM HOUSE
NEW YORK

All rights reserved under International and Pan-American Copyright Conventions.
Published in the United States by Random House, Inc., New York, and
simultaneously in Canada by Random House of Canada Limited, Toronto.

Library of Congress Cataloging-in-Publication Data

Alexander, Shana.
    When She Was Bad / Shana Alexander.
        p.   cm.
    ISBN 0-394-57606-3
    1. Myerson, Bess—trials, litigation, etc.   2. Trials (Bribery)—
    New York (N.Y.)   I. Title.
KF224.M94A44   1990
345.73'02323—dc20   89-42772
[347.3052323]

Manufactured in the United States of America

2   4   6   8   9   7   5   3

First Edition

Book design by Debbie Glasserman

FOR JEAN HARRIS

THIS BOOK GREW OUT OF A PHONE CALL EARLY IN 1988 from Marcia Gillespie, executive editor of *Ms.* magazine, inviting me to write an article about the woes of Bess Myerson. For nearly twenty years, the onetime beauty queen had been a high-ranking New York City political figure, and had recently fallen from grace with a thud. At sixty-four, she and her twenty-one-years-younger boyfriend stood accused of trying to fix a judge, and all three of them were facing trial together in the fall.

I told Ms. Gillespie that I had not been following the story in detail. A messenger arrived with a thick folder of clippings. When I read them it seemed to me that the story had three main characters, not one; three very modern, highly accomplished New York women of different ages, none of them young. A central truth in each woman's life was the same. She enjoyed a much-admired public existence, and she had a dismal private life. Each woman in a different way had seemingly been brought low by love.

One, Myerson, was a public figure. One, Justice Hortense Gabel, was a respected judge. The third, Nancy Capasso, was a full-time housewife and mother of five.

Nancy Capasso was the least well known of the three. She turned out to be a spirited and remarkably forthright woman of forty-seven. At our first meeting she confessed there had been times during her ex-husband's seven-year love affair with Bess Myerson when she had literally contemplated killing him. Feelings of murderous fury surged up seemingly out of nowhere, as she was brushing her hair, or driving a child to the dentist, and she found herself seriously plotting Andy Capasso's death. When these fantasies overwhelmed her, there was but one sure cure. She would shut her eyes and silently repeat over and over to herself, "Jean Harris . . . Jean Harris . . . Jean Harris."

I know Jean Harris well. She was the subject of an earlier book of mine that described the events leading up to the night of March 10, 1980, when she shot and killed her lover, Dr. Herman Tarnower, and what followed. Or should one say, is still following? Mrs. Harris, a lifelong schoolteacher, was tried and convicted— tragically and unfairly—of murder, not manslaughter, and she is now in a maximum-security prison beginning her ninth year of a fifteen-years-to-life sentence. She does not become eligible for parole until 1996, by which time she will be seventy-four years old— if she is still alive, a doubtful proposition. In prison she has had two severe heart attacks. The sole person empowered to intervene in her suffering, by recommending clemency, is the governor of New York State, Mario Cuomo, who so far has been disinclined to interest himself in her case.

Since she was sent to prison, Jean and I have kept in close touch, and after nine years of letters and phone calls and occasional visits, she has become a close and indispensable friend. She is a constant source of wit, insight, understanding, and comfort, and of course she puts my own problems into instant perspective.

By the time the Myerson/Capasso/Gabel trial got under way, I had published the article, and had also decided that the story was really about four New York women and what they would and would not do for love. The fourth one was Justice Gabel's interesting daughter, Sukhreet. Together, the quartet seemed a subject worthy of a book, and I was having my usual tortured time writing it. One day I complained, "Jean, this new book is a tough one. I think the main defendant hates me."

The previous Monday morning in the courtroom, during a recess, Myerson and I were walking up the center aisle when she suddenly shouted at me, "You bitches are all alike!" The trigger for her outburst was a just-published article about her by another writer that most people in the courtroom including me had read over the weekend.

"I know she's overwrought, but this was wild," I told Jean. "She's fascinating, but not a nice lady, I'm afraid."

"No, she's *not* nice," said Jean. "She's tough. She's like a lot of the women in here. She's learned you have to grab, to hang on, to get what you want in life.

"I just hope you won't write that you feel sorry for her," Jean added, "or that she's pathetic. That would be the worst, most hurtful thing you could possible say."

THE BOOK TURNED out to be more agreeable to write than I anticipated, thanks entirely to the marvelous and generous help of two very able people. In a great stroke of good fortune, Bob Loomis, an old friend, is now my impeccable and elegant editor. A new friend, Temma Ehrenfeld, took on the burden of digging up and checking out the mountainous research required. As our work went on, I saw that not only were Temma's files thorough and well written, but she was shrewd and kind-hearted and graced with an unusual empathy for others. I could not have done my job without both of these people working overtime, and my gratitude is beyond measure.

December 1989
New York, N.Y.

CONTENTS

WHEN SHE WAS BAD

Among the ancients, three goddesses were revered above all the rest: *Venus*, goddess of beauty; *Minerva*, goddess of wisdom; and *Juno*, goddess of wifehood and queen of Parnassus.

All was serene on Parnassus until the arrival of a minor diety, *Eris*, goddess of discord, who proved a very troubling fairy indeed. Eris brought with her a golden apple, the so-called apple of discord. When she threw the apple to determine which of the three was "the fairest," all hell broke loose, and men and women have been squabbling ever since.

In this modern retelling of the story, the part of Venus is played by Bess Myerson, and of Minerva by Judge Hortense Gabel. Nancy Capasso plays Juno, and the role of Eris is superbly realized by Sukhreet Gabel. As for the apple, that is the symbol of the grimy, blighted playground where the drama takes place.

APPLE OF DISCORD

I

THIS IS A TALE OF NEW YORK CITY. IT COULD HAVE happened nowhere else but New York, the shining Apple, and at no other time but now. New York, alas, is not what it used to be. Today, in the last gray twilight of the 1980s, so much of the city is a blasted landscape of drugs and AIDS and filth and crime, a place where hospitals and schools have broken down, where homeless adults roam the streets and crumbling walls hold tens of thousands of abandoned children. Today anybody can see that the Apple is rotting. The wonder is not the decay, but that it all happened so fast. Only a few years ago, say 1971, it was still possible to believe that New York was in good hands, and would somehow find ways to solve its problems. In 1971 the hands belonged to handsome, noble-hearted Mayor John Lindsay, a politician so admired by the citizenry and so confident of his own powers that midway through the year he became a Democrat in order to challenge President Nixon in the next election.

Take an ordinary time in 1971, say late March, and look at what was happening in the richest, tallest, most vigorous city in the world. The month blew in cold, gray, and damp, hailstones off the Hudson; "seasonable" was the weatherman's term. The new Gallup Poll reported Democrats preferred Ted Kennedy for '72 over Muskie or Humphrey. The other night, before a capacity Garden crowd, the New York Knicks took a 2–1 lead over the Atlanta Hawks in the NBA first-round playoffs. Joe Frazier was still in St. Luke's hospital after the head pounding he took from Muhammad Ali last week in defense of his heavyweight title. In City Hall the pols were arguing over how to respond to Governor Rockefeller's leanest budget yet. In Queens, Mrs. Alice Crimmins, a cocktail waitress, was standing trial for the murder of her two small children. Two other trials were on the front pages. In California a jury was debating the gas chamber versus life imprisonment for Charles Manson, and in Fort Benning, Georgia, a court-martial was preparing to convict Lt. Rusty Calley for the My Lai massacre.

The sex-and-pop-culture scene was in its usual ferment. A book called *Everything You Always Wanted to Know About Sex, but Were Afraid to Ask* had been on the best-seller list for sixty-two weeks, closely followed at forty-eight weeks by *The Sensuous Woman*. One-time shockers like *Sex and the Single Girl* today seemed tame indeed. Next Sunday the ever-earnest *New York Times Magazine* was boldly publishing an article on the emergence of lesbianism, wondering whether it was "an illness."

Books like *Future Shock* and *The Greening of America* led the non-fiction list. Wall-to-wall epics like *Waterloo* and a revival of *Lawrence of Arabia* swept across the big screens. Tiny shorts called "hot pants" were the newest fashion rage. On TV, Archie and Edith Bunker ruled the airwaves, and "Bridge over Troubled Water" had just been named most popular song of the year.

One Tuesday twenty-five hundred mourners turned out at Riverside Church for a memorial service for Whitney Young, the former director of the National Urban League, who had died in Nigeria at forty-nine. Among them were Coretta Scott King, Governor and Mrs. Rockefeller, Senators Kennedy, Muskie, Javits, and Buckley, Representative Shirley Chisholm, and Cardinal Cooke, as well as Mayor Lindsay. Also on Tuesday, Ford Motor Company began recalling nearly all of its Pintos. Spurred by Ralph Nader, consumer power was a growing force in America. On Wednesday, the *Today* show aired a scoop: a two-hour Barbara Walters interview with President Nixon discussing Tricia's forthcoming wedding. The president had been elected on a promise to wind down the war in Vietnam, and now his popularity was at an all-time low. Every month he brought home a few thousand more troops. But his stubborn refusal to name a deadline for full withdrawal simply increased the turmoil in Indochina with no corresponding gain on the home front. Last month South Vietnam had begun its "incursion" into Laos. As for the Paris peace talks, they had been deadlocked since the month he came into office, January 1969. All this had produced a burgeoning antiwar movement, which the president interpreted as criticism of his personal popularity rather than his foreign policy. Hence the *Today* show appearance, which prompted the columnist James Reston to observe, "There is something very wrong and very sad when a President has to ask to go on the *Today* show for two hours."

In opposition, Democrats had organized a "Barnstorming for Peace" campaign, and this week four New York Democratic congressmen were staging a series of antiwar rallies throughout the city's five boroughs, drumming up support for the Vietnam Disengagement Act, which, if passed, would halt all funds for the war on December 31. The group made fifteen stops in Queens alone, where they were joined on the platform by freshman Queens city councilman Donald Manes and first-term congresswoman Bella Abzug.

On Thursday John Lindsay opened a school in Bedford-Stuyvesant, chaired a Board of Estimate meeting at City Hall, and made an appearance in Forest Hills with his popular commissioner of consumer affairs, Bess Myerson, at one of her new walk-in consumer-complaint offices. She had opened the first one last week, in Forest Hills, Queens, and another this week on Delancey Street, with Bella Abzug standing beside her at the ribbon-cutting.

No member of the Lindsay administration was more popular in 1971 than beautiful Bess, not even the mayor himself. Her 1945 victory as Miss America, followed by her lucrative years on television game shows, eight as the star of *The Big Payoff* and nine as a panelist on *I've Got a Secret*, had made Myerson a beloved public figure and a national celebrity. Privately she was the wife of Arnold Grant, a wealthy and brilliant show-business attorney. It was early 1969 when Mayor Lindsay had named Mrs. Bess Myerson Grant, as she was then known, to be the city's first commissioner of consumer affairs. The new agency combined the old Weights and Measures department with the Licenses department, and it was responsible for licensing more than one hundred types of businesses in New York City.

When she accepted the $25,000-a-year post, about one eighth of her TV salary, a few soreheads had grumbled that Bess was "whipped cream" and "window dressing." Cynics said that Republican Lindsay had appointed a Jew who had campaigned for Hubert Humphrey in the last presidential election because he was thinking about running for president next time himself, and feared trouble with Jewish voters, many of whom were critical of his support of integrated housing, and of his policy of decentralizing the schools, which were controlled by the predominantly Jewish teachers' union and the Board of Education.

Publicly, Bess said simply that "Lindsay wanted to make sure the department was as visible as possible." Privately, she had expressed misgivings about her lack of experience as a businesswoman. Her husband, as always, encouraged her, and they went off together to Palm Springs with a trunkful of books on consumer law, works with titles like *Thumb on the Scale.* There, for four weeks beside the pool, the onetime honor student crammed her lovely head with consumer facts and figures, and at the end of each day Arnold quizzed her.

Bess Myerson Grant swiftly became not only the most visible New York City official after the mayor, but possibly the busiest. Daily press releases flew from her office, and she appeared on several talk shows each week attacking such abuses as "shamburgers," unlicensed auto mechanics, and unsafe baby rattles. She set up a twenty-four-hour consumer hot line. She sent the Consumobile, a beat-up blue-and-orange truck staffed by volunteers, touring the outer boroughs and dispensing information. Her department's official motto was "Wise up!" and tacked to the wall of her orange-

and-yellow office was a newspaper astrologer's advice: "Do nothing that jeopardizes your reputation."

In the department's first four months, it issued thirteen hundred summonses, most of them to grocers who short-weighted foods. The gorgeous commissioner always accompanied her inspectors on well-publicized raids of grocery stores. By the end of 1969, Mayor Lindsay had signed the toughest consumer law in the nation. It gave the city the right to prosecute any business or person victimizing the public through deceptive trade practices. In the old days, the city had just handed out fines. The new law also gave Myerson enforcement and rule-making powers. Soon more than $5 million was being repaid to defrauded consumers each year.

By 1971 Consumer Affairs was one of the few city agencies in the black. A fiscal crisis gripped the rest of the Lindsay administration, but Myerson's department collected $4.66 million for the city in license fees and fines. The commissioner had also brought unit pricing and open dating to city supermarkets, and now she was busy setting up the walk-in complaint centers, yet another of her popular innovations.

There were a few dissenting voices, to be sure. Gail Sheehy was publishing a series of articles on Manhattan prostitutes in *New York* magazine that later would form the basis of her book *Hustling*. One article, "The Landlords of Hell's Bedroom," posed the question "Who are the hypocrites, calling for a cleanup of New York City, but owning the hotels where hookers work, or closing their eyes to the massage parlors which are being used for purposes of prostitution?" It pointed out that the city officer in charge of licensing these places of business was Bess Myerson, and cited police-department complaints about her office: When the cops reported violators of the licensing laws to the commissioner, either she would not act to issue a summons to hold a hearing, "or her deputy commissioner, Henry Stern, would simply fail to hold a hearing." In short, said Sheehy, "it was a rollover at the Department of Consumer Affairs."

But this was only one audible croak in an otherwise universal and rising chorus of praise. In mid-March Myerson personally opened two new neighborhood centers. In Forest Hills on Friday, March 19, flanked by Queens councilman Donald Manes and Mayor Lindsay himself, she dedicated the first government-financed consumer-complaint office in the nation. On Delancey Street on Sunday, she dedicated another, sharing the platform with Bella Abzug. Without question, the New York commissioner of consumer affairs had made herself the city's most adored public official.

Privately, it was another story. Privately, in March 1971 Bess was in the last stages of a prolonged and cruel divorce battle with Arnold Grant. The Grants had divorced once before, in Mexico in 1967, then remarried. Before their second marriage, Grant had persuaded Bess to sign a prenuptial agreement renouncing all claim to alimony, maintenance, or support in the event of a second separation or divorce. Bess was now claiming the agreement was unenforceable under New York law, and seeking $3,500 in monthly temporary alimony plus exclusive possession of what had once been Grant's apartment, a luxurious, art-filled maisonette on Sutton Place.

In return Grant had filed an extremely nasty affidavit he said was based on material obtained from his wife's diaries, which he had stolen. Grant's assertions in his own behalf had a peculiarly unpleasant tone. "Soon after our divorce in 1967, she prevailed upon me to allow her to return to my home to recuperate from a claimed illness," he wrote. "She wanted to occupy the guest room only for a few weeks and would then leave for a scheduled professional engagement abroad. Once ensconced in my home, however, she lost little time in finding her way to my bed. For the next thirteen months, she behaved as a most accommodating mistress." In conclusion (point 81 in his affidavit) Grant told the court, "Her distorted picture of me as a monster, and her hate, would be painful if I did not find myself in the illustrious company of so many others about whom she feels the same way—her family—her friends—her employers and co-workers—and the institutions about which she gives the impression she is devoted—and her own, possibly merited, feelings about herself."

But Bess's purported diaries, if authentic, were in a class by themselves, detailing a daisy chain of marital infidelities, and enumerating various schemes to get her hands on Grant's money. If Grant "would die I would have the safety + security of a house . . . and I could then reach out to new experiences." Elsewhere she confided, or quite possibly fantasized, that John Lindsay was a "lousy lay."

Although the divorce proceedings were private and the court records sealed, the legal battle ground on for nearly a year, during which information leaked out from both camps, and the gossip columns were filled with innuendo. It must have been a harrowing time for a public official so much in the public eye. Bess icily refused all comment on her private life, and she had surrounded herself with a female Praetorian Guard of staunchly loyal friends. These friends thought it likely that the private pain and stress brought on by her marital woes were what had triggered an episode of shoplifting by Myerson in 1970 at Harrods department store in London for which she was fined £40.

At the ceremony to open the Forest Hills community complaint center, the commissioner informed the crowd as a seeming afterthought that henceforth she was to be known as Bess Myerson, and no longer as Mrs. Arnold Grant, from which it could be inferred that the bitter domestic struggle was inching toward resolution. Indeed, Bess's request for $3,500 temporary alimony had been denied a few weeks earlier when the judge agreed with Grant that his wife had become wealthy in her own right. And in mid-April the divorce was finally granted after Bess withdrew all claims for separation, alimony, and counsel fees and a property settlement.

A block and a half up Centre Street from the county courthouse where *Grant* v. *Grant* was grinding along was another, far shabbier courthouse, home of the Manhattan civil courts, where small-time civil and criminal matters were dealt with. One of the dozen civil judges sitting in late March 1971 was a small, frail-looking, middle-aged woman in thick glasses. That week Judge Hortense Gabel was presiding over a suit in which an accountant was suing a delicatessen over tainted applesauce.

After a noteworthy career as a real estate lawyer and innovative expert in housing for the poor, and also as New York City's commissioner of housing and rents in the 1960s under Mayor Robert F. Wagner, Hortense Gabel had been appointed to the civil-court bench by Mayor John Lindsay. A year earlier, he had appointed Myerson to Consumer Affairs, and it was scarcely surprising that the judge and the commissioner were acquainted. Very few women held public office in 1970, and both Myerson and Gabel were graduates of Manhattan's all-female, tuition-free Hunter College. Both later became active in alumnae activities and in Jewish affairs.

Judge Gabel's long record of public service was distinguished and totally unblemished. But her life, too, had its worrisome private side. Her vision, poor at birth, was slowly deteriorating, and for some years she had been concealing a heart condition that, if known, might bar her from appointment to the state bench, and even result in the loss of her present assignment. Hortense Gabel could not bear to stop working. Law and politics had been her whole life, and besides, the family needed the money.

"Horty" and Dr. Milton Gabel, a dentist, had lived for twenty-five years in the modest, four-room, rent-controlled apartment where they raised their only child, Julie Bess, now twenty-one. Even more than her husband, Horty was tormented about the future of this unconventional, feisty, and lovely daughter, who as a teenager had taken up the study of Sanskrit and changed her name to Sukhreet, an Indian name meaning "One with a Tradition of Happiness." She was a brilliant student, expensively educated. After dropping out of the United Nations School at fifteen, she would easily complete four years' worth of undergraduate work at New York University in a little over two years. She would spend academic summers at Oxford University and Johns Hopkins University, working toward a Ph.D. in international relations. Recently she had told her parents that she had once more dropped out of school, because she was in need of money. But not to worry: She already was hard at work at a new job from which she confidently expected to net an amazing $50,000 a year. She would call again soon.

Sunday, March 28, 1971, was a beautiful day of sunny skies and afternoon temperatures in the low fifties. At the home of Dr. and Mrs. Lawrence Yaeger in Jamaica Estates, Queens, a small family wedding was about to take place. The judge was in the den putting on his judicial robes. Standing in the pale-yellow living room and looking rather ill at ease were the parents and sisters and a few friends of the groom. Beside them stood the bride's parents and the Yaegers and their two small children.

Waiting in the curve of the piano, where the actual ceremony was to take place, were the bridal couple and the bride's three children, the two older ones exactly the same ages as the two Yaeger kids, eleven and nine. The children held hands, and the bride and groom held hands, and all five people were smiling. They had all waited five years for this day, while the bride's Jewish mother got used to the idea of her daughter Nancy marrying an Italian. Meanwhile Nancy's children had come to adore their new stepfather, Carlantonio Capasso, whom everybody called Andy. He was a small-time sewer contractor who, with Nancy's help, now owned his own business, called Nanco in her honor. His trucks were stenciled NANCO on the sides, and NANCY was painted in big letters above the front fender. Nancy and Andy's close friend and neighbor Donald Manes, the newly elected Queens councilman, had offered free advice on how to set up the business. He had even come up with the judge when the couple decided the time had come to make it legal.

Today Nancy looked extremely pretty, tan and sexy in her Oscar de la Renta dress bought at a Queens discount-fashions store. It was brown silk jersey with a white jersey bodice, and her long thick dark hair hung down her back almost to her waist. She and Andy were the same height, five feet ten, and she thought he looked sensational dressed up in his new dark suit. Normally he wore work clothes, and when necessary he drove the bulldozer himself.

Nancy and Marlene Manes served on the PTA together, and Marlene was Nancy's closest friend after Judy Yaeger. But the bride didn't mind that the Maneses couldn't make it to the wedding. Donnie was in politics now, and that had to come first. "Donnie *makes things happen*," Nancy often said. "That's what he loves most." Now he as much as anyone had made this wedding happen. The judge was just coming in. Judy Yaeger hit the button on her tape deck, and strains of Mendelssohn's wedding march filled the sunny room.

Sunday afternoon was always Sukhreet Gabel's busiest day, after Saturday night, and just now she was diligently working away. She was employed at Kay's Place, located in an old brownstone on West Fifty-seventh Street. Kay's Place was one of the massage parlors that Commissioner Myerson had so far failed to close down. Sukhreet told herself that she didn't really mind the nature of her work. It was no worse, after all, than when she had done nursing work in a senior citizens' home and had to give people enemas and body rubs all day long. What's more, the money was terrific, and all cash. A standard hand job cost $75, of which you had to turn $40 back to Kay, but you got to keep all your tips—extra money, paid in advance, for special requests. Her present customer, the third today, had paid the extra $15 to have her work topless. Bending lower, she momentarily freed one hand from her work and unfastened the hooks on her pink lace brassiere.

2

BEGINNINGS

ESS MYERSON IS AN ENTIRELY SELF-MADE WOMAN, and she has not had an easy time of it. She "did it my way," as the song says, from the very beginning, and at times the cost was fearful. As Miss America 1945, impossibly leggy and breathtakingly lovely in her too-tight white sharkskin bathing suit, Bess Myerson at twenty-one gave the nation a ripe new image of American beauty and of emancipated womanhood. In her slow and steady rise from the Boardwalk of Atlantic City to the corridors of City Hall, this brainy, disciplined, witty, and well-spoken woman made herself heroine, mentor, and role model to millions of American women. To millions of men, she embodied perfect wifehood, or sisterhood. Connoisseurs of perfect motherhood or daughterhood probably looked elsewhere, but they were a small minority in the general torrent of adulation.

Everyone will be famous for fifteen minutes, said Andy Warhol. But between her debut as a bathing beauty and her swan song as a celebrity defendant in a front-page criminal trial, Bess Myerson endured nearly forty-five years of American celebrity, not something to be taken lightly. Back in 1980, age fifty-six and running as a candidate for the United States Senate, she described herself to voters in personal rather than political terms: She spoke of her working-class origins; the anti-Semitism she encountered as the first Jewish Miss America; her two broken marriages and messy divorces; her various careers; her recovery in her mid-fifties from a near-fatal bout with cancer. "I've finished bringing myself up," she concluded. "I'm a survivor."

What made her feel qualified to run for the Senate?

"Because I'm better than most people I know." Implicit: "And I know everybody."

These were not the answers of someone seeking to be liked. Most people do want to be liked, and women, particularly women of Myerson's generation, had been so thoroughly trained to seek approval, to put themselves second, to walk a pace behind, that they could not step out. They were crippled by a near-lethal case of the Disease to Please. The four words they most dreaded hearing were "I don't like you." Such women regarded these words as the vampire does the crucifix. But not Bess Myerson. By age fifty-five, if not sooner, she had made herself impervious to criticism, fearless of the negative opinions of others, a seeming woman of Teflon.

Then, in the last decade of her remarkable history, the years between fifty-five and sixty-five, when most American women of her age were settling gently into gardening and grandmotherhood, Myerson's never-serene life went into a kind of wild overdrive. She experienced new heights of public power and public scorn. She discovered new depths of private hell and perhaps private passion. There was real public failure, her very first, when voters decisively rejected her senatorial bid. This was swiftly followed by real romance, if not also her first, at least her first in many years, with a rich and vigorous lover twenty-one years her junior. He was Andy Capasso, a genial, expansive, and amazingly successful sewer contractor. And *this* was followed by an invitation from Mayor Koch to become New York City's commissioner of cultural affairs, a classy post that provided an $83,000 salary, a high degree of visibility, and the prime Manhattan status possession, a full-time limousine with car phone. In time the besotted Capasso, who had already given her a Mercedes-Benz and a toolbox full of good jewelry, took steps to divorce his wife.

Myerson's great happiness was followed by megadisaster. In 1987 her lover was convicted of tax fraud. Weeks later she was forced to resign her commissionership in disgrace after accusations that she and Andy had tried to influence the Capasso divorce judge. This was Hortense Gabel, a seventy-four-year-old woman with a record of blazing rectitude who, weeks after Myerson's resignation, was herself forced into sudden retirement. The so-called bribe, if that is even the correct term for what had occurred, was minuscule compared to the wholesale corruption rampant elsewhere in the city. By then, eleven top officials of the Koch administration had been forced out of office; five were already behind bars. All Myerson was said to have done, by contrast, was give Judge Gabel's daughter a piddling $19,000 city job as Myerson's personal assistant. The offer may have been ill advised, but there was nothing on the face of it that was illegal. Yet in the hands of the city's Savonarola-like federal prosecutor, Rudolph Giuliani, the mere appearance of evil, in tandem with the undisputed coverup that followed, was crime enough to get this unlikely trio of miscreants—an aging beauty queen, her mob-connected boyfriend, and an enfeebled little-old-lady judge—indicted on federal conspiracy charges.

Well known to readers of the city's tabloids were two other facts. The government's star witness against them all was to be the judge's brilliant, unconventional daughter, Sukhreet. Second, the defense line was that all the trouble had been stirred up by Capasso's vengeful, venal, diabolical ex-wife Nancy.

On October 15, 1987, the regal and willowy Myerson, her chunky beloved, now clad in prison denims, and the defrocked and purblind old judge stood together in a federal courtroom for their arraignment. After hearing themselves officially described as criminals, they were led off for mug shots and fingerprinting. Trial was at least a year away. In the interim, it would not be too difficult for Andy Capasso and Judge Gabel to retreat into the obscurity they had formerly enjoyed. But what of the big-time defendant, the one who had survived nearly forty-five years as an American celebrity? What was she supposed to do for the next year? Hide her head in shame? Go to a fat farm? Take up needlepoint? Not this self-made survivor. Contingency plans were already in place.

A year or so before, in anticipation perhaps of this difficult day, Myerson had hauled out her scuffed old scrapbooks—a tonnage of big-league personal publicity comparable to that amassed by Elizabeth Taylor or Charles Lindbergh—and found herself a solid professional author as collaborator. Working overtime, the two women had swiftly crafted a book that they would hold in dual copyright, a detailed description of some things that had happened at least forty-one years earlier. Its full title was *"Miss America, 1945: Bess Myerson's Own Story* by Susan Dworkin," and it alternated chapters of autobiography by Myerson with chapters of historiobiography by Dworkin. When it was published, around the time of the arraignments, most reviewers said it was very good as far as it went, which was not very far. Neither writer took the story one day further than 1946, an oddity considering that so much had happened to Bess *after* 1946, but an oddity in which it was not difficult to discern some criminal attorney's unseen hand.

Just three days after the humiliation of her arraignment, Myerson, with mad bravado, took off solo on a grueling fourteen-city, six-week book-selling publicity tour packed with as many broadcast and newspaper interviews as mortal flesh could endure. She was alone except for a representative of her publisher, who lugged massive amounts of photographs and other promotional materials designed to "place" the book for potential buyers whose memories did not extend as far back as 1946. The literature enumerated three momentous events that had taken place in the summer of 1945. In June in Europe the Nazis had surrendered to the Allied forces. In August in Tokyo Bay the Japanese had surrendered to General MacArthur. And on September 9 in Atlantic City, New Jersey, before a solid wall of newsreel cameras, a tall, radiant twenty-one-year-old from the Bronx had been named "Miss America, 1945."

This happening had been the very first major news event of the new peacetime world, her book materials explained, and it made Bess Myerson, "along with Einstein and Hank Greenberg, one of the most famous Jews in America." True enough perhaps, on both counts, but putting it in just that way exemplified and foreshadowed what was to become the lifelong Myerson style. The line was eye-catching, thought-provoking, prideful, intensely personalized, and not outstandingly modest.

BESS MYERSON'S FATHER was a small child when word swept through his Russian village that another pogrom had begun. He survived the rampage entombed by his parents under the floor. Inside his black hole, he could hear boots pound, dishes crash, his mother screaming, and the little cousin buried beside him gasping for air. By the time the cossacks left, little Louis Myerson had nearly suffocated and his cousin was dead.

Eighteen-year-old Louis Myerson passed through Ellis Island in 1907, and worked as a handyman, housepainter, and carpenter. In 1915 he married Bella, twenty-three, a beautiful, wild Russian girl who must have had her own childhood memories of Russia, but never spoke of them. Bella, and *her* mother, Besseleh, the very tall one, the one from whom Bess got both her name and her unusual height, had been born in Odessa, and Bella had lived there until she was ten.

She never really learned to read and write properly, either in Yiddish, which the family spoke at home, or in the language of her frightening new adopted country. She was toiling in a shirt factory on Manhattan's Lower East Side when she met Louis Myerson.

Bess's father was by then a dedicated, self-employed housepainter. "It's a common story," Bess recalls, "watching him go off to work, and coming home at eleven o'clock at night. She's not educated, she didn't speak the language at all, she didn't have any skills or talent, she can't work, she can't help. She resents my father's fiscal limitations. She was angry about it. Every time he came home with a letter from Marlene Dietrich—he did wonderful homes here in New York—she'd look at [the letter] and say, 'Where's the check?' "

Gentle Louis and shrewish Bella raised three daughters in a tiny apartment in the Sholem Aleichem Cooperative Houses in the Bronx. The parents slept on a fold-out couch so their daughters could share the only bedroom. Claustrophobic as the arrangement was, each daughter remained at home until she married.

Two years after their first child, Sylvia, had come a son, their beloved "Yosseleh," little Joseph, and then they lost him to diphtheria when he was only three years old. Bella nearly died of grief. She was unable to eat, sleep, or look after her husband and child. Only Louis's threat to cart her to an asylum persuaded her to resume her household responsibilities. Bella's grief gradually destroyed her: Her hair went gray, her teeth fell out, her hearing deteriorated, and she was plagued by persistent buzzing sounds that only she could hear.

Bess was the baby who came next, seven years after Sylvia. She was the child meant to assuage her mother's inconsolable grief, and she could never overcome the guilt she felt at not being the son her mother had longed for. The birth two years later of frail and asthmatic little Helen only seemed to make Bella worse. Her bitterness was black and her irritability constant. Having no interest in such traditional Jewish concerns as religion, culture, or politics, she took it all out on her family.

The five-story, walk-up Sholem Aleichem Cooperative Houses, fifteen linked red-brick buildings curving up the side of a steep hill along Sedgewick Avenue, was an unusual place to grow up. Built in 1926–27 by a group of idealistic, left-wing, working-class Jews newly arrived from Eastern Europe, these were among the first co-op buildings in New York City. Across the street was a park and later a playground, and in summer people used the rooftops as a "tar beach." Down the hill was the much larger Amalgamated housing project, founded by the largely Jewish Amalgamated Clothing Workers Union, and to the west was another Bronx Jewish co-op, this one built by old-country communists. The Sholem Aleichem founders thought of themselves as blue-collar members of the Jewish intelligentsia. Of primary importance to these people was "culture," which meant the preservation of Yiddish traditions and the Yiddish language, and it was no accident that they named their new home in honor of Sholem Aleichem, meaning "Peace Be with You," the pen name of the Yiddish-speaking people's greatest writer.

The original buildings included a large hall for community lectures and dances, a stage, a piano, and a cafeteria for banquets and birthday parties. The founders showed their respect for artists by providing three studio apartments specifically designed to house a sculptor, a painter, and a musician. But for most Sholem Aleichem families the cultural emphasis was on music, dance, and literature rather than the visual arts. The few original residents still alive remember a continual series of poetry readings, concerts, bazaars, and holiday parties. The famous Vilna Troupe, a Yiddish theater group, appeared regularly in the auditorium.

But the founders' primary motive seems to have been to design a setup for "collective living" so as not to let themselves be too quickly stirred up and dissolved in the big American melting pot. A few atheists and agnostics were among the 237 Sholem Aleichem families, but no Orthodox Jews. Politically, perhaps 80 percent of the families were socialists, people who today would be called democratic socialists, and the others were more to the left, protocommunists of a pre-Stalin, Marxist variety. There was also a small but vocal group of anarchists, perhaps twenty-five in all, who held an annual ball on Yom Kippur, the Jewish Day of Atonement, to show their contempt for religiosity; and there were also a few deeply religious families. "What we all shared," recalls one of the original residents, "was love of Yiddish, and a social conscience."

Irish families lived on one side of Sholem Aleichem, and Italian families along another, as some still do today. There was scant overt conflict, but the members of each ethnic group still kept largely to themselves. The Jews, families who had lived for generations crowded into the ghettos of Russia and Eastern Europe, were used to living squeezed closely together with people of their own kind. In Sholem Aleichem they had in fact built themselves a kind of ideal ghetto without walls on a bare Bronx hilltop. When the place first opened, there were few neighbors, no bus line, and no school. There was only a large park, a reservoir, and, at a distance, a garbage dump shrieking with sea gulls.

When Sholem Aleichem was first set up, each family paid for its apartment, perhaps $40 to $50 per room, plus $12 per room per month for upkeep. The apartments were all walk-ups, but most were spacious and bright, with nine-foot ceilings, oak parquet floors, and large closets. It was a "closed community," and if one family got in trouble and couldn't keep up its payments, others quietly helped out. "Those who had shared with those who had not, no questions asked," one woman recalls. "You couldn't pay your rent one month, it was ignored."

But with the advent of the Depression, many families could not pay even these meager rents, and the bank started evicting unemployed people. A rent strike was declared, one of the first ever in New York City. For once, socialists and communists united, and every single Sholem Aleichem family joined in. Bess Myerson remembers carrying a picket sign after school when she was eight or nine years old.

The Myerson apartment was in Section C, on the corner of 238th Street, and both the living room and bedroom overlooked the park across the street. Bella had two sisters and two brothers and their families living in other Sholem Aleichem apartments, and Louis's two brothers and their families also lived there, so Bess grew up surrounded by close family members. But in fact all the adults looked after one another's children, and in those days no family ever locked its front door, so there was constant visiting in and out of the apartments and up and down the stairwells. In a sense, it was an idyllic place to grow up. There were always plenty of other children to play with, always someone to take care of you if you hurt yourself, always organized games in the park across the street, and cultural projects in the auditorium and library. None of the kids who grew up there remember any problems with alcohol, drugs, or crime. A few boys sneaked cigarettes, or drank the Sabbath wine, or constructed homemade firecrackers. As for sex, one woman says of the girls, "Some did. Some didn't. Boys always seemed to be on the make, but you did not give a girl a reputation, as a matter of courtesy. If a girl made out with a boy, he'd keep her secret."

Another woman recalls, "The houses were a *shtetl*, where everyone felt safe. During the day all the doors were open. You walked right in. The doors were open at night too, but then you rang the bell. Unless you heard a child cry. Then you walked in. Every adult was every child's parent. If you misbehaved, the nearest adult whopped you on the behind. And when your mother heard about it, she whopped you again."

Philip Shapkin, today an expert in demolition work, grew up in the Sholem Aleichem co-op, and remembers Bess well from when they were teenagers. He has not seen her since, but all during the "BessMess"—as the city's tabloids came to refer to the entire affair—Shapkin was certain she was "an innocent political target. I can't abide anyone who thinks of knocking her. My faith comes from growing up in this ghetto where we honored friendship." Like many Jews in the Bronx today, probably like most of them, he says simply, "She's our Bess."

As kids, neither Philip nor Bess had enough money to take a bus to a real beach, and he recalls many afternoons with her on the "tar beach" rooftops when he was fifteen and a half and she was seventeen. She let him put oil on her back, "but Bessie was no flirt," he says firmly. "She was very beautiful, with magnificent long hair. But she wasn't impressed with her looks, or self-centered. She was down-to-earth, smart, and she had a great command of language. And she was nice."

Sometimes he would hear her playing piano through an open window, and he'd call out, "Bessie! Play 'In a Persian Market.'"

"And you know what? She always would."

Growing up in such an atmosphere, it is not surprising that 90 percent of the Sholem Aleichem children took music lessons. Poor, illiterate, tone-deaf Bella Myerson decided that her three daughters must all grow up to be piano teachers. That way they would never have to become dependent on unreliable husbands. Somehow the family acquired a grand piano, and Louis, who could make anything with his beautiful long-fingered hands, sewed together old carpet samples into a floor covering so that the neighbors would not complain of the day-and-night thumping of continual piano practice in apartment 4-B.

Sylvia and Bess were forced and scolded into hours of piano practice from the age of nine. Bella shouted at her daughters like a camel driver, bellowing "Wrong!" at intervals from the kitchen, even though she could not tell wrong notes from right. Bess had genuine musical talent, and soon she was taking music lessons and performing in piano recitals. Music became her means of escape from the ghetto, and her teenage idol and mentor was her piano teacher, a beautiful, stately, cultivated, and serene woman who lived in a gracious apartment near Central Park West, and who was different from Bella in every way. When she killed herself many years later, Bess could not summon the courage to appear at the funeral.

Her tall teacher had helped her feel a little better about her own ever-lengthening legs. Bess was taller than all the other girls in her class, and most of the boys. Her shame had deepened when she was assigned to play Olive Oyl, Popeye's homely toothpick of a girl-friend, in a school pageant. Bess sobbed and wept to no avail. No one understood her anguish, least of all her parents. Decades later, long after she had grown to magnificent womanhood and been crowned Miss America, officially the most beautiful woman in all the land, Bess kept a snapshot of herself as Olive Oyl tucked in the back of her wallet. To everyone else she was the most beautiful girl alive; to a part of herself she has remained always Olive Oyl.

Bess's musical ability got her admitted to the famed High School of Music and Art in Manhattan, which had been set up by Mayor LaGuardia and accepted students on merit basis only. Her dream was to become a symphonic conductor. But there were no woman conductors in those days. Indeed, there was not one female player in any major symphony orchestra.

Bella was never a warm-hearted or even an enthusiastic parent. Bess describes her as a terrible housekeeper, an atrocious cook, a bitter *kvetch* who barked one-word commands—"Practice!" "Homework!"—without noticing what her daughters were doing. Whatever cuddling and kissing and encouragement the girls got came from their father. Whatever good words Bella had to say for them—and there were many more than the girls realized—she spoke only behind their backs, to neighbors and relatives. She boiled meat until it was unrecognizable, and she served glasses of warm, liquid Jell-O in the belief it would prevent cancer. She disapproved of makeup, boys, and fun. She was angry, ignorant, harsh, and stingy. She never gave to charity. She would permit her daughters to buy only marked-down clothes.

In one of Bess's well-polished stories of her miserable upbring-ing, her mother asks the neighborhood grocer, "How much for grapefruit?"

"Two for fifteen cents."

"I'll take the one for seven," she replies.

Bess remembered her late teen years as happy ones. For the first time, she was praised for her schoolwork. For six summers, she worked as a swimming teacher and later a music counselor at camps in New Hampshire and Vermont. She reveled in the freedom of being away from Bella. She found out she was a talented sports-woman, good at tennis and horseback riding as well as swimming. She loved meeting girls from well-to-do Jewish families in New Jersey, Manhattan, and Long Island, girls who wore cashmere sweaters and spoke without Bronx accents. And the delicious food! So different from Bella's boiled-gray pot roast, and the hot cereal with dry, undissolved lumps.

All three Myerson sisters worked in summer camps at various times throughout their high school and college years. All three grew up to become accomplished and good-looking young women. But in these midteen years Bess's truly exceptional beauty emerged. Dressed in white shorts, without makeup, her hair in long pigtails, she conveyed the impression that the goddess Diana had suddenly reappeared in the woods of New England. Like Diana, Bess was virginal, shy. In fact, like Bella Myerson, she was downright prud-ish, as well as sexually ignorant and dormant.

FAR ACROSS THE Bronx from the Sholem Aleichem Houses, in a respectable neighborhood of business and professional people, was a group of middle-class, one-, two-, and three-family stucco or red-brick dwellings clustered around Prospect Avenue. The inhab-itants were a mix of mostly Italians, Germans, and Jews, people who had passed through Ellis Island a generation earlier than the Myersons. In one red-brick house lived an Italian family, a rabbi and his family, and the family of Reuben J. Wittstein, a real estate and negligence lawyer, whose wife worked as a bookkeeper. The Wittsteins had two daughters, and the older one, Hortense, had been born with a congenital eye defect. Though she was not blind, her range of vision was only about four feet, and at first her parents educated her at home with a tutor. The child was not sent to school until the fourth grade, by which time she was a grave, bright-eyed ten-year-old with chipmunk cheeks and thick glasses. At about this time the family moved from the Bronx to Washington Heights, just north of Columbia Presbyterian Hospital. This neighborhood was more solidly Jewish, but little Horty's two best friends were both Irish, and both boys. After P.S. 115, Horty went to sprawling George Washington High School and, despite her vision problem, did moderately well. At Hunter College, she studied social studies and found a mentor in her tough but brilliant sociology professor, who recommended her for Columbia Law School.

"I assumed I'd be a lawyer because that's what Father did," Hortense Gabel said. Her sister, Sybil, three and a half years younger, studied economics at New York University.

Reuben Wittstein's law office was at 360 West 125th Street, in those days still a white neighborhood on the edge of Harlem. In 1922, Wittstein, an unusually broad-minded man for his day, took on a black law partner. Two years later he would invite a woman to join the firm. As for Hortense, she turned out to be a brilliant student at Columbia, and in 1937 she too joined the family firm, which had moved to 42nd Street, and now changed its name to Wittstein & Wittstein, to acknowledge and honor her presence.

HUNTER COLLEGE WAS known as a center of liberal arts, and it had an excellent music department. It also had a reputation as "the best poor girls' school in the city," and attracted the cream of women students from all over New York. In 1941, one member of the freshman class was five-foot-ten-inch Bess Myerson. She had enrolled first in night school so she could study piano by day, and possibly earn a scholarship to a fine music school like Curtis or Juilliard. But she soon realized and accepted the fact that her considerable musical talent was insufficient to sustain a performing career. After she switched to day classes at Hunter, Bess earned $5 an hour as a photographer's model, far more money than she could ever command as a piano teacher. She also worked as a rehearsal pianist, and clerked in department stores. Her college years were unremarkable, and she seldom speaks of them. She majored in music, her grades were consistently good, and every day she found time and money for a piano lesson with her beloved teacher. But her social life was scant. Most young men were away at war during that period, and when she graduated in 1945 with a B.A. in music, she listed no extracurricular activities in her yearbook. She also was the only class member who did not tell where she lived.

THE WAR THAT made life difficult for Bess made it exciting for the young lawyer Hortense Wittstein. She had been research counsel for the New York State Chamber of Commerce since 1937, working on an investigation of mortgage foreclosure practices. The war brought an acute apartment shortage to New York City, and in 1943 the federal government imposed rent control to stop the zooming cost of housing. At the same time, Hortense, now a diminutive young woman of thirty with the same chipmunk cheeks and heavy glasses, became an assistant corporation counsel to the city. That summer, at an Adirondacks vacation hotel on Lake George, she met a tall, shy, good-looking dentist from New York City. Milton Gabel was in the U.S. Army Reserve, and had been called up after war was declared. When he was sent to Fort Huachuca, near Tuscon, Arizona, Hortense decided to accompany him, and they found a Tucson judge to marry them on June 17, 1944. Dr. Gabel was later transferred to Fort Hood, Texas, where he proved to be an unusually popular army dentist. Hortense Gabel kept busy writing a real estate column for the local newspaper.

THE SUMMER THE war ended, while Bess Myerson was away at camp, her sister Sylvia, now a speech therapist, entered Bess's photograph in a beauty contest staged by a radio station. Paul Whiteman and Danton Walker were the judges, and to everyone's surprise, Bess won. Next came the Miss New York City contest. When she won that, Atlantic City was inevitable. This year, 1945, was the first time that the "Miss America Pageant," as it was tonily called, carried with it a $5,000 scholarship, enough money to pay for the graduate education in music that Bess could get no other way.

Bess had always thought of Sylvia more as a wise, kind, assistant mother than as a sister, and throughout her life she would always seem to need such a person close by her. She was terrified of being alone, and made sure one especially close woman friend was always in the big-sister role. Membership in her female Praetorian Guard changed, but Bess always saw to it that Sylvia's shoes were filled. For now, Sylvia would become her road manager. Sylvia's husband would stay home to mind their two young daughters.

The bewildered Myerson parents signed a long and involved contract binding their daughter, should she be chosen winner, to one year of servitude on the road plugging the products of the pageant's commercial sponsors. Free ball gowns were contributed by a kindly garment maker who guessed that a girl from Sholem Aleichem might need them. This windfall marked the start of Bess's lifelong pursuit of free, wholesale, or cut-price apparel. For the moment, it was just one more good omen in the modern-day Cinderella story by then under way.

Shortly before the Myerson sisters boarded the train for Atlantic City, what today would be termed a "photo opportunity" was arranged in the office of Mayor Fiorello LaGuardia. While the newsreel cameramen were setting up, the Little Flower asked Bess sotto voce what a high-class girl from his own pet High School of Music and Art was doing entering a vulgar Atlantic City leg show.

She was explaining about the music scholarship when a cameraman in the rear of the pack called out for the mayor to please stand up.

"I *am* standing up, dammit!" LaGuardia yelled.

The non-Jewish world heard of *schlock* with the advent of the big TV game shows in the early 1950s. *Schlock* was the merchandise the shows gave away, all the refrigerators and "dining-room suites" and trips to Hawaii; the toothy TV "hosts" who handed the free stuff out became known as *schlockmeisters*.

But many non–Yiddish-speaking people about Myerson's age had become aware of the word *schlock* a few years earlier, in the 1940s, when the word was often associated with the bathing-beauty contest held each September in Atlantic City. At about the same time, young women first became aware of another exotic, exciting word, *sharkskin*, that being what the beauties wore—white one-piece sharkskin bathing suits. They became aware of "American beauty roses" because that's what the contestants carried as they paraded the Boardwalk.

Today the Boardwalk and the pageant and the *schlockmeisters* and American beauty roses and the sharkskin-clad beauty queens are all part of the same stock of postwar teenage memories. The best remembered of the beauty queens, in fact the only one most people recollect at all, is the 1945 winner, Bess Myerson. Partly she is remembered for her extraordinary beauty and charm, outstanding even by Miss America standards. Jews remember her for being Jewish, and proudly so. In a sense they felt she was a daughter of all Jewish people. Mostly, of course, Bess Myerson is remembered because she has not long been out of the newspapers from that day to this.

It was the Boardwalk hotel owners who first dreamed up the notion of holding a Miss America pageant each September. The idea enabled them to get several weeks' extra business and fill their cavernous and otherwise empty caravansaries once the big summer crowds had decamped after Labor Day.

The organizer of the pageant in Bess's day, and for many years thereafter, was a Florida woman named Lenora Slaughter, who may have been the original steel magnolia. Her avowed intent was to upgrade the annual event from the tawdry bathing-beauty contest it had been since 1923 to a classier bathing-suit parade that would feature tonier girls, a talent contest, and a grand prize of a college scholarship rather than the near-worthless six-month Hollywood contract of old. Slaughter, a former employee of the St. Petersburg, Florida, Chamber of Commerce, came north with her homegrown professional standards intact. She at once recognized that upgrading the contest would mean more money for everybody, starting with the commercial sponsors, the bathing-suit and wristwatch and sharkskin manufacturers who footed the bills.

Lenora had a mesmerizing, hypnotic effect on her girls, including Bess. She made them feel regal, truly queenly. It was no great trick to send a bevy of fearful, ambitious, unworldly girls whirling into soaring flights of fantasy about the glorious future that lay ahead once the crown was theirs and the ermine-trimmed robe placed around their white shoulders. Bess's fantasies included a large new apartment for her parents, with an elevator and a new grand piano; a maid to help her sister care for her two young children; and good false teeth for her mother, to replace the ones that had fallen out after baby Joseph died.

She imagined herself traversing the land as Miss America, helping the big corporations that sponsored the pageant to sell their products. But more important than anything else, she imagined herself pleasing not just her family and friends and employers, but people all across America.

But Ms. Slaughter was a pragmatist as well as a spinner of dreams. Well before the Miss America Pageant, she scouted local beauty contests to identify potential Atlantic City contenders, and potential problems. The shock must have been great the night before the voting in the Miss New York City contest when Ms. Slaughter had quietly approached Bess and urged that she change her name to Betty Merrick, a name less identifiably Jewish. Bess had the pride, and the good sense, to refuse.

"It didn't worry *me* that Bess was Jewish," Slaughter said many years later, but indications are that the picture was different forty-five years ago. Even among her sister Miss America contestants, Bess Myerson was obviously head and shoulders—in both senses of the term—above the others, and an almost certain winner. She was not only a knockout to look at, she played both piano and flute like a professional. Well before the voting, dire warnings began circulating among some of the backers that "if this Jewish girl becomes Miss America, it will be the end of the pageant!" The night before the votes were cast, several of the more important judges received anonymous phone calls asserting that a vote for Myerson would guarantee that they would never preside over another pageant.

It was past midnight on the early morning of September 9 that Bess Myerson stood on the stage of the Atlantic City Auditorium with forty-seven other white-bathing-suit-clad young women, heard her name spoken on the public-address system, and stepped forward to receive a jeweled scepter in one hand and a bunch of long-stemmed red roses in the other, have a scarlet silk cape draped round her shoulders, and a rhinestone crown placed upon her lovely head.

ONE DAY AFTER Bess Myerson was crowned Miss America in Atlantic City, in St. Clare's Hospital in New York City a healthy, squalling infant was born to Josephine and Michael Capasso, the owner of a small-time construction company. The Capassos had two daughters, Sallie and Rosalie, but this baby was their firstborn son and they were overjoyed. They christened him Carlantonio Capasso even before they took him home from the hospital.

3

MARRIAGE AND

MOTHERHOOD

THE END OF THE WAR WAS A HEADY, GIDDY TIME all across the nation. No one celebrated that event with greater gusto than Hortense and Milton Gabel. The dentist and his wife were avid for his discharge and return to civilian life. Horty had always dreamed of being a writer, and had much enjoyed her stint working as a reporter while her husband repaired army teeth. But there was never any question that law, particularly housing law, would remain her passion. Now that the war was over, Hortense was even more eager than Milton to get home to the town they loved best, New York City.

BESS MYERSON'S FIRST weeks as Miss America must have been devastating. Instead of embarking on a regal procession through the finest hotel suites and corporate boardrooms in the land, she began her reign with two appearances, for $50 each, on the Steel Pier in Atlantic City. Next she took off on a few weeks of shabby vaudeville to which Lenora had precommitted the winning contestant. Homesick and scared, Bess did four shows a day, always in her bathing suit, amid people she remembers as broken-down vaudevillians without talent or charm.

Bess already was fed up with being a sex object. But worse lay ahead. Her prize required her to tour the country on behalf of the pageant's five commercial sponsors. Before this tour, Bess had always lived within the all-Jewish world of Sholem Aleichem, or in the cosmopolitan, strongly Jewish worlds of the High School of Music and Art and Hunter College. But now, outside of New York, she encountered religious and racial prejudice for the first time. She began to appreciate the prevalence of anti-Semitism in the nation when three out of her five sponsors suddenly pulled out, including the important Catalina Swim Suit Company.*

In the South, she was booked into theaters where restrooms were labeled WHITE ONLY, and where blacks were allowed to sit only in the balcony. In one town she had been scheduled to make a promotional appearance at a country club that did not admit Jews. She did not know the club was "restricted" until, at her arrival, the hostess stammered that there had been "a terrible mistake."

As winter came on in 1945, something happened that saved Bess Myerson's soul. She was invited by the Anti-Defamation League of the B'nai B'rith to tour the nation's high schools speaking out against religious and racial intolerance of all minorities, not only Jews. As a beautiful young woman of working-class background, she was just the sort of person who could most readily capture people's attention, the league believed, and work to change the institutionalized prejudice that still held the nation in its grip.

Bess loved the assignment. It appealed to her sense of idealism, and her need to do something useful. Until her stint as Miss America ended, Myerson spent about half of her time speaking on racial, religious, and political tolerance to high school students, Kiwanis clubs, Rotary clubs, women's groups, 4-H groups, anyone who would listen. She received $25 per performance.

....

* After her victory, Bess began to receive voluminous mail, and her mother, Bella, threw much of it away unopened. Bess has always wondered whether an invitation from Catalina might have been among the discards.

"You can't be beautiful and hate," her standard speech began, "because hate is a corroding disease and affects the way you look. . . . You can't hide it—ever. It shows in your eyes. It warps your expression. It affects your character, your personality." It was a weird Dorian Gray theory of personality development, a curious amalgam of moralism and narcissism, which may be why it went over so well with her young audiences.

Then Bess received the greatest opportunity any aspiring pianist could hope for: an invitation from the great New York Philharmonic! She was to appear as the orchestra's guest soloist at Carnegie Hall. Carnegie Hall! It was unbelievable. The city's music critics thought the invitation a vulgar publicity stunt, and cheerfully anticipated disaster. Bess decided on Rachmaninoff's Second Piano Concerto, and drove herself into a frenzy of practicing.

At the performance she played very well. The applause was thunderous, and the shouts of "Brava!" were mingled with cries of *"Mazel tov!"* For by now, her celebrity as Miss America had made Bess Myerson the special heroine not just of the Sholem Aleichem Houses, but of all the Jews in America. In an incredible accident of timing, she had won her title in the same year that the shocking facts and sights of the Nazi concentration camps and their systematic extermination of six million Jews became known to the world. At that horrendous moment in human history it seemed somehow redemptive that here, in America, a Jewish girl should have been chosen fairest in all the land.

In Carnegie Hall her admirers filled every last seat. When the applause finally ended, fans and friends fought their way backstage, and a clutch of neighbors from Sholem Aleichem rushed to throw their arms around Bella Myerson. "Your daughter was *marvelous!*" they chorused.

"I don't know why," said Bella. "She never practices."

Bess tells this story today with the practiced skill of a Milton Berle. It is one of a repertoire of wry, witty, well-told anecdotes she has built up to deal with the pain of having had someone like Bella Myerson for a mother. For Bessie never rebelled. She was always a dutiful daughter. As much as her mother denied her, she never talked back; she almost always obeyed, and she always, always tried to please. But everyone knows that a wicked fairy stands waiting with a magic curse whenever a true fairy princess is born into this difficult world, and it was Myerson's curse to suffer from birth the dread Disease to Please in its most focused, virulent form. At bottom, there was only one woman in the world whom Bess Myerson ever really wanted to please, and that was the one woman she never could.

Working for the Anti-Defamation League had salvaged Myerson's wounded pride, and began a lifetime of impassioned service to Jewish causes. "There is a Jewish word for what I got from my ADL work: *koved*, pronounced like 'covet,' " she wrote in her book. "It means stature in the community. . . . I knew if I brought *koved* to the family, I would make my father happy and maybe even more important, I would make my mother happy. . . . My mother loved it when I toured for the ADL. The Miss America [fan] letters she had thrown away."

Nonetheless, no one was happier than Bess when her year as Miss America finally came to an end. Despite the money, the fame, the *koved*, and the worldly experience her tour had brought, she wanted no more of any of it. Her dreams were much more fundamental. With the end of the war came the era of Togetherness, the period when the highest aspirations of every young woman were marriage and children and, alas, it (literally) went without saying, faithfulness within marriage. Not surprisingly, Bess bought the whole thing. Her career, even her career as Miss America, made her vaguely uneasy. Though the rise of the new feminism and the so-called women's movement was still a good twenty years in the future, Bess, in her bourgeois 1950s attitude toward herself, in fact prefigured one of feminism's shrewdest observations: Men in our society are made anxious by failure; women, at least women of her generation, are made anxious by success.

In the spring of Bess's Miss America year, Lenora Slaughter had insisted she return to Atlantic City to appear at a toy convention. There she met a tall and good-looking army captain. He began to pelt her with flowers, candy, and gifts. Soon he was always at her side, attentive, devoted, and openly adoring. Just home from four years fighting Japan, Allan Wayne had prosperous Jewish parents (the family name originally had been Wayneschenker) who lived on West End Avenue, not far from the elegant studio of her beloved piano teacher, and light-years away from the walk-ups of Sholem Aleichem.

"I knew that when my year ended in September, I'd be home . . . with my parents. Who was going to look for me there? How was I going to meet somebody? I began to think that if I didn't marry Allan, there wouldn't be anybody else suitable to care for me."

Myerson's book contains no description, nor even a mention of her wedding to Wayne. But among its dozens of photographs is a small one of a radiant bride in a gown with a long train, arm in arm with her smiling new husband, who is clad in a rented cutaway. They stand, knife in hand, beside a tall, fancy wedding cake in front of the marble fireplace of an elegant and ornate room.

Like many impulsive postwar marriages, this one was quite miserable, and Bess tells her readers almost nothing about it. Because of the housing shortage in those years, they lived with Allan's parents in their big apartment, and Allan worked for his father in the toy business. Bess gave birth to their daughter, Barbara Carol, now known as Barra, on New Year's Eve, 1947. The senior Waynes doted on their first grandchild. Bess resumed giving piano lessons, and occasionally played piano on local radio and TV shows.

TWO YEARS AFTER Bess and Allan's baby was born, the union of Hortense and Milton Gabel was also blessed with a beautiful daughter. They named her Julie Bess. Though they rarely spoke of it, the Gabels had almost given up hopes of a child. Hortense was thirty-seven. For several years she had been working as a volunteer for the much-admired Rabbi Stephen S. Wise, founder of the American Jewish Congress. Through her friendship with the crusading rabbi and his daughter, she became involved in what would become the ruling passion of her professional life, discrimination in minority housing. Her interest had been piqued at a dinner party where she was seated next to Rabbi Wise. He was talking about the need to have a New York State committee that would work to prevent such racial discrimination. Hortense enthusiastically volunteered her services. A year later, despite her pregnancy, Hortense was working as a founding director of the National Committee Against Discrimination in Housing. This was an umbrella group for more than twenty agencies around the country that were concerned with the issue. Hortense's imposing task was to design the pioneering legislation that was required at every level, local, state, and national. At the same time, she was organizing community action programs. The work was very demanding, and she relished every moment of it. When it was completed, she began drafting a highly critical report on Robert Moses, then the single most powerful man in New York City and New York State. One of the many hats Moses wore was that of director of the mayor's Slum Clearance Committee. Gabel's report described the disastrous impact that Moses' policies were having on the already desperate housing problems of the city's poor. She accused Moses of creating new slums faster than he demolished old ones, and she appeared before the Board of Estimate as a representative of seventeen civic groups protesting Moses's plans for Washington Square.

Though it did no good, Hortense waged a spirited fight. "I've visited a lot of bad slums," she told the writer Robert Caro while he was researching his brilliant biography of Robert Moses, *The Power Broker*. "But I've never seen any worse than the Title I slums when the developers start milking them." By "developers" she meant Moses. She described visiting one slum site, "and, as any woman instinctively does, when I went into the bathroom, I glanced into a mirror to see if my hair was straight. And when I looked . . . where the mirror ought to be, I found myself looking straight into the next apartment."

Throughout the early 1950s, Hortense Gabel continued to lead the reformists who opposed Moses' "public works" as making things worse than the conditions they were created to relieve. Moreover, she was the sole city official willing to meet with and brief the band of crusading city reporters who were trying to expose Moses as the arrogant, dictatorial old man he had become.

From the very beginning, when the fair-housing movement was young, Hortense Gabel fought steadily against racial discrimination. Later, as a New York City housing official, she would launch imaginative, innovative rehabilitation projects, at the same time holding the line as a staunch defender of rent control. In the third stage of her career, as a housing consultant to the Ford Foundation as well as to many states and municipalities across the nation, she would supply technical assistance to all sorts of community and church and civic groups that were starting housing projects, as well as to individual states setting up housing agencies.

Her merits have long been recognized. The lifelong housing activist Anita Miller, now chairman of Amerifederal Savings Bank, a large mortgage institution, said recently, "Public housing built high rises. Urban renewal tore them down. There was nothing in between. Gabel filled the gap with the idea of rehabilitating neighborhoods. Before her, everything was tear it down, tear it down, tear it down. There was tremendous disruption and dislocation."

IN THE LATE 1940s, television was beginning to become important as a mass medium, and one of the first people to be seen regularly on local TV in the Big Apple was the beautiful pianist Bess Myerson. By 1951, she had her own show. On the last day of that year, Barra's fourth birthday, Bess appeared on her first national network program as hostess of CBS's *The Big Payoff*. Billed as the "Lady in Mink," she handed out the *schlock* to the lucky winners on the popular game show, and soon became the Vanna White of the 1950s. The pay was very good, and it was not long before Allan Wayne had become her business manager.

In addition to eight years as the "Lady in Mink," Myerson was soon appearing on many other TV shows. In 1954 and 1955 she was hostess for NBC's *Philco TV Playhouse*. For fourteen years, from 1954 to 1968, she appeared on the annual Miss America Pageant broadcasts, as co-commentator at various times with Doug Edwards, John Daly, and Walter Cronkite. She only gave this up, she later told a *New York Times* writer, "when I looked down the roster of entrants and saw that none of them were born the year I won." For eight years, 1960 to 1968, she was also commentator at the Tournament of Roses, which precedes the Rose Bowl.

As a TV celebrity, Myerson was a rousing success. As a wife, mother, and daughter, things had not gone nearly so well. During her reign as the "Lady in Mink," her father-in-law became ill, and Allan began drinking heavily. After the senior Wayne's death, his son's drinking increased, Bess said later, adding that alcohol made him impotent and subject to horrible war nightmares and outbursts of violence. Soon he was terrorizing not only his family but Bess's TV associates. When she decided to leave him, her parents objected. You do not leave even a bad marriage—you work things out, they said.

On her 1987 book tour, nearly forty years later, Bess spoke to a reporter from the *Long Island Jewish World* of this difficult period in her life. "I went home and said to my father, I have to divorce this man. I mean he is brutal, he is destroying himself, and I took him to a doctor, and the doctor said . . . 'If you don't leave him, he's going to destroy you and your child.' What was more important to me than my child?

"And my father said to me, 'You can't divorce him. You go back and *you* make it better.' "

With a catch in her voice, the pain and exasperation still seeming so fresh, Bess told the reporter she asked her father, " 'How much more do you want me to practice? When am I going to teach you and show you that I'm really okay?' And my mother said, 'You can't get a divorce. You just put new drapes in the living room.'

"Do you know what I felt like? Like they pulled my toes out and whatever energy or strength I had was gone, and I suddenly realized, at age 31, they're not there for me . . ."

Like all celebrities, Bess Myerson has been asked the story of her life many times. She does not always tell it the same way. Often she leaves out the part about her parents and moves on to her prolonged and bitter fight with Allan Wayne. Her husband demanded sole custody of Barra, but what he really was after, she said later, were her considerable savings from her TV work. Myerson had managed to put most of this money in a safe place, and now Wayne wanted it, claiming he had earned it for looking after her affairs. Wayne's lawyer told her lawyer that if she would turn over her savings to her husband, she could have a divorce and sole custody of their daughter.

Bess has told several writers that during this period of her life, her husband's wartime experiences caused him to suffer from "post-traumatic stress syndrome," a condition that would be unknown to medical science for another decade.

The Waynes separated for the first time in 1956, and Bess accused her husband of alcoholism, shell shock, and abusive behavior. They reconciled for a while, then split for good. Bess filed assault charges, and demanded to keep $100,000 of her money. Later, she told still other writers, she was finally forced to surrender all the money in the divorce settlement in order to keep her child.

IN 1955, NEW YORK governor Averill Harriman named Hortense Gabel counsel and first deputy administrator to the New York State Temporary Housing and Rent Commission. It was the highest legal post held by a woman in the state. Something of the unusual intellectual tone of the Gabel household may be inferred from the fact that that same year, on their daughter's sixth birthday, her parents gave her a junior membership to the NAACP.

Later, Julie Bess recalls, her parents would sit in the living room of their modest, rent-controlled apartment reading the day's newspapers and listening to show tunes on their phonograph. Those from *Oklahoma!*, *Carousel*, and *The King and I* were favorites. Julie Bess meanwhile would be in her parents' bedroom perusing a collection of great-art picture books that they had picked up when first married. While leafing through these art books, she liked to listen to *The A&P Treasury of the World's Greatest Music*, a collection of classical greats that her parents bought for her one by one at the supermarket.

Milton Gabel, a natural athlete, used to take his daughter roller-skating and ice-skating, and he tried to teach her tennis and other sports. She was clumsy and slow, no good at any of it. It did not help that his favorite expression, which she says he repeated almost daily to his wife as well as his daughter, was "Good, better, best. Never let it rest. Till your good is better, and your better best."

Hortense Gabel had a pleasant voice and entertained her daughter, when she had time, with a seemingly endless repertoire of rollicking school and camp songs, Gilbert and Sullivan, and pop hits of the twenties and thirties. She was also an accomplished whistler, and was wonderful at making up bedtime stories. Dr. Gabel lacked imagination, so the child always asked him to tell her true stories of the days when he was a little boy. He almost always told the same story, she says, and it "used to break my heart." Still, she kept asking to hear it.

The story: Right after World War I, Milton's parents began vacationing in the Catskills, boarding with a local dairy farmer because they could not afford the big summer hotels. Little Milton especially loved feeding the farmer's pigs, which lived in a mudhole. He poured slops into the hole and watched them eat it. The branches of an apple tree overhung the hole, and sometimes apples fell in. The boy loved to watch the pigs diving deep into the mud to fish out apples.

Each time little Julie Bess heard the story, she imagined her father was thinking of her as one of the pigs. Her face was porcine, she thought, and "I felt round, pink, and snuffly, like I lived in a mudhole." When she grew up, she decided her father had not been thinking of her, but he was still outspokenly critical of her sloppy living habits.

IN 1958, BESS MYERSON became a weekly panelist on a second game show, *I've Got a Secret*, along with regulars Henry Morgan, Betsy Palmer, and Bill Cullen, and Garry Moore as host. The program would last fifteen years on CBS, sealing Myerson's place as a national celebrity. Nonetheless, a fellow panelist recalls, "Bess was unbelievably insecure in those days. One week our task was to bring to the studio something we had baked ourselves." In an era before the whole nation had gone cookery-mad, this was a bold assignment. Bess was so scared of looking less than accomplished that she brought in something very fancy, like a napoleon, which she must have bought at a fancy bakery because it could not possibly have been homemade.

Bess was also an energetic, impassioned, even obsessive fundraiser for the new State of Israel. A chum of the period recalls, "Offer Bess anything, an English muffin, and her first question was always the same: Is it good for the Jews?"

Somewhere along the line, Bess began to refer to herself publicly as "Queen of the Jews." The reference was to the biblical Queen Esther, the beautiful savior of the Persian Jews whose story Jews celebrate on the holiday of Purim. Of course there has always been more than a touch of self-mockery in the sobriquet, but many people did not pick it up, so that later in life, when Bess was no longer so popular, so admired, so adored, much of the public scorn directed against her was in retribution for her *chutzpah* in proclaiming herself queen.

She had many love affairs, and on one trip through Israel was accompanied by the movie actor Jeff Chandler, born Ira Grossel, and best known for his portrayal of the Indian chief Cochise. Chandler was one of the great loves of Bess's life, and ever after the model for her favorite type of man: tall, dark, handsome, younger, and "Jewish-looking," with crinkly gray hair.

In 1959, Republican Nelson Rockefeller replaced the Democratic governor Harriman in Albany, so Hortense Gabel moved back to the Apple, which was still controlled by the Democrats. In May, in front of 150 family friends and relatives, Mayor Robert F. Wagner swore in Gabel to a three-year post as his assistant for housing. The press questioned her newly created job in a period of budget austerity, and she defended herself strongly, saying her work would return to the city much more than her salary in increased real estate tax revenue because she would improve housing stock. Streamlining city work on slums and eliminating overlap in functions of various agencies would also save money, she contended. Deputy Mayor Paul O'Keefe said that Gabel's job of coordinating agency work on cleaning up slums was "vital," and that the city's long-range financial health depended on shoring up housing.

The best-known effort at this time was called the Bloomingdale Project. It ran from 99th Street to 104th Street, and from Amsterdam Avenue to Riverside Drive. Gabel convinced the City Planning Commission, then dominated by Moses, to designate this fifteen-block area for extensive rehabilitation, thus qualifying it, with Board of Estimate approval, for federal funds. The plan called for restoration of buildings through strict code enforcement and for rehabilitation of existing housing by present owners or by the city's Housing Authority. Tenant participation was also emphasized. Upgrading of housing would include converting two buildings on 103rd and 104th streets, each of which had seventy-seven single-room-occupancy units, to twenty-four apartments each. Tenants could help by serving on committees and advising the city. This gave them a stake in the results, helping build pride in the neighborhood.

Gabel worked out of an office in City Hall. "It's the most exciting job I've ever had," she told a reporter. She bragged about her husband, "a dentist who believes in my work and is extremely handsome." Of their ten-year-old daughter, Julie Bess, she said, using quintessential NewYorkliberalparentspeak, "She's proud of me. But she also expresses her own individuality." Knowing that her mother was an ardent Democrat, the child had said, "Mother, I have to tell you that I'm a Republican . . . and I'm also for the Cleveland Indians."

This could be a child who is merely smart and cute, and it also could indicate a daughter who is struggling to differentiate herself from an overpowering mother. Hortense would say later that she herself came from a very enlightened, progressive household. As she put it, "My mother's chief rival for my affection was F.D.R." That sounded as if Hortense too may have been a resolutely nondependent daughter. Another likelihood is that both these daughters were needful of more plain and simple mothering—wider, warmer laps—than either one ever found.

At election time, it was Gabel who masterminded Wagner's tough stance on rent control, which in turn helped him win reelection. In 1960 Gabel moved up to the national level. She was named consultant to the United States Housing and Home Finance Agency, and began serving as administrator and secretary to the U.S. Department of Housing and Urban Development, a post that she held for the next six years.

Privately, Hortense and her family were going through a difficult time. She had begun a series of eye operations in hopes of saving her failing sight. Then, in August 1960, tragedy struck. Hortense's nine-year-old niece, Betsy Jailer, daughter of her younger sister, Sybil, drowned while away at summer camp. Eleven days after the child's death, Sybil's husband, the brilliant Joseph Jailer, M.D. and Ph.D., collapsed and died of a heart attack.

Julie Bess Gabel was attending a different summer camp, and was not told of her cousin's death. She was disappointed and hurt when her parents failed to show up for her eleventh birthday. She did not know that on that day they were attending little Betsy's funeral. Her uncle Joe Jailer's death came just before the end of camp. When the campers arrived at the Port Authority bus terminal, no one was there to meet Julie Bess. She waited an hour and a half for her parents to arrive. Only then did she learn that both Betsy and Joe were dead. Horty and Milton were late getting to the bus station because they had been attending Joe's funeral.

The three Gabels drove straight from the bus station to the Jailer home in Scarsdale. Julie Bess remembers her aunt Sybil coming down the stairs "looking like Medusa, and giving me a look of utter hatred," probably, she thinks now, because she was alive and Betsy was dead.

The grown-up Julie Bess has understanding but not much compassion for the events of that dreadful summer. "Betsy I hated," she says frankly today. " *'Ding dong the witch is dead'* was my reaction to her drowning. I couldn't have been happier."

The year following the tragedy was a truly awful time for everybody. The three Gabels moved in with Sybil and her remaining child, Jim, nine months older than Julie Bess. Hortense and Milton had to commute into the city to work, which they hated, and their daughter had to go to a new suburban school, which she hated. She also decided that a Jailer family servant loved Jim "because he was an orphan," but hated her. She remembers the woman punching her, she says, and twisting the flesh of her upper arm until it was black and blue. She never told her parents. Her mother seemed oblivious anyway, totally wrapped up in commuting and in caring for the grief-stricken Sybil.

Julie Bess seemed to grow up incapable of sympathy or even comprehension of the pain felt by the adults around her. The perfect egocentricity of childhood survived intact and, at thirty-nine, she would still blame her mother. "How could she bring a child into that House of Death? That was child abuse."

Three years later Sybil married Wayne Phillips, then special assistant to Robert C. Weaver, head of the federal Housing and Home Finance Agency, and Hortense's mentor and boss until his move to Washington. Sybil worked in the HHFA New York City office. The wedding was held in the Gabels' apartment and presided over by Algernon Black, leader of the Ethical Culture Society. Six years later, the marriage ended in divorce.

The Wittstein sisters are still close, and Julie Bess says they are now both alcoholics. (Because of her own genetic history, she says, and because alcohol would not mix well with the drugs she must take to control her emotional depression, Julie Bess does not touch alcohol, nor any other drugs.)

The year after her cousin's death, Julie Bess remembers that she became the first girl in her class to menstruate. No one had prepared her, and she thought the blood was a sign she had cancer. She left her stained panties at the top of the laundry hamper, where a kindly servant found them and told Hortense. But mother and daughter never had any discussion about sex, then or later, Julie Bess says.

Hortense Gabel's job was growing ever more demanding. The following summer, on July 5, Mayor Wagner ordered Gabel to lead a "shock attack" on a single block of West Eighty-fourth Street, between Amsterdam and Columbus avenues, in the wake of a Fourth of July riot involving four hundred people there. The area had been slated for rehabilitation a year earlier. Gabel summoned landlords and said, "We want your buildings cleaned up now—and I don't mean a *schlock* house job."

Six days later, she opened her housing department's first branch office, at 135 W. Eighty-fourth Street. It was a big day: She led a team of city officials to a conference with community leaders at the Protestant Episcopal Church of St. Matthew and St. Timothy, just east of the "pilot block." The session was chaired by the Reverend James A. Gusweller, who had declared a few days before that "this place needs a concerted drive of all city departments—health, fire, police, narcotics, housing, and sanitation—and to require landlords to obey the maximum-occupancy laws. . . . That's what the mayor promised two years ago and nothing has happened."

"This is no headline-seeking stunt," Gabel said. "We don't plan to be here just for the summer. We are here to stay."

Gabel put three people in the office full-time and detached building inspectors from their regular duties to do emergency inspections in the pilot block. She also ordered a census of neighborhood welfare clients, and appealed for volunteers, especially Spanish-speakers, to translate. Within a week, she herself was putting in regular afternoon office hours at the new office. When she found sixty-three remaining violations in one building thirty days after her announcement to landlords, she persuaded a magistrate to levy a record $1,000 fine on the owner.

TWO YEARS BEFORE tragedy struck the Wittstein sisters, Bess Myerson had met Arnold M. Grant, a brilliant financial and tax attorney, politically liberal and active, who was a member of all the right clubs and knew just about everybody in show business and politics. Among his personal clients were Johnny Carson, Darryl Zanuck, Bing Crosby, Mary Pickford, Gary Cooper, Lana Turner, and Orson Welles. He was a director of many motion-picture and theatrical corporations, was active in Jewish philanthropies, and had served as TV-and-radio chairman for the presidential campaign of his hero Adlai E. Stevenson. A precise, demanding, and often extremely charming man, Grant was slender, elegantly turned out, a few inches shorter than Bess, and sixteen years older.

"Arnold was a *great* suitor!" a close friend of the time recalls. He and Bess first saw one another on the dais of a dinner honoring Ed Sullivan, and Arnold managed to insert into his prepared remarks his wish "that this lovely lady to my left might have dinner with me later this evening." She did; she fell. As a shrewd and successful theatrical attorney, Grant knew Myerson would be a great asset to him. She felt the same way about the powerful, well-connected lawyer.

One of the most effective ways Arnold wooed Bess was by providing her with her own limousine and a tall, handsome black chauffeur. When she appeared at the theater to do her TV show, the chauffeur entered behind her, carrying the huge and elaborate fairy-princess-style gowns she favored.

"Bess in those days was such fun! So witty and bright!" another friend says. "But she has always wanted to get ahead, to climb the ladder. And she also had a great need for men, both for emotional security and for money. She loved money. Arnold Grant was a very wealthy man. And sweet. And he gave her entrée into a total new world."

Many of Bess's friends were less than enthusiastic about her newest boyfriend. "Arnold Grant was such a crook!" one says. "But like all the other men Bess was attracted to, he was powerful, and she was so hungry for power. He wasn't handsome, not at all the Jeff Chandler type, but he walked in an aura of power."

Grant and Myerson kept company for four years before they married. Arnold took over all of "21" for their engagement party, and it seemed that every show-business luminary in New York City turned out for the occasion.

On May 2, 1962, Myerson married her Pygmalion and moved officially to his luxurious home on Sutton Place. Grant, who had a grown daughter by his first marriage, now formally adopted fourteen-year-old Barra, and she became Barra Grant. (The day before the wedding, Allan Wayne had died of what his former wife has variously described as "suicide" and a "cerebral hemorrhage.")

Bess's friends said she seemed to enjoy "playing the grand lady, giving dinner parties in rooms decorated with rare Japanese objets d'art that Arnold had brought home from the war. One night everybody got into a terrible fight, with Arnold boasting about his stolen Japanese artifacts, and the others saying he ought to call his law firm 'Booty, Plunder & Loot.' "

Frequent guests still talk about "Arnold's extraordinary maisonette! So incredibly mannered! Lettuce-green silk damask walls, and the greatest china, in vitrines, everything specially lit. The place lacked the wit of a Tiffany window but, oh boy, it sure had the merchandise."

HORTENSE GABEL HAD served nearly two years as consultant to the Housing and Home Finance Agency, and she was still working for the Department of Housing and Urban Development. One week before Bess Myerson married Arnold Grant, Gabel received a three-year appointment as New York City commissioner of rent and rehabilitation, which meant she was administering the largest quasi-judicial agency in the city or state. Robert Wagner was still mayor, and Gabel was a key member of his Executive Policy Committee on Housing. She sometimes dined with the mayor and his family and various civic dignitaries at Gracie Mansion. But the Gabels' social life remained essentially modest. The chic, two-story Grant maisonette with its lettuce-colored walls was way beyond the purview of the purblind little housing expert and her nice dentist husband.

4

Long before she finished college, a good-looking and fashionably dressed young woman named Nancy Roth knew her way around every atelier on Manhattan's Seventh Avenue, and she could tell you the label in a cloak or suit or gown at fifty yards. A green-eyed Marjorie Morningstar from Queens, Nancy had been born in 1940, the only child of Ruth Turim and Harold Reis, who was in advertising. Before Nancy was of school age, her parents were divorced and Ruth married George Roth, a jolly Hungarian wholesaler of dressmaking supplies. "He would import-export Japanese stuff. *Tchotchkes* for chain stores," Nancy said. When he formally adopted her, Nancy Reis became Nancy Roth. But she liked both her fathers, and remained in touch with Reis after he remarried and became an adman for Levelor blinds, living in Woodstock, New York.

Nancy described herself as an entirely average Jewish teenager, educated in Queens public schools, including two years at Jamaica High School. Her childhood was so quiet you could hear a pin drop, she later said with a smile. "Guess that's why I created all this commotion later on."

When Nancy was twelve or thirteen, her teachers decided she was intellectually gifted, and she transferred to Halsey Junior High School, which then had the only gifted-child program in Queens. In her last two years she transferred to the new Martin Van Buren High School. She was merry, popular, a good student, and was elected vice president of student government. Statuesque, with a gorgeous body, she had many boyfriends but no serious romances.

At sixteen, she enrolled at Skidmore College in Saratoga Springs, New York, and her stepfather advised her to study teaching or nursing, "so I could work anywhere. I knew I didn't want to be a teacher, so I wound up with a B.S. in nursing. I guess I thought I would love to be Florence Nightingale. Now, I wish I were a lawyer!"

In Nancy's day, Skidmore did not have the grand campus it later acquired: "It was a tiny girls' school, in old houses." During and after getting her degree in nursing, Nancy worked as an aide on the OB-GYN service at New York University Medical Center and at the Columbia University psychiatric institute. But the only later use she made of these skills was to read the "Nurse Nancy" stories in the Little Golden Books to each of her five children while they were growing up.

In June 1959, Nancy was a tall, vivacious nineteen-year-old just graduated from college with honors and feeling somewhat at loose ends. One summer's day, shopping for a bargain, she visited a wholesale coat manufacturer on Seventh Avenue. Espying this smart, sexy, very good-looking, and obviously well-brought-up Jewish girl in her showroom, the wife of the coat maker also saw good value. She contrived to introduce Nancy to her son Howard, just graduated from Dartmouth. Nancy, no fool, had already met Howard at a Dartmouth ski weekend. That's how she happened to *be* in this particular wholesale showroom.

"But then I married rich Mr. Herbert. And I couldn't deal with his family," Nancy said later. "At Dartmouth, Howie was president of his fraternity, a rah-rah guy. But the minute he was with his family, he became a different person. Just namby-pamby. And we had no money—though they had plenty!"

Nancy, like so many nice Jewish girls, like Bess Myerson in fact, fifteen years before, was a virginal Sleeping Beauty–type who drifted into matrimony without undue forethought. Marriage was what nice girls did. She had no thought for the future except what she calls "my plan. By the time I was forty, I knew I was going to be 'a lady,' but I had no clear idea what that meant, either." Bubble-headed as it may sound today, this is an honest self-portrait of many girls of her age and class. They were the same cashmere-sweatered, materialistic fillies Bess had seen and envied as a counselor at summer camp.

In fact, Nancy was raised to be a prime specimen of the so-called Jewish-American Princess. When she was growing up, "my mother went to the A&P, and she played bridge. That was her life. I did it the same. I was always home for my five kids until Andrea, the littlest, went to school. I never thought about working. My mother never worked. If my own kids were that way now, I would kill them."

Nancy Roth wed Howard Herbert in 1959 in the marriage-license bureau of New York City Hall. Later his parents threw a big party at their handsome Long Island home. Within a year Nancy's first child, Helene, was born. Steven and Debbie followed. By the time Nancy Herbert was twenty-four, she was a busy housewife who spent all her days looking after three children under the age of four. In the evenings she served dinner to her husband, a man she describes today with disarming candor as "your average boring Jewish businessman." It was a quiet life.

BESS AND ARNOLD GRANT became veteran world travelers, always going first class, and usually with another couple. A foursome made matters convenient for dining, golf, and so on. On their first big trip, the honeymoon, they went to Venice with Ruth and Ilya Lopert, a producer and top distributor of foreign-made films in the United States. The Loperts were slightly older, cultivated Euro-peans, and to them the new bride seemed still a very uncertain, unworldly young woman. When Grant sent her to buy expensive Venetian linens and glassware for their home, she had the shop-keepers deliver all her tentative selections to the hotel for her hus-band's approval.

Ruth Lopert had a sense that Bess was a woman who had, until then, experienced scant sexual pleasure, and Ilya had told his wife that his friend Grant was much experienced in that area and also well endowed. On the women's first shopping expedition, Ruth could scarcely wait to ask, "How's the honeymoon going?"

"Well, I've had plenty of honey, but I haven't seen the moon yet," Bess replied enigmatically. Ruth believed that Bess "woke up sexually" with Grant and that she "didn't have it so good again for many, many years."

All her women friends talked about Bess's many lovers. "But she was always very condescending to them behind their backs," says one. She was even condescending to Arnold. She used to tell her friends that every woman needed at least three men: one for sex, one for money, and one for fun; you could never find them all in the same man. However, this never stopped her from trying. And trying.

Arnold was patiently teaching his wife the complex customs and folkways of mid-century Manhattan society. Bess not only was ignorant of fish forks and salad plates and vintage wines and gam-bits of simple dinner-party chitchat; she knew almost nothing about basic housekeeping: cooking and serving food, cleaning house, or dealing with servants. Grant employed a beautifully trained French couple who looked after everything, but their very presence seemed to turn Bess rigid with fear. She would wait until their day off and then invite a friend over to join her in raiding her own kitchen, like naughty boarding-school girls on a spree, hunting for good things to eat.

When not in California or traveling abroad, the Grants spent summer weekends at Deal, New Jersey, where Arnold owned a large, sprawling house complete with tennis court and swimming pool. Arnold played golf at the best (Jewish) country club, Holly-wood Golf Club, while Bess stayed home and improved her tan and her tennis. These weekends were business as well as social occa-

sions, and there was always another couple or two along as house-
guests.

One sunny morning on the tennis court, Bess suddenly grabbed
hold of her woman partner and said, "You know why I really
married Arnold? So I could supply wonderful mornings like this *for
us!*"

In those days it had never even occurred to most of Bess's female
friends that she might be bisexual or lesbian. Much later, while in
the throes of divorce, Grant said to a number of these women,
"Bess is so beautiful. But she has only ugly women for friends.
Harsh, crude women," he added, and named a few. "I think she's
basically a dyke."

But Grant was then overwrought, and certainly he had made no
such suggestions while the pair was happily married. His reason-
ing, and timing, suggested he had no actual evidence. And other
women, including friends Bess roomed with all over the United
States and Europe, maintained they noticed nothing. Or almost
nothing. She did not appear to want to make love to them. She did
have all sorts of provocative ways, with both sexes. Most women
she met felt these had little or nothing to do with sexual desire; men
disagreed.

There were stories like the one in which Bess told a friend in her
most imperious, Queen-of-the-Jews voice that she was going into
the bathroom to put on her makeup. "Sit with me," she com-
manded.

"And then she put on her makeup completely in the nude!"

When the friend told this to her psychiatrist, he said dryly, "And
you noticed *nothing*?"

She was disturbed, of course, which is why she brought the story
to her psychiatrist. Many straight women acknowledge attraction
to other women that they do not act upon; and they keep the signals
clear. Bess did not. Deliberately or not, she was confusing, ambig-
uous. Nor did she seem to notice or mind making women friends
uneasy. She appeared to enjoy it.

Married or single, Bess did seem to have a difficult time being
alone, and the stress became greatest when she was making the
transition from private person to public celebrity, or vice versa. In

private, she used no makeup or artifice whatsoever, and appeared proud of her remarkable, flawless beauty. When it was time to get ready to go out to some public function, she frequently asked someone to sit beside her and watch her in the mirror while she dressed and performed her toilette. It was a strange, lifelong habit. Over the years, she invited close friends, new acquaintances, employees, near-strangers, servants, children—mostly women, but sometimes men—to remain with her while she got dressed, or undressed.

Then there were the touchy-feelies. Bess Myerson was always physically imposing, not merely because of her unusual beauty and height, but because of her habit of standing extremely close, often too close for the comfort of the person she was talking to. As she talked, she patted, stroked, and fondled the other person, often holding both hands in hers, and making unusually intimate revelations about herself, inviting reciprocal confidences from the other. Some people, mostly men, found this intense approach seductive, even irresistible. Others, mostly women, especially small women, were intimidated or repelled, and would as soon be embraced by an octopus. In both cases, what appeared to be a bid for unusual intimacy was probably a bid for territorial dominance, something similar to what the male lion intends when he urinates on thornbushes.

Standing, Bess loomed, crooning little endearments or unwanted words of encouragement to the person who was at eye level with and precariously close to her bosom. Seated, it was no better. She bent her long lovely body at the waist, grabbed the other person's hands; eyes locked. The other felt not loved but entangled. Sometimes she let one hand go, but only to make things worse—pat one's cheek, perhaps, or touch one's hair, the low, intimate voice talking, talking. People who knew Bess were used to this behavior, her "touchy-feelies," and endured the pats and murmurs without complaint. The experience could be so strange, it took a long time to realize that something else might have been going on. The person who grasped one's hands so tight, so tight, could have been a little girl, frightened, and holding on for dear life. Or it could be simple dominance behavior, like a stag in rut.

Myerson's usual approach to someone she was bent on ensnaring was to grab hold and utter some variation on the theme of: *Let's stick* together. *It's you and me, babe, against the world.* Coming from a woman with such a powerful aura, with so much natural charisma, this approach was in fact very seductive. Said a woman friend who knew Bess well, "Her attitude has very much to do with her view of men and women—that at bottom we women are alone in the world, and we have to do the most we can to defeat or outsmart or outrun the men. Basically she hated men."

Myerson could be seductive with either sex, and women meeting her for the first time often wondered if she was lesbian. A female TV personality who knew Myerson a long time once said, "I always felt there was a helluva lot of sexual confusion there. Very much patting, breast-touching, and so forth. But mainly I remember her as being very ambitious, and always trying, without success, to use the show to launch herself into something else."

Many of Bess's friends were undergoing Freudian psychoanalysis, and from time to time one would suggest the same therapy for Bess. She had had some psychoanalysis in the late 1950s, but her doctor had died and she was reluctant to seek a replacement.

In the 1960s a particularly close friend, the big sister of the hour, made rather a pest of herself on the subject, and Bess agreed she could certainly use professional help. "It was so obvious she needed therapy. All the outer things in her life were working wonderfully, yet she was clearly dreadfully unhappy. She could not bear her own company, and would go to any extreme to avoid being alone, even for one evening. So one day I told her, 'I've got a wonderful recommendation for you from my shrink.' "

"I'm ahead of you," Bess said, smiling. "I've just found a very good psychiatrist, and he's already invited me to his house on Cape Cod for the weekend!" This was Theodore Isaac Rubin, M.D., who thereafter became Myerson's therapist and subsequently remained her very close friend and adviser. In addition to seeing patients individually, Dr. Rubin headed a therapy group that met several nights a week. He was also director of the Karen Horney Clinic, a psychoanalytic institute, and was a prolific writer of both technical papers and popular works.

In 1959, Myerson's first TV show, *The Big Payoff*, was canceled amid the burgeoning quiz-show scandals of the era. It had all begun to unravel when the handsome and distinguished English professor

Charles Van Doren of Columbia University revealed that he had won $129,000 on *The $64,000 Question* because the producers had secretly fed him the correct answers to keep him on the show. The shocking news eventually touched off a congressional investigation, in the face of which CBS president Frank Stanton canceled all the network's big-money quiz shows, including *The Big Payoff*—even though that show handed out merchandise, not cash. His intent, he said, was to forestall federal regulation of broadcast programming, inasmuch as quiz shows were "inherently prone to hanky-panky" and could not be properly policed.

But Bess still had her Tournament of Roses and Miss America Pageant assignments, and *I've Got a Secret* weathered the scandal period and for eight years remained among the more popular quiz shows in the nation. Viewers came to regard the panelists as bright, glamorous members of their own families, and similar good feelings warmed the show's performers and producers.

Said the award-winning TV producer Judy Crichton, then a staff researcher on the show, "Henry Morgan was always so funny and irreverent. Garry Moore was the world's nicest man. Betsy Palmer was very married. She lived in Englewood, New Jersey, was pretty, blond, and fluffy, and always went home after the show. We always felt there were two Besses: the go-home-to-the-Bronx-and-sing-around-the-piano Bess, and the driven woman who *had* to be the most beautiful, the most talented . . . to be right . . . to win."

Says another longtime staff member, "Despite working and socializing together for so many years, on and off the show, one had no sense of her interior core. You really knew Henry; you really knew Garry; you never knew Bess. This was the case despite that awful business of her premature confidentiality that was always vaguely embarrassing. I remember her as continually luring you into very personal conversations that carried you beyond where you wanted to be. For example, she used to debate marrying Grant with really just anybody."

The same women saw Arnold Grant as "a compulsive perfectionist. One never felt she loved him. He was a mean fellow, with an extraordinary need to be right." One example of this occurred in 1963, when a rookie cop arrested Grant for jaywalking while strolling from Sutton Place to his office at Park Avenue and Fifty-second Street. Enraged, Grant sued for false arrest and spent three years and thousands of dollars appealing the case all the way up to the U.S. Supreme Court, which declined to hear it.

THE NEW YORK STATE Temporary Housing and Rent Commission ruled for twelve years as rent overseer in New York City. On May 1, 1962, the newly created New York City Rent and Rehabilitation Administration took control of 64 percent of city dwellings. (The state retained control over the rest.) Hortense Gabel had been appointed head of the new agency in April and she remained until 1965. Gabel ran into a storm as soon as she took office. Governor Nelson Rockefeller had shifted responsibility for rent control from the state to the city in order to dump a political albatross before his reelection campaign in the fall. The city had been set to take over administration of rent control on May 1, 1962. The day before the transfer of power, state rent-control officials approved scores of increases. A city investigation was launched, and by early August the city reported that at least twenty rent inspectors and examiners were suspected of graft and bribery. Governor Rockefeller had also asked the district attorney to investigate the charges. By that time one Bronx couple who owned six houses with 150 apartments had already been charged with perjury and conspiracy. They were among those who had received last-minute rent increases.

On August 9, the state rent administrator, Robert Herman, defended his handling of the case, saying that he himself had ordered that rent increases on the apartments be revoked. Gabel said she was "appalled at Mr. Herman's statement," going on to say that during the last two weeks, teams from her main office had examined the Brooklyn and Bronx offices to see how they had been run under state aegis. "The degree of sloppiness which I found in processing cases, the gaps in evidence upon which a rent increase could be granted, beggar the imagination," she said. Later she added that there actually had been five rent hikes in one of the buildings owned by the Bronx couple, and hikes in seven other buildings based on "phony invoices and doctored checks."

Gabel announced a complete shake-up of her agency's Brooklyn

and Bronx offices, to "include transfer of personnel." She promised
to close loopholes in the handling of applications for rent increases,
and to recheck some increases granted by the state. The state's basic
procedures had been sound, she said, but "sloppy operation" made
graft possible. "If you have a tight ship the chances of chicanery are
infinitely less than if you have a sloppy operation. You can imagine
how easy it is to slip a paper into a file that is disorganized."

The first breach in rent control came during Governor Rockefeller's administration. The state passed a "vacancy decontrol"
law, meaning that any unit that became vacant could move to
free-market rent. Gabel tried without success to limit the law only
to luxury apartments. The vacancy decontrol law was eventually
repealed, but not before thousands of units were permitted to escape rent control.

The rent-control debate centered on the city's claim of low vacancy rates, which critics on both sides said was biased by the
choice of certain statistical methods. Another argument was that
rent control took away incentives to maintain buildings. Gabel
denied there was any such evidence, arguing that no rent-controlled
city—Chicago, for example, or St. Louis—had worse and more
costly slums than did New York. She said she could force landlords
to maintain buildings by threatening to reduce rents. She repeatedly had to deny claims such as the one made in October 1962 by
the largest city tenants' organization, Organized Tenants, Inc., that
there was "great danger" of losing rent control because of the sur-
plus of luxury apartments, the number of which had sharply increased. (Rent control is pegged by law to a vacancy rate of 5
percent or less, indicating a housing "emergency" or shortage,
which is the rationale for the law.)

Gabel said, "There isn't a chance in hell that vacancies in luxury
housing will push the ratio over the top. . . . I want to reassure the
tenants of this city that this cannot happen. It's a matter of arith-
metic and humanity."

As administrator of rent and rehabilitation, Gabel had a chance
to put her commitment to poor people and poor neighborhoods into
action. Every project she worked on employed some unusual creative strategy. She was the first to try interest subsidies for low-
income housing, with government making up the difference, and

also the first to try rent supplements. Housing activists in the 1980s would agree that Hortense Gabel was the driving force behind everything that had evolved over the previous twenty years in non-profit efforts at rehabilitation and in saving abandoned housing, not just in New York City, but across the entire nation.

One of her major concerns in rehabilitation was to avoid putting people out of their homes for too long. What a simple idea—to move temporarily displaced residents into nearby vacant apartments. But apparently Hortense Gabel was the first to do it. Developers often used prefab kitchens in new buildings; Gabel was the first to use prefabs to renovate an aging building in two days.

Gabel invented the idea of a revolving fund of city "seed money" that could be drawn upon by community groups seeking to renovate. Suddenly a small group of residents could use city money to option an old building, hire an architect, hire an engineer. Once the building was financed, the seed money went back into the fund. Before the seed fund was established, the only money available was what one authority called "a federal program with no way to access it. The feds would not release funds without a feasible package to be approved beforehand. This meant the would-be rehabilitators needed an option on the building and a detailed breakdown of the cost of the work. Bank loans were only available after you got federal commitment."

Gabel's seed fund enabled a black community group in cooperation with a Jewish agency to restore a large number of buildings between Park and Lexington avenues and from 116th to 124th streets, on the edge of what used to be called Spanish Harlem. The area had been virtually bombed out, with no heat and no water, and only a few families remaining, living in the worst possible conditions.

THE YEAR 1965 was a fluid time in New York City politics. Traditionally, Gracie Mansion had been occupied by a Democrat. But three terms as mayor of the Apple had so dulled Robert F. Wagner's appetite for public office that he had declined to run for a fourth. So the winner of the Democratic primary, Abraham Beame, a modest Brooklyn accountant who had risen through clubhouse party ranks to become city comptroller, looked likely to be the next mayor. But though Beame enjoyed the ritual backing of the Democratic party all the way up to President Johnson and Vice President Humphrey, the actual voters in New York's five boroughs cared less.

The situation caused senior Republican eyes to brighten, glance about, and swiftly focus upon John Vliet Lindsay, the charismatic Republican congressman who for the past six years had represented Manhattan's East Side "silk stocking" district. Lindsay himself was not at first enthusiastic about changing jobs. His own eyes were focused on the White House, not Gracie Mansion, and he was inclined to agree with Charles R. Morris, author of a thoughtful work on governance, *The Cost of Good Intentions*, that the job of mayor of New York City "seemed too grinding, too tarnishing, and the sheer weight of detail inevitably too belittling."

In due course, the Republicans, led by Governor Nelson Rockefeller, made Lindsay the sort of offer he couldn't refuse: a campaign war chest of a then-unheard-of $1.25 million. What's more, Lindsay knew by then that he could count on vigorous support from the unions and from powerful Liberal party leader Alex Rose. Major newspapers were behind him, and Lindsay's outspoken positions, particularly on civil rights and Vietnam, were beginning to attract increasing numbers of liberal Democrats. Indeed, as Election Day approached, the political situation in New York had become *so* fluid that rank-and-file Democrats, particularly in Greenwich Village, appeared to be swarming ahead of their leaders in all-out support of the Republican/Liberal candidate. On the day before the election, forty-year-old Edward I. Koch, leader of the Village Independent Democrats, bolted his party to support John Lindsay. It would turn out to be the closest New York City mayoral race in a quarter-century, and when it was discovered that Lindsay had won it by only 102,000 votes, defeating both Beame and William F. Buckley, who had run a poor third on the Conservative party ticket, Koch's role in the outcome was impossible to gainsay.

At City Hall, Hortense Gabel resigned her job as rent administrator. She was a loyal Democrat, and the new Republican mayor would want to appoint his own people. Over the next three years,

Gabel was a private housing consultant to various states and municipalities, and perfected the knack of sleeping on airplanes. She prepared legislative state housing programs for New York, New Jersey, Kentucky, and West Virginia; she helped design new community-housing proposals in Michigan, Georgia, and South Carolina; she consulted on housing programs for Detroit, Chicago, Los Angeles, Seattle, Nassau County, New York, the Appalachian Regional Commission, and the Ford Foundation. But though she traveled a great deal, she was rarely away from home for more than two or three days at a time.

John Lindsay was sworn in as mayor of New York City on January 1, 1966, a tough year. The very next day the transit workers went on strike, paralyzing the city, and their union chief called the mayor a "pipsqueak." Lindsay had inherited a budget crisis that nearly resulted in city employees not getting paid. He licked the budget, and then dealt with more strikes, by nurses and doctors in city hospitals and by lifeguards on city beaches. He managed to keep the lid on the city's black ghettos simmering in summer heat by personally walking the streets of Harlem and Bed-Stuy, thus forestalling the kind of wildfire riots that had swept through the Watts section of Los Angeles, and would devastate Detroit and Newark. His most heroic moment came when he walked alone into an angry mob of blacks and Puerto Ricans demonstrating against a proposed industrial park in Canarsie, Brooklyn. As Lindsay walked on, a bunch of teenagers fell back silently, then surged forward and lifted the mayor onto their shoulders while cheers spread through the crowd.

IN 1966 HORTENSE GABEL had been elected a delegate to the New York State Constitutional Convention to take place in Albany the following year. She was the Democratic/Liberal party candidate of Manhattan's Twenty-sixth District and, along with Brigadier General Telford Taylor, U.S. prosecutor at the Nuremberg Trials, she won the endorsement of *The New York Times*. The convention agenda, which the *Times* called "staggering," included legislative reapportionment, judicial reform, greater home rule for cities, and

church-state relations. The last was the pivotal issue. Both Catholics and Democrats wanted federal and state money to aid parochial
schools; the Republicans did not.

In Albany, Hortense Gabel renewed her longtime acquaintance
with the beautiful, generous-minded Marietta Tree, also an elected
delegate, who had been serving as the first U.S. woman ambassador to the United Nations. Over the years Tree had contributed
money to and made her exquisite town house available for fund-
raising parties to benefit the housing and civil rights causes in which
she and Gabel had long been interested.

During the six-month series of Albany meetings, Gabel and Tree
became close friends. They discovered they both had teenage
daughters whom they adored but nonetheless found faintly embarrassing. Children of the sixties, the two young women looked fairly
bizarre to the more conventional-minded delegates when they visited their mothers. For the past three years, Hortense's daughter
had dressed exclusively in Indian saris and worn a red dot on her
forehead. She had even changed her name, from Julie Bess to
Sukhreet. Her obsession had begun when an Indian schoolmate at
the United Nations School gave her her first sari and taught her
how to drape and fasten it. Penelope Tree was then a spindle-
legged, trendy, and extremely successful fashion model who favored skimpy, outlandish dress and outsize false eyelashes that she
wore on her lower lids because they were "easier to put on there."

Marietta, the wife of the wealthy Ronald Tree, was just becoming interested in urban planning and architecture as a result of the
convention agenda. "Day and night for six months we sat next to
each other, and Horty was my best tutor," Tree said later. "She
gave me reading matter. She'd know all the issues in depth. But her
knowledge was more than merely theoretical. She knew just whom
to go to for moral support, for political support, and for expertise."

After her convention tutorials with Gabel, Marietta Tree studied
city planning at Columbia University's school of urban studies,
following which she joined a well-known British architectural and
city-planning firm. Its founder, the late Richard Llewelyn-Davies,
was a world-famous city planner, who designed several well-known
new towns in Britain and in the States. By the time Tree became
a New York partner and opened the firm's New York office,

Hortense Gabel was in private practice as a housing expert, and Gabel and the Llewelyn-Davies firm worked closely on many projects, including ones in Watts and Detroit. The firm was staffed with seasoned urban planners from the London office, and the word soon went out in the troubled areas where Horty was working: "Don't speak to a honky unless he has an English accent."

AT AGE FIFTEEN, when Sukhreet Gabel took to wearing the sari, she also started playing hooky. Eventually she dropped out of school altogether. It didn't suit her, she said. She was bored. She found a full-time job as a guide to the Indian pavilion at the New York World's Fair, and worked the entire May-to-October 1965 season. By the time the fair folded its tents, she had learned to speak a little Sanskrit, and had devised a long-range plan.

She planned to apply to the nursing school at Bronx Community College. It was the only two-year program in the nation, she had discovered, that was accredited by the American Academy of Nursing. Both her parents were against the idea. She was too smart for nursing, they said. But Sukhreet was avid to earn money. Having been unhappy in high school, she knew she wasn't ready for college. Her goal was to amass a grubstake as rapidly as possible and then use it to finance a trip around the world.

While she waited, Sukhreet determined to get some practical experience and took a job as an "infant care technician" at St. Clare's Hospital. The date was September 1965, just twenty years after Andy Capasso had been born in that very ward.

BY 1966, THE popularity of *I've Got a Secret* had peaked, and Bess Myerson the public figure was nationally known. But the private Bess Myerson was scarcely known at all. Among her oldest friends were a pair of talented sisters who both had come to know her well. "Give me one word to describe Bess," one sister recently challenged the other.

"Hunger," was the instant reply. "Voracious hunger, always. And no compassion in her eyes. Her eyes are a bottomless pit. I think of a big, gaping, open mouth needing to get fed. She needs to be stroked, to get compliments. But it's never enough. She's perpetually hungry.

"Another striking thing is her constant lust for power, her perpetual search for the most important person in any room. Talk to her at a party, and she'll nod and say 'yes' and 'no,' but barely be looking at you. She tries, but she's worse than anyone I've ever known at hiding the fact that she is not hearing you or seeing you. She is always watching to see if someone more important just came in. She *lives* in anticipation."

And then at last, in 1966, at a party in Greenwich Village, someone very interesting came in, and Bess was introduced to Edward Irving Koch, by now safely back in the Democratic fold as leader of the liberal-minded Village Independent Democrats. Tall, bald, shy, and shrewd, Koch was an intensely ambitious Jewish bachelor, a lawyer of Bess's exact age and background, from as humble a Bronx family as her own. In him, eventually, Bess would find someone who could appease her constant hunger, at least for a while.

5

SHE STEPS

OUT

JULY 1965 WAS HOT AND STICKY. EVERY MORNING after her husband left for work, and she had finished feeding the baby, Nancy Herbert sat at the table in front of her kitchen window, where the good breeze came in, and dawdled over a second cup of coffee. The pretty new house was just off the Long Island Expressway near Union Turnpike and Utopia Parkway, with a Tudor-style second story, white brick below, and a corral fence. This part of Jamaica Estates was originally one large hillside property recently leveled and cut into eight lots, and workmen were still installing new sewer lines. Every day Nancy watched the big yellow bulldozer chew up dirt and asphalt. As summer came on, the good-looking young driver took off his shirt. Nancy admired his muscles glinting in the sun. One morning he walked up to the kitchen door. The car in her driveway was in his way, but he would be happy to move it if she gave him the keys. The baby gurgled in her high chair.

"Hey, how come you never ask me in for coffee?" he asked with a grin when he returned the keys.

Nancy smiled back. "So have a cup of coffee," she said, and unlatched the screen door.

AROUND THE TIME that Hortense Gabel left her job as city rent administrator to make way for the new Republican administration of Mayor Lindsay, Bess Myerson left Arnold Grant. Grant was a difficult person to live with, and frankly, so was his wife. The couple split for the first time in October 1965. They were back together by the following May. But by Christmas, 1966, Bess was in Mexico, filing for divorce. A Mexican divorce is a satisfyingly large document with bits of red ribbon and gold seals that, in the United States, can be literally not worth the paper it is written on.

Not long after the divorce was final, Bess moved back in with Grant, and they remained together on and off for a couple more years. They remarried in 1968, but not before Bess had signed the prenuptial agreement waiving all financial claims against her husband should the second marriage come apart. It did, and on July 14, 1970, Grant filed for divorce, asserting his rights under the agreement, and stating that Bess had gross assets of $1 million. He produced financial statements showing that, contrary to Bess's claim that she supported her aging parents with $5,000 to $10,000 annually, she had given them less than $2,500 in 1967 and 1968, and $1,200 in 1969. Court battles over money and property, and accusations of gross infidelity, went on for nearly two years, fueled by Grant's possession of some of Myerson's love letters, as well as her extremely frank and cynical diaries.

Myerson was a compulsive diarist. She wrote every night about her feelings. Sometimes she stopped whatever she was doing—even a tennis game, or a sightseeing tour—in order to go and confide her feelings to the locked pages. She said things like "Atlantic City is the toilet of America," and that she hoped Arnold Grant would die so she could get the money. The pages were filled with references to other men, and women, including her psychiatrist and dear friend Theodore Rubin, and to her wish to leave Arnold and her longing for his death, yearnings that appear to have set in only a few weeks after their second marriage. But the diaries are most pathetic in their constant disparaging references to her unhappy self, her horror of being alone, and her sense of utter emptiness about her own life.

During their second divorce, Grant gave her diaries to the *Daily News*.

OVER THE SAME five or six years that the Grants' marriage was unraveling—1965 to 1971—the plot was thickening, and only occasionally curdling, between Nancy Herbert and her macho bulldozer driver. Nancy's confidante at the time, and still her closest friend, was Judy Yaeger, then a housewife. "Do I remember Andy!" Judy says. "How could I forget him? He was just adorable."

That fall the Yaegers had bought the house diagonally behind the Herberts. Larry Yaeger was a surgeon. Each family had a five-year-old daughter and a three-year-old son, and the two young mothers were soon inseparable.

One day Nancy saw Andy's driver's license and was astonished to find he was only nineteen. He looked like a man, not a boy. But at least he had finished high school. Now he was working for his father, Mike Capasso, the sewer contractor.

"He was not *my* taste in gorgeous hunks," says Judy. "I like Paul Newman. Andy was an Italian street kid. Look at Ken Wahl in *Wiseguy;* he has the flavor of Andy. Also, Andy listens. And he's a flirt, in a subtle way." Most important, perhaps, "Andy was just always there."

Within a year Howard Herbert had moved out, and eventually he obtained an easy Mexican divorce. Nancy had no difficulty getting custody of their three children. For the next few years Andy continued to live at the nearby Forest Hills Inn. "But he was around a great deal," says Judy. She remembers a very appealing young man, naïve and inexperienced, socially bashful, "and madly in love with Nancy. Madly!" Capasso was always very fond of Nancy's children, and entirely at ease with them. He treated them like his nieces and nephews.

"You wouldn't believe the shyness, the air of innocence Andy had then. And he was in *awe* of Nancy. She was quite a piece of work, you know. Your typical JAP—intelligent, funny, bright, alert, and rather gorgeous. My husband used to say, 'Your problem is that Nancy Herbert is your friend and she's teaching you how to spend money.' "

Andy was very impressed with the older, well-educated, knowing woman, as well as seemingly in love. "As for Nancy—well, who the hell had ever met a nineteen-year-old sewer man? They were not around at Skidmore. But there was such sweetness about him then, it's just hard to believe he's behaved the way he has."

Andy's behavior, then and now, might not have seemed bad, or even unusual, to an Italian woman, but it was incomprehensible to nice Jewish girls like Nancy and Judy. Like the rest of him, the behavior reflected his machismo. The Latin male behaves in certain ways, and Capasso was not only Latin, he was Neapolitan. He is loyal to men and flirtatious with women, of whom two at a time is an acceptable, even traditional number—one a wife, one a mistress.

Andy, a third-generation sewer man, had never gotten along with his father. During Andy's boyhood his father had kept his family on an economic roller coaster—sometimes driving a Cadillac, sometimes too broke to buy food or pay the electric bill. Andy vowed to bring stability and prosperity to his mother and sisters, even if it meant destroying his father, which it almost did.

Judy Yaeger describes Mike Capasso, Andy's father, as "a little gnome. Andy looks like Clark Gable compared to him. He was a little rat out of the sewers." Andy often spoke to Nancy about his contempt for his father, and what his father did to his adored mother, a woman Judy called "the barefoot and pregnant type, always in the kitchen." For one thing, Andy's father had kept a mistress for forty years, a Jewish woman. Her existence was known to his wife and children, but never discussed. That's the way most Italian women are. "We have too much pride," they say.

The last time Judy saw Mike Capasso was at a Passover seder at Nancy's house. "He talked on and on about his Jewish girlfriend. He was quite open about it. Frankly, it made me very uncomfortable."

Nancy was not an original investor in Nanco, founded in 1968. But when Andy's father couldn't meet his payroll, she gave him

$11,000, which she had had in a savings account since the age of nine. "Needless to say, I never got it back," she says bitterly. "If I ever write the story of my life, I'm gonna call it *All Women Are Assholes*."

Early one morning, during the period after Herbert had moved out and when Andy was staying in Nancy's house from time to time, Nancy rang Judy's doorbell. "She was crying, and injured. Her thumb was in bad shape. My husband was a general surgeon, and he thought it was broken." The damaged thumb had to be set with a pin through it, and then encased in an elbow-high plaster cast.

Nancy first insisted she had fallen down the basement stairs while throwing out the Christmas tree. "Believe it or not, she's a kind of private person," says Judy. "I didn't even know she was involved with Andy until Howie moved out."

Eventually Nancy confessed that Andy had done it. The provocation? Always the worst crime in Andy's book: talking out of turn. In Andy's world, women did not discuss business or sex, at least not in front of the men. Nancy had learned that a relative of Capasso's had a girlfriend, and she had let the news slip to the man's wife. Andy had become enraged. Nancy, ignorant of the traditional Italian attitude about such matters, had unwittingly broken the unspoken code of *omertà*, and Andy had reacted like the primitive roughneck he was.

The thumb had to remain in a cast for several months, and that winter the only coat Nancy could wear was the sable one Andy had given her; it had a wide sleeve.

Sable coat! From a sewer worker? "Andy always told her it fell off a truck," says Judy.

"In those days Andy was very kind to me," Judy adds. "My marriage was in trouble. He knew—as I didn't, then—that my husband was involved with someone. He'd seen them together at the Forest Hills Inn. Andy went and talked to my husband. He made an attempt to patch things up between us. He didn't have to do that. He didn't tell *me*. He would *never* do that. That's not the Italian way. But he did go and talk to Larry. And I was grateful . . ."

During Nancy and Andy's first winter together, the house just across Grand Central Parkway from the Herbert house was bought by Donald and Marlene Manes. He was an engaging and politically ambitious Queens lawyer, she a teacher/housewife, and they had children the same ages as the Herbert and Yaeger kids. Nancy and Marlene Manes served on the PTA together, and the two families became good friends.

The previous year had marked the start of Manes's political rise. At thirty-one, he had been voted a member of the City Council in the same election that had made Lindsay mayor. More than twenty years later, during the unraveling of the corruption scandals that embroiled the Koch administration, it would be revealed that Manes had obtained his council seat illegally. In those days a city councilman was required to reside in New York City, but before they came to Jamaica Estates, the Maneses had lived out in Jericho, Long Island. Manes had falsified his papers and listed Marlene's parents' apartment in Electchester, a Flushing, Queens, housing development put up by the United Electrical Workers, as his own.

A few months after Nancy and Andy met, a major eruption occurred in the long-smoldering family feud between Andy Capasso and his father. The lifelong feud divides the family down the middle. The younger sister, Rosalie Mazzalupo, a teacher married to an architect, and the former Josephine Corillo, their mother, side with Andy; sister Sally sides with her dad. Sally's son "Flash" eventually became his uncle Andy's general manager. Since 1979 Andy and Mike have not spoken. There is such bad blood between them that they vow they will never speak, even though everybody knows Mike is very ill with emphysema.

At age twenty Andy quit working for his father and took a job with a competitor as an equipment renter and bulldozer operator. Three years later he started his own company, Nanco, with rented equipment. Until he could afford office space, he kept his books and records in his room at the Forest Hills Inn. Then he went to see a man called Jack Farber.

Self-made bankers are rare. One of the rarest is Jack Farber, a genial and charming man born in 1910 who is president of the Flushing National Bank, the nation's largest privately owned national bank, valued at $80–$100 million. Farber owns it all. There are no stockholders. Farber's father started out in life as an itinerant peddler, and Farber himself started out as a caddy. He earned enough money on the golf course to put himself through Lafayette College, class of 1931, and Brooklyn Law School, at night, sitting in the empty seats of absent students who, unlike Farber, *had* paid their tuition.

Flushing National Bank was formed in 1963 by local merchants with $1 million in capital. Farber took it over in 1965, by which time it had gone into the black in only twenty months, a very rapid success rate. Farber refers to his bank as the "House that Jack Built."

In 1968, Farber recalls, "this guy walked in to see me. He had dirty fingernails and torn overalls. He wanted to borrow money on his bulldozer." Farber, a keen judge of character, said he would make the loan on one condition—that the man's wife come in and co-sign the note. Nancy Herbert signed. She was not yet Andy's wife, but she was an officer and employee of Nanco.

Andy was an unbelievably hard worker, starting at 6:00 A.M., and not quitting until 8:00 P.M., after which he'd clean off the equipment for the next day. He ran his company well and paid his debts on time. By 1970, Nanco was solid enough to be bonded, which meant it could bid on city contracts.

Farber was happy to remain Andy's banker for a decade or so. But about 1979, Farber gently told Andy that he was getting too big for Farber; perhaps it would be best if he found someone else. In fact, Farber had decided he did not like some of the "connections" he'd heard Andy now had, and so he made a seat-of-the-pants decision to cut loose from this particular client. Farber and Nancy remained friends. Andy met Bess Myerson the following year.

Capitalism is catching. The year after Jack Farber bankrolled Andy Capasso, Nancy Herbert and Judy Yaeger decided to go into business together as maker-marketers of handmade accessories. Nancy handled the finances, and Judy was the designer. "We were young and poor, but Nancy knew her way around every store and every showroom in New York."

Yaeger & Herbert was born as a consequence of Nancy taking Judy to the wholesale showrooms of Coblentz to shop for handbags. When they got home, Judy crocheted an appealing little handbag in metallic yarn. Next day they took it to Bendel. "I love it!" the buyer raved. "I'll take a dozen in gold and a dozen in silver."

Donald Manes drew up incorporation papers at no charge, and Yaeger & Herbert was off and running. "I would make the sample," says Judy. "Then I would *schlepp* the yarn to our bunch of grandmothers who did the crocheting. They were so happy to be able to earn some money they would kiss our feet. Andy helped us to pack boxes and *schlepped* them to airfreight."

The tyro entrepreneurs were written up in the fashion pages of *The New York Times*, and the business prospered until Nancy and Andy married and moved to the new home they'd purchased in Greenvale, Long Island.

In the months before the wedding, Nancy's mother used to call Judy and wail, "You can't let her do it! You gotta *do something*. How can my daughter marry this sewer man?"

"Actually my parents did like Andy," says Nancy. "After they got over me running off with an Italian. In those days Andy could charm the bow right out of your hair."

"It had nothing to do with Andy's being Italian and Catholic," says Judy. "To her mother it was a class problem. Andy was a high school person, and she was Skidmore."

"It wasn't just my mother," says Nancy. "*I* wasn't so sure. Andy didn't have any money. It was not the smartest thing to do. Also, I was a snob in those days." She had had a crush on a Princeton premed student whom she met on a Fire Island beach while she was working as a mother's helper and he had a summer job at the local drugstore. Jerry invited Nancy down to Princeton for football games. He came to her senior prom. All the other girls "were very impressed with us because I was valedictorian, and he was premed and an Orthodox Jew. Now he's an OB/GYN someplace mid-Island," she laughs.

In the end, the deciding factor had nothing to do with money or class. Nancy heard Andy had taken up with an airline stewardess. Then one day she walked in on them in Andy's hotel room. She laughs again with rueful hindsight. "So that pushed me into it." It might have pushed another sort of woman out of it. But Nancy was not analytical or calculating; she was passionate and naïve. Without marriage, there was no commitment on either side. After marriage, things would be different.

After their small wedding at Judy's house, both families and what Nancy calls "some of my husband's Italian friends from the sewer business in East New York" went to a party at a Roslyn, Long Island, restaurant, after which the couple retired to their new home in Greenvale, a honeymoon at that point seeming superfluous.

The Herbert children were ages eleven, nine, and seven, and Andy twenty-six the year he became their stepfather. It would be difficult to overstate the gusto with which he took on the job. His devotion and generosity were entire, and the children adored him. He paid for all their expenses, including some private schooling and, later, college. He was always available for Little League, for teacher-counseling sessions, for long talks and picnics and family vacations. He bought a car for each child when he or she came of age. When Steven was old enough to be bar mitzvahed, he wanted his stepfather to participate, so Andy learned to recite all the necessary Hebrew prayers.

In turn, Nancy had been very much a part of Nanco from the beginning. When Judy saw that NANCY was painted on the fronts of all the trucks, "I thought it was like hanging your baby's shoes on the rear-view mirror." The Greenvale house had a real office in it, and Nancy did a lot of work there. Judy remembers going along with Nancy one time to submit a bid, a sealed contract, on one of Andy's jobs.

Managing Nanco was a full-time occupation, but Andy still found time to do some work on the house. It was a very pretty, modest, sweet, and charming house, says Judy. The family lived there two years. By the end of the first year, Nancy was pregnant. That same year, 1971, their friend City Councilman Manes was elected Queens borough president. Three years later he would be named Queens Democratic leader as well.

Michael Capasso was born in 1972, and his sister, Andrea, in 1974. By that time the Capassos had moved to estate-size quarters in posh, sedate Old Westbury. The family could be described as ferociously upwardly mobile, unabashedly nouveaux, and très riches. They had bought a very large Georgian house on three acres with seven bedrooms, eight baths, and extensive gardens. Andy's men put in a tennis court, and the whole family took lessons. They even had their own pro. Daughter Debbie Herbert got so good that in her freshman year at Emory University in Atlanta, she was made captain of the tennis team.

Andy was making real money, and Nancy saw her faith in him justified. By 1976, Nanco had twenty-five employees and $4 million in annual sales. The year before, Andy had bought the family a beachfront condominium in Westhampton Beach. Later he bought a winter condo in Palm Beach, and still later, a second Florida condo.

The Capassos sometimes flew friends along with the family to their Florida home. Everybody traveled first class. Nancy particularly enjoyed the vacations with the Manes family. "Donnie was meat and potatoes, he was grass roots. He liked having a million balls in the air, a real circus! He was like a big teddy bear, the most jolly, funny, happy man! When we were in Palm Beach it was always a laugh a minute."

The Capassos saw somewhat less of the Maneses after leaving Jamaica Estates, but they had a new neighbor. Two blocks from their Old Westbury house lived Andy's good friend and patron Matty "The Horse" Ianniello and his family. Mafia watchers identify Ianniello as then a *soldato* and later a *capo* in the Genovese organized-crime family. Born in 1920, he was six feet tall and weighed well over two hundred pounds, hence "The Horse." Active principally in New York and northern New Jersey, Ianniello had long been known as a top money-maker for the mob, so much so that his importance was always greater than his rank. He was a specialist in loan-sharking and pornography trafficking, with sidelines in restaurants, nightclubs, and garbage dumping. Andy Capasso was a frequent visitor to the Ianniello home at all hours of the day and night. Nancy saw her neighbor far less frequently, but she describes him as "a very sweet, dear man."

When Judy Yaeger was divorced, not long after the Capassos got married, she decided to go to law school, and eventually became a top-flight Manhattan matrimonial lawyer. When later asked, as she often was, about Andy's rather sudden wealth, she replied with a question of her own: "How does somebody who is a city contractor, which means he's working with closed bids, make money? He has *connections*. Too bad, but only someone with *connections* can succeed in that business."

Connections would appear to be a euphemism for mob, or Mafia. It is certainly true, one of the well-known sordid facts of Apple life, that anyone involved in construction in New York City has to pay off the mob. "It's simple," says the writer Nick Pileggi, perhaps the shrewdest of modern Mafia historians. "The mob controls two unions that are necessary to any construction project—the hod carriers and the teamsters. The hod carriers, Local Six and Local Ten, the guys who put bricks and mortar in wheelbarrows and wheel them to the bricklayers, are run by the Genovese family. Teamsters Local Two Eighty-two members deliver anything you can think of to a construction site, from lunch pails to steel girders. Importantly, they deliver cement. Teamsters Two Eighty-two is controlled by the Gambino family. So if someone was looking to build a cement plant, say, he'd have to deal with both Genovese and Gambino. That's the way it is."

The Capasso marriage was generally a happy one, but its tempo was scarcely *legato*. They fought with some regularity. Judy Yaeger describes them as "explosive fighters. Then they loved to make up. With Nancy, there was a teasing quality to her fighting. Once she provoked him by stealing a thousand dollars from his pants pocket."

"I went out and bought a ring to cheer myself up," Nancy later acknowledged. "Andy was never easy," she added. "But we had some wonderful, four-star vacations . . . that's the only time I knew where he was! Andy could be cute and loving. He could also be disinterested, disinvolved, and disappear. . . ."

IN THE YEARS that the Capassos were getting married and the Grants getting unmarried, the life of Hortense Gabel was busier than ever before. As a public servant, she had set up a city technical-assistance unit of the sort that was vitally needed by small community groups that wanted to deal with housing problems. Now, as a consultant to the Ford Foundation, she could provide such assistance across the country.

"Kennedy and Johnson had just invented the liberal mortgage," says Lou Winnick, a housing expert who brought Gabel to the Ford Foundation, "and hundreds of nonprofits sprung up to take advantage of it. Horty would give them advice on calculating rents, getting the mortgage, setting up the organization. It was all very complicated and people were making all kinds of blunders. HUD had a very high loss rate in mortgages: undercollection of rent, construction cost overruns—everything."

In the same period, Gabel was advising other states on how to set up their own housing programs. She had always been good at dealing with government and finding ways to get money to the people. She was efficient at running meetings and drawing people out so that they didn't feel bossed around.

By spring 1968, about the time that the Capassos formed Nanco and Bess Myerson remarried Arnold Grant, Gabel was in San Francisco helping set up a new housing agency, the Center for Community Change. She recalls working very late in her office one night, and bursting into tears at the news that Robert Kennedy had been shot. She was invited to attend his funeral, but decided that finishing her work for the center was the best memorial to him, a decision she later regretted.

The Center for Community Change was a national charitable organization funded by churches and foundations, Ford in particular. It provided technical assistance to community groups of poor people working to improve their neighborhoods, and this assistance consisted of getting government funding, helping negotiate with government agencies, meeting government requirements, and providing expertise on housing and job issues.

Andrew Mott, vice president for urban development at the CCC, and Gabel's deputy, calls her "the most extraordinary person I've ever met in my life. Her career was incredible. She is a true heroine, one of the great national leaders in the housing field," despite the odds of being a woman in a man's field, and despite having been classified as "industrially blind" at birth, which meant she had double vision past four feet.

Gabel was the "best boss I ever had. I've never seen anyone more effective in meetings. If she said a meeting was an hour, the work was done in an hour. . . . She had an ego, but she was sensitive to other people, not self-centered, and not naïve at all about housing issues."

At CCC Gabel worked on three major programs. In Watts, she helped a black group negotiate with the state's highway department. Instead of destroying several hundred houses in the path of a proposed freeway, the department agreed to move them to vacant lots, where they were renovated. CCC negotiated a combination of state and federal funds for the project. Mott believes this had never been done before. Houses were also shifted to make room for the expansion of Los Angeles International Airport.

In Chicago, she helped a black group, the Woodlawn Organization, negotiate with the University of Chicago to cooperate in developing land next to the school. The university not only loaned Woodlawn $800,000 to develop the land, but also sold the land to the group in a separate financial arrangement.

In South Carolina, Gabel worked with the Presbyterian Church to develop eleven hundred acres outside of Columbia into the racially integrated new town of Harbison. The setup was similar to scatter-site housing in New York City in that the town was to have both low-income and middle-class residents. The local church, a black congregation, owned the land and asked CCC how to integrate a project there. Harbison was one of the earliest "new towns," and the only one in the South. Earlier ones, in Columbia, Maryland, and Reston, Virginia, built by private developers, were racially integrated but didn't have as many low-income people as Harbison did. John de Monchaux, a consultant to the project, later became dean of the MIT School of Architecture and Planning. He describes Gabel as "extraordinarily creative, humane, and quick-thinking. She's a problem-solver."

Gabel soon became vice-president of CCC, which added administrative home-office duties to those involving the major projects in South Carolina, Los Angeles, and Chicago. At the same time, she was completing a complicated housing report commissioned by Nassau County, Long Island. To endure all the exhausting travel this required, she learned to keep herself going with truly prodigious quantities of coffee and cigarettes.

6

PLOTS

THICKEN

IN FEBRUARY 1969, MAYOR JOHN LINDSAY AN-
nounced he was naming Bess Myerson Grant to
head the city's new Department of Consumer Affairs, equivalent to giving her cabinet status in his
administration. The $25,000-a-year salary repre-
sented a major financial sacrifice, but in her zeal to
serve the city she loved she was giving up her television income entirely,* she said, something between $125,000 and $200,000 a year.

President Lyndon Johnson had set the precedent
for appointing a consumer watchdog when he selected Betty Furness. Indeed, Furness had been
Lindsay's own first choice, but she turned down his
offer for two reasons. Mainly, after two years in
Washington, she wanted to spend some time with
her new husband, Les Midgley, producer of Walter

*Well, not entirely. Much later it was revealed that Grant had negotiated ongoing "consult-
ing" fees from Colgate-Palmolive and certain other commercial TV sponsors, and these
continued to pay off a decade or more after Bess had left the air.

Cronkite's evening news show. Second, she had been tipped off that the "new" department, which was really a consolidation of two old departments with a new label stuck on, was probably rife with corruption. Why should she risk being the person sitting there when the lid could blow off at any moment? Furness quietly advised Myerson to turn it down too. Instead, Bess went on to win national acclaim in the job.

She started small. One day, New Yorkers woke up to find the former Miss America on TV explaining why Mr. Clean cost more in the big, so-called economy-size bottles than in smaller bottles. But in the next four years, Myerson would become the most visible city official after the mayor. The press, recognizing her as good copy, printed just about anything she had to say. Soon she was on the screen three or four times a week, going after parking garages that damaged cars, butchers who sold phony veal cutlets, and "computer schools" that had no computers. She dared to attack the Better Business Bureau for siphoning off complaints from her agency. She even went to Washington to denounce Good Housekeeping's so-called seal of approval.

When Myerson took over the department, 350 employees, 160 of them inspectors, were working in or out of the first three floors at 80 Lafayette Street. Like a new football coach, she infused and energized the place with team spirit. She set up a handpicked Consumer Action Team (CAT), swiftly nicknamed Grant's Guerrillas. They were mufti-clad inspectors who daily made surprise raids in high-complaint areas of the city. She set up a telephone hotline and now, for the first time, New York's always vocal populace—the gulled, the diddled, the benighted, foolish, and wise—found there was a place they could complain to twenty-four hours a day.

Myerson's assistant from day one was Henry Stern, then a young lawyer on the city payroll, subsequently president of the City Council, and today a veteran municipal servant and New York City's parks commissioner. Betty Furness says Stern was the "brilliant Svengali" who really ran the department.

With becoming modesty, Stern says Bess Myerson is "the most remarkable person I ever met. Even then, she was into art, into furniture design, into music, into clothing—she was knowledgeable in so many fields. And she was so persuasive with merchants!

Partly it was her beauty, of course. But still, she has a gift of persuasion that's unique, an almost uncanny ability to reach people."

Not everybody was charmed. Organized foodbiz fought back hard, claiming, not unreasonably, that Myerson "sensationalized" the issues. A blast in *Modern Grocer* accused her of not doing her homework before she "blew her top." But Bess was learning fast and well. By the end of her first year, Mayor Lindsay had signed the Consumer Protection Act, which was adjudged toughest in the nation. It gave the city the right to prosecute any business or person found to be victimizing the public through deceptive trade practices, and it provided legal avenues for class-action suits and claims for mass restitution. This last could make fraud unprofitable as well as illegal. Instead of merely handing out modest fines of $15 to $100, the city could now sue merchants on behalf of victimized customers, and could collect and disburse funds.

In the beginning, the press still treated Myerson as Miss America. She was praised for not refreshing her lipstick during the day, and her measurements were cited in interviews. Friends were quick to warn that her celebrity image threatened to trivialize her work, and they urged a lower profile. Instead, she chose to use her image and allow a lot of personalized publicity. "Building image: I worked on that all the time," she has said. "After all, image was the product I sold."

In one early interview, she emphasized her image as an amateur. "Some of the things I accomplish are because of my innocence rather than my astuteness. I am not a serious politician, and I just don't have time for political red tape. If we need something here, I'll often pay for it myself rather than wade through the bureaucracy." So saying, as cameras clicked, she wrote out a personal check to a Harvard Business School student who had complained at not being paid for time spent conducting a supermarket survey.

Highlighting her image as a forty-five-year-old workaholic, Bess said that her new job had changed her way of life. The perennial "night person" who never rose before 10:00 A.M. now showed up at 8:00 meetings at Gracie Mansion. She confessed to reporters that she had given away all her opera and symphony tickets so she could get to bed early. Each evening between 6:30 and 7:00, she added, she would speak to either her sisters or her parents. On an at-home night, she went on, she liked to read something from the Grants' own Kennedy library; she and Arnold had collected every book ever written by or about that image-wracked family. She also said in October 1969 that she was taking medication several times a day in consequence of a "serious intestinal operation" she'd undergone the year before.

After she was finally divorced from Arnold Grant in April 1971, and her daughter, Barra, had moved to California, Bess said she often returned to her office late at night in T-shirt and blue jeans to read letters from citizens who had been swindled.

BY SPRING 1969 Sukhreet Gabel, whom we last saw in the maternity ward of St. Clare's Hospital, had had a year of nurse's training at Bronx Community College, mostly low-paid drudge work. When she wasn't bathing patients and emptying bedpans, she lived in a tiny two-room apartment in her parents' building.

Sukhreet has always said that the "natural nurse" in the family is her father. When he walked the dog every day, he went a couple of blocks out of his way to buy the newspaper from a stand owned by a hunchback. Though famous as the family cheapskate, he always gave the newspaper vendor a little extra, saying, "Don't bother with the change." When the hunchback went to the hospital, Milton Gabel visited him there.

Hortense Gabel had finally quit her terrible cigarette habit, but not in time to avoid a severe heart attack in the late spring of 1969 that would require a year's convalescence. During that time, doctors made it clear that her life was going to have to change drastically, and that her traveling days were over.

When Milton Gabel called his daughter to report Hortense's heart attack, he asked her to wait a day or two before visiting. At New York Hospital, she found her mother semicomatose. Sukhreet recalls emerging from the sickroom and seeing her aunt Sybil sitting with a friend in the waiting room. Both women were "all dressed in black, like two vultures, or crows."

"She's very sick," said Sukhreet, "but I think she's going to make it."

"You don't know how sick she is," cawed the two black crows.

Sukhreet felt insulted. "I was dating a cardiovascular surgeon who had taught me how to read an EKG. I'd spent that very day nursing someone with a similar case."

Sukhreet's optimistic prognosis proved correct. Fourteen months later, her mother was able to return to work, and a less arduous regimen had been found. On August 15, 1970, Mayor Lindsay awarded Hortense Gabel an interim appointment as a New York City civil-court judge, filling out the unexpired term of another judge, who had retired. Her courtroom was in the civil-courts building at 111 Centre Street, just across the way from Bess Myerson's offices at 80 Lafayette Street.

Sukhreet had in fact dropped out of nursing school in spring 1969, after one year's training, finding the work every bit as boring as her parents had predicted. In March 1970 she found a well-paying, year-long job as a United Nations tour guide, then did her brief stint in a mob-owned massage parlor. She quit that because professional work as a sexual mechanic was ruining her private life. "After seeing a man ejaculate four or five times in a day, you didn't want to see it again at home. You'd even prefer sex with a woman, or masturbation," she said.

By the early spring of 1971, Sukhreet had amassed $7,000 and was ready to set off on her long-dreamed-of trip around the world. Her itinerary was a travel agent's dream: ten days in California, ten days in Hawaii, a month in Japan, two weeks in Taiwan, two weeks in Hong Kong, a month in the Philippines, a week in Burma, two weeks in South Vietnam, followed by nine glorious months in India and Pakistan, months so vital and nourishing to her inner spirit that she does not want to talk about them. Someday she will write a book.

NOW THAT BESS was single again, she could do what she wanted with her evenings. She spent many of them amid a new group of friends, the close, lively circle that orbited around the leader of the Greenwich Village reform Democrats, Congressman Ed Koch. Among them were Bess's deputy Henry Stern and his wife, Peggy, and Daniel Wolf, editor and part-owner of *The Village Voice*, and his wife, Rhoda. Another member of the group was Herbert Rickman, a nonpracticing attorney active in Village politics. Like Koch, unmarried, but unlike Koch, an admitted homosexual, Rickman was a useful escort for and companion to Bess, and they swiftly formed an intense friendship. His Bronx background was not unlike her own, and they particularly enjoyed speaking Yiddish together.

"We're like an extended family," Rickman once told a reporter. "We see one another at least once a week. We go to the movies together. We go to Chinatown to eat together, or to the Parkway or the Lower East Side. Sometimes we have dinner at one home or another. Eddie is a great cook in that apartment of his on Washington Place."

A few years later, when Koch was elected mayor of the Apple, he appointed Rickman his "special assistant" responsible for liaison between City Hall and the gay community, the troubled garment industry, the theater world, and other special-interest groups. A jubilant Myerson held the Bible at his swearing-in. When Rickman praised her for being his personal confidante, adviser, and interior decorator, Bess replied, accurately, "I'm like the housemother."

Being housemother and pals with an extended family of smart, sophisticated political activists suited Myerson's temperament. She found being a dedicated career woman far more congenial than being a dedicated wife, and blossomed in her new role. She was fortunate too in the caliber of her professional associates. Consumer Affairs began to attract a young, appealing, energetic, and idealistic staff, and Bess deployed them well. Most of her executives were under thirty. Four were smart, sassy-looking female lawyers who wore long hair, miniskirts, and chain belts. Her number two, the dedicated Stern, was thirty-four when he started working for Bess. Her executive director, Simon Lazarus, was twenty-eight. Bruce Ratner, who eventually succeeded her, later alleged, "I remember doing investigations that Lindsay didn't necessarily like, but she never let that get in her way." Philip Schrag, another then-young lawyer who was the department's first consumer advocate, confirms that Myerson was not in the least a figurehead. "She mastered all the information, and she made final decisions and judgment calls. I was awed by her gutsiness and intuitiveness. She was a great hero."

Once Myerson had gained enforcement and rule-making powers,

her department began to hold well-attended public hearings. Her speeches promised strict enforcement, and her staff delivered. The following year, Myerson did even better, introducing unit pricing and open dating to city supermarkets, despite vigorous opposition from the New York State Food Merchants Association, which warned it would add $50 million to the food bill in labeling costs alone. By the end of that year, she had set up the neighborhood complaint centers in Forest Hills, East Harlem, West Harlem, and on the Lower East Side.

A year-end interview in *The New York Times* pictured the commissioner at a desk dominated by a paperweight Sisyphus pushing a huge boulder uphill. The reference was to the Lindsay administration's fiscal crisis, which meant that Consumer Affairs's $3.5 million budget had not been increased in two years. What's more, paid staff had declined by about 14 percent, and some employees earned less than the poverty-level wage of $5,000. The department's consumer-education section was now entirely staffed by volunteers, and Bess bemoaned that she could deal with only one in twenty complaints that came her way. Nonetheless, it was a huge consumer-affairs operation for its time, and a clear demonstration of Lindsay's commitment to consumer issues. Despite the budget crunch, creative innovations to help consumers continued. That year the legal department had published a free brochure: "How to Sue in Small Claims Court."

Myerson took her marching orders from Lindsay's press secretary, Tom Morgan, and he recalls her as "wonderful, smart, cooperative, efficient, and effective. She was not only very competent, she was always on the team."

As consumer-affairs commissioner, Myerson's powers to inspect and fine and prosecute all derived from the City Council. Over the years, she was careful to maintain excellent relations with council members, and as a result, the council never turned down any of her requests for new laws and regulations. Her show-biz glamour also served Lindsay well, and he often asked her to stand in for him at public and administrative functions. She did it beautifully.

In 1972, to raise money, Bess went back into commercial television with a syndicated daily morning show, *What Every Woman Wants to Know*. Each program included interviews with consumer advocates, a product demonstration, and a brief editorial that the *Times* described as often very tough, and "occasionally radical." Heretofore silent on issues of special concern to women, Bess now used her show to plead for nationwide laws legalizing abortion.

The program had commercial sponsors, primarily Du Pont, but it also advertised an exercise salon, a patent medicine, and a school for refrigerator repairmen. Some thought it unseemly that a public servant appear on a sponsored show. Bess said she had chosen commercial over public TV because it paid better and reached a wider audience. She also denied that she was doing the show to keep her TV career alive as a job option in case Lindsay became a lame duck before the next election, in 1973.

All of Myerson's personal television fees were channeled back to her department through a nonprofit fund, an arrangement origi- nally made by her former husband, Arnold Grant. Myerson acting alone has never been known to turn back anything. When she made a series of private, high-level appeals for bonds for Israel in the homes of wealthy Manhattanites, for example, she was known for always stopping first in the kitchen to collect her fee before entering the living room to deliver her pitch.

By midsummer 1971, Myerson was of sufficient national impor- tance to rate a major cover story and takeout on "a consumer's best friend" in *Life* magazine. In hindsight one can see that the period from the *Life* story, in July, to her resignation from the Department of Consumer Affairs, in March 1973, marked the zenith of Myer- son's civic popularity and professional success. Thereafter the curve led very, very gradually at first, and then precipitately, downhill.

ONE OF THE millions who pored over the *Life* story with interest was a young housewife in Greenvale, Long Island. Nancy Capasso was happy in her new home, and expecting a baby. She and Andy had pooled their money to buy the Greenvale house, her contribution being $25,000, her share of the profits on the sale of the Herbert house in Jamaica Estates. Her marriage was going reasonably well. There was an occasional wild fight, but the making up afterward was always very sweet. Her only real complaint was that Andy did not stay home at night, and some nights did not come home. The first time this had happened was only three days after their wedding. Andy offered no explanation of where he had been, and made plain to Nancy that he considered it bad form of her to ask.

One who almost certainly did not read the *Life* article was twenty-two-year-old Sukhreet Gabel, who was spending the summer in the Philippines. A month after Sukhreet took off, Judge Gabel published her third housing study since going on the bench. This one, a result of her service on the Temporary Commission of Local Government of New York State, was a pioneering national study of reasons why ghetto landlords abandon their buildings, and the patterns such abandonment takes. She had earlier published a monograph on New York City's rehabilitation experiments. Another housing study, prepared for the Fund for the City of New York, had recommended setting up a new public corporation to advise small landlords on their problems.

Bess Myerson continued doing a spectacular job at Consumer Affairs. Says Esther Kartaganer, deputy to Betty Furness, who eventually took over the department, "She had an itty-bitty budget, and she really was Saint Bess. The people there loved their jobs. So what if the boss was a little nuts? Then Betty Furness followed in her footsteps, and she became Saint Betty." But it was Saint Bess who had established the department's image: energetic, creative, vigilant, and incorruptible.

Another old friend, Amy Green, a former beauty editor and department-store executive, recalls Myerson as "fanatical about the consumer job. She put every fiber of her being into it. She always loved New York—the energy that comes up through the streets here, the fact that it's a war. She loved the difficulty of New York, and the challenge of making it better."

As for the private Bess Myerson, opinions have always been rather sharply divided. Green, a loyalist to the end, knows several people who asked Bess for help, and "she was always there financially, and spiritually, for her friends." Green's key words for Bess are *proud* and *decent*. "*Proud* means you have self-respect and don't air your private problems in public. *Decent* means that she was a victim. Decent women always get it in the neck."

Do they? Some of Myerson's longtime friends see her pattern of repeated victimization by men differently. Says one, a man, "She had so much beauty and sexual desirability, she could have had any man she wanted. *Any.* She has what every man looks for: beauty, sensuality, brains, dependability, wit, responsibility. So you could describe her life as a quest for Mr. Wrong. You could say she feels a guilt that deserves and demands punishment. For some reason, one often finds this quality among actresses and desirable women. They frequently make self-punishing relationships."

Another friend of Bess's is a stunning and successful business-woman and TV producer. One day the two lean-limbed beauties were tanning themselves on the beach. "We didn't know one another all that well," the friend recalls, "but suddenly Bess was telling me the entire story of her life, a very, very detailed account of her travails, her sufferings, her torments as Miss America. She kept saying, 'If only I could be like you!' Then she'd tell some more of her troubles. Then, again: 'If only I could be like you! Then I could really have *done something* with my life,' et cetera. Believe me, it was very, very flattering to have this absolutely gorgeous dame saying these things to me."

Except that this friend, like others who have heard the same patter, got a strong sense that it was all another of Bess's rehearsed routines, that she had told the same story many times before, and that "at bottom she was entirely insincere. So, when the pitch finally came, and it was always to invest money in one of Bess's projects, I backed away."

This woman was scarcely alone in her negative attitudes toward Myerson. Many members of Mayor Lindsay's high command could not abide her. Says one, speaking for many, "I found her arrogant, overbearing, and a person who would not play by the rules. She overran her budget, then tried to blame others. She hired people she didn't have a 'line' for. . . . But she was a star, so she got away with all of it."

Why is Myerson so actively disliked in so many different quarters? A longtime friend of hers, the distinguished psychoanalyst Dr. Erika Padan Freeman, once mused aloud: "She is disliked by some for 'class reasons.' She was not very well brought up. She didn't go to Sarah Lawrence. The sort of people who did go often disliked her for her abrasive behavior, devoid of little niceties, which was shaped by the class from which she came.

"She is also disliked for being someone who one day gives you a big hello, and the next day doesn't know who you are. But remember what this celebrity-loving nation does to our celebrities. First we make them into false gods. Then we give them no privacy. Instead we take an attitude—you are ours; you are *not entitled* to privacy. So, when one does not say hello, it need not be snobbery. It could be an attempt to preserve a shred of privacy. Or it could be she's not wearing her glasses. Or that she's in a bad mood. Or it could be her inadequate upbringing. She was never taught: Don't ignore your old friends just because you are surrounded by new friends. This could explain her well-known behavior at large parties. She holds on to you, literally, with her famous grip on your hands or shoulder. Then she is distracted, and moves on to the next person, and you feel dumped. Many people do this, focus on only one person at a time; politicians are famous for it. Bess is famous for it.

"To seduce and dump became Myerson's style. She was known for it. She did it to everybody. People who are upwardly mobile tend to do this, and so do people who have no original sense of peer group, no solid social base. Clubmen and Junior League types don't do it; they don't have to. They live among people they have known all their lives.

"Also, high-powered women in particular tend to be abrupt, or to seem so. They don't have the social network of the ladies-who-lunch. One time I was receiving an award at a dinner near Columbia University, and I asked Bess to be there. It turned out that Bess was receiving an award of her own that same evening, at the Plaza Hotel. Nonetheless Bess did a long *schlepp* to my dinner party, with no limo. She had to run back quickly, because she too was being honored that night. But she stayed long enough to make a charming little speech. As usual, she had been willing to extend herself and to lend the glitter of her name to help a good cause, no matter how personally inconvenient. Glittering names are not easy to get, especially when there is no great glamour to the cause.

"Yes, Bess rarely gives parties, and she entertains purposively, like Bill Buckley. But all politicians do this. Some have a bit more grace, some less."

IN AUGUST 1971, Republican mayor John Lindsay had switched political parties and, on December 28, in Miami, Florida, he declared his intention to run for president. No one understood Lindsay's state of mind better than Theodore H. White, who wrote,

> To Florida he brought the inner torment of six years as Mayor of New York, as well as the exaggerated reputation of the city's breakdown that the national media had hung on him. John Lindsay had lived with street killings, and knew the statistics of what loose guns and Saturday-night specials were doing to his town. He had learned what sorrow, sadness and tragedy were milled through the abortion walk-ups of his city. He knew the havoc of drugs, the pestilence of mugging, the crackle of race tension; and the institutional poverty of a great city starved of money, reckoning that each raid on Hanoi cost as much as might renew a slum block in the South Bronx. Above all, he was convinced of his historic duty to bring an end to the exclusion of blacks in a white society.*

Lindsay's sense of mission and his uncommon humanity notwithstanding, many of his political advisers opposed his presidential bid on purely pragmatic grounds. It would pit the brand-new Democrat against such established party stalwarts as Senators Muskie, McGovern, Jackson, and Hubert H. Humphrey. Even if Lindsay should stage an upset and win in Florida, there was still no guarantee that labor leaders and other Democratic heavyweights would rally to support his candidacy. A Florida state senator summed up the situation well when he said, "In America, a candidate without a chance has a chance. This is particularly true in Florida."

Even in Florida, Lindsay's support was less than solid. One bloc of voters badly in need of shoring-up was the Jewish population. Political entrail gazers had long whispered that Lindsay's hiring and

---

* *The Making of the President—1972* (NewYork: Atheneum, 1973), p. 90.

spotlighting of Myerson had been aimed at strengthening his shaky support among New York's Jewish voters, who mistrusted the mayor's policies on housing and education.

The people around Lindsay were always sharply divided on Bess. Her detractors described her as "a thoroughly evil woman. Yes, she was hurt early. I think it was the terrible anti-Semitism which she encountered as Miss America. At a point when she was at her most vulnerable, her dreams were crushed and spat on." Others, more cynical, had always suspected that Myerson over the years exaggerated her youthful head-on collision with anti-Semitism to gain sympathy among Jews. For them, the proof was her behavior in regard to the Florida trip.

Lindsay decided to announce his presidential bid there only after Myerson volunteered to accompany him to the heavily Jewish precincts of Miami and Miami Beach. Without her promise to walk with him among her people, they say, the WASP mayor never would have been so foolish as to make the excursion into possibly hostile territory. At the very last moment, they say, she canceled, and Lindsay had to make the scheduled shopping-center visit alone. The crowd was small and the reception mixed; several times he was heckled by visiting or former New Yorkers. Later, a Piper Cub flew along the beach towing a banner: LINDSAY SPELLS TSURIS (Yiddish for troubles, grief). All chances of a presidential bid—if indeed he ever had any, which is questionable—were shot down.

To the Lindsay people, Bess's nonappearance was disloyalty of the most reprehensible kind. He had been her patron/sponsor; he had made her his commissioner. They either did or did not have a more intimate relationship. Stories abounded. Certainly it is true that when a dazzlingly beautiful woman turns on the thousand-watt charm to get something she wants, then turns it off again, a man can never forgive her. At any rate, Lindsay, who is foremost a gentleman, has for years refused to discuss her.

Anti-Bess people believe Myerson canceled the trip "for reasons of cold ambition. She did not want to impair or erode her tremendous standing with Jews by appearing with the despised WASP Lindsay." These Jews were her own constituency, when she was ready to run. And the Queen of the Jews wanted to preserve their adoration intact.

Henry Stern sees the whole matter differently. "She didn't go because she realized this was not for her. She didn't want to walk down the beach. She told me, 'No. That's Atlantic City all over again. I won't play that game.'

"I think at one point she said she would go, and then thought better of it," Stern adds. "She realized he wasn't going anywhere as a candidate, and it would be ridiculous for her to support him.

"But the Lindsay people *were* very angry." They decided to punish Bess by firing her invaluable deputy Stern, using the excuse that he was alienating the business community. One by one, four applicants for Stern's job came to the commissioner to be interviewed. Says Stern, "Bess managed to work it so that not one of them wanted the job!" Thus did she reward her faithful Henry, in a manner reminiscent of Portia's trickery in *The Merchant of Venice*.

IN 1972 HUNTER COLLEGE set up its hall of fame. At a dinner in the old Americana Hotel ballroom, Judge Hortense Gabel became one of its first one hundred inductees. Bess Myerson, ineligible because she had already been honored singly by her alma mater, took a prominent part in the gala ceremonies and the anointment of her sisters.

In April 1972, one year after setting out on her world tour, Sukhreet Gabel flew from India to London, then returned briefly to New York to check up on how her mother was doing. She need not have worried. Hortense's health was apparently holding up and, the previous December Mayor Lindsay had reappointed her to the civil court. In June she would win election to a full ten-year term to begin January 1973.

In the summer of 1972, Judge Gabel spent a few weeks in Reno, Nevada, attending meetings of the National College of the Judiciary. She also worked with the Joint Center for Urban Studies of the Massachusetts Institute of Technology and Harvard University from 1973 to 1975. In the fall of 1973, she became founder and chair of the Hunter College Institute for Trial Judges. Her institute brought together fifty judges and scholars to explore the interfaces of the judicial process and the social sciences. Topics included juvenile delinquency, the criminal justice system, the environment, poverty, anthropology, insanity and criminal responsibility, and the role of the trial judge. In cooperation with the New York Psychoanalytic Institute, the Institute for Trial Judges also sponsored seminars for judges and psychoanalysts.

EARLIER, IN MARCH 1973, John Lindsay had announced his intention to seek a third term as mayor. Bess Myerson resigned from Consumer Affairs the next day, saying that she thought it time to return to private life. She wanted "time to reflect," and planned to write a book. She left at the top of her form. Her department had its biggest payroll ever, despite the city's fiscal crunch, and 100 full-time volunteers. It operated on a $4 million yearly budget, and handled a stunning two hundred thousand complaints annually. In her four years, Myerson had built the biggest consumer-defense operation in the nation. Chicago, by contrast, had a budget of $925,000 and 93 workers. And the federal government had a mere 35 employees, and $810,000 to spend.

The role of official shopper for the city had been a perfect fit for Myerson. She could behave naturally, as Bessie from the Bronx, rather than pretend to be a rich girl. What's more, for the first time it allowed the Bella part of her nature to express itself in a positive way. As commissioner of consumer affairs, Bess was perpetually on the prowl for the seven-cent grapefruit, and she was being paid to do it. Most of all, Bess had got more *koved* for this job than for anything she had ever done.

7

IN SICKNESS AND

IN HEALTH

FOR SOME TIME, ADMIRERS HAD BEEN URGING BESS to run for higher political office. A friend remembers driving with Bess and Supreme Court Justice Arthur Goldberg up to the crowded Grand Concourse in the Bronx on a sunny summer's day, "and my God, I opened the car door and, Whammo! They almost tore her clothes off. 'It's Bess! It's Bess!' they shouted. It was total *worship*. No wonder she got this idea she was Queen of the Jews, that she was invincible, that she could do no wrong."

Myerson has always been a great walker, and the sidewalks of New York, or at least of Manhattan, all of them, are the queen's domain. Wherever she went after she left DCA, ordinary people stopped her on the street to say, "You ought to be mayor of New York." Though not certain, it is likely that Myerson attended the United Nations street fair, a block party with entertainment and ethnic foods that was held in front of the Museum of Modern Art on the sunny spring afternoon of April 5, 1973, days after her resignation. It was just the sort of festive, high-minded civic fete that showed Myerson off to her best advantage.

One who was there for sure was the former U.N. guide Sukhreet Gabel, just back from her second year of world travel. This time she had flown from New York to California and joined up with a group of "hippies" who were driving to New Orleans. From there she flew south and traveled for three months all over Mexico, then on to Belize, Guatemala, Venezuela, Curaçao, Trinidad, and one or two other Caribbean islands. Back home, and lonely, she had come to the block party hoping to meet an interesting man. She was standing in front of a group of Trinidadian drummers when she noticed someone tall, blond, and handsome. "I like drum music," she said.

He'd never heard it before, he said. His English was extremely poor, but he managed to get across that he was Jan Revis, a junior diplomat at the Dutch mission to the United Nations, and had been in the United States just four days. They discovered they could communicate in French, and repaired to a nearby bar, where Sukhreet told him about her visit to Trinidad, and some of her other adventures.

Sukhreet was again living in the tiny two-room apartment in her parents' building, and had begun working toward a B.A. degree in political science and international relations at the New York University "School Without Walls." She knew she was an excellent student, and thought she could complete all the work for her degree in less than two years. During this time she had brief affairs with a couple of her professors, and she continued off and on to see Jan. He had made it clear early in their relationship that he was not interested in marriage. He said he would be leaving the U.N. in two years for reassignment elsewhere, and did not envision taking a wife along.

IN 1974 THE GODS appeared to be smiling down on three of our four heroines. Hortense Gabel was moved up from New York City civil-court judge to also being an acting supreme-court justice of the State of New York, a political boost that at once increased her prestige, her authority, and her salary. She and Milton were very proud that their daughter had now received her college degree from NYU. Out on Long Island, Nancy Capasso's fifth child, Andrea, was born, and Andy Capasso was beginning to make serious money.

Bess Myerson was again making big money as a private citizen. She was a well-paid consultant to both Citibank and Bristol-Myers, and a board member of Warner Communications, while carefully preserving her identity as the consumer's friend. For the next five years she contributed occasional columns to *Redbook* magazine, and broadcast consumer programs on several networks. She wrote a syndicated consumer-affairs column, "Listen, Bess," which ran in the New York *Daily News*.

Once Sukhreet had obtained her college degree, the next thing she wanted was Jan. That would prove a far more difficult matter. She cajoled and joked and wheedled; nothing worked. She pleaded with him, sometimes tearfully. "Why not at least get engaged? You can always break it." But it was no good. One day, on the street, she felt about to burst into tears and stepped into a dark church to get control of herself. She sat quietly for a while, and made herself face the fact that begging or pursuing Jan further was no use. Time to dust herself off and move on.

Without further ado, she arranged to return to Britain and enrolled in an Oxford University summer graduate program on British politics and society. In the fall she would transfer to the Johns Hopkins University School of Advanced International Studies in Bologna, Italy, and concentrate on European studies, African studies, and international economics. The program entailed six months of study in Bologna, to be followed by six months in Washington.

When Jan found out that she had left town, and where she was, he was astounded, she said later. He wrote letters begging her to come back to New York. She refused. The players in love's old power game had switched sides. Now she was the cool, aloof one. Jan finally telephoned her in Italy and proposed marriage. She told him she wasn't at all sure she was interested, and perhaps would visit friends in Oxford to get advice. On the same trip, she went to Holland to meet Jan's father, a professor of German, whom she believed was quite attracted to her himself.

The Johns Hopkins program in Washington was a disappointment. Schools of international affairs are designed to develop two kinds of people, international bankers and foreign-service officers. Hopkins's strong point was languages and economics, neither of which interested Sukhreet. She had always found languages easy to learn—she spoke half a dozen—but boring to study. Seventy-five percent of Hopkins's graduates went into international banking. Nonetheless, she was determined to stick it out, a determination made easier by the fact that she needed to spend only three days a week attending classes in Washington and Baltimore. She spent the other four days in New York, with Jan, at his apartment.

While Bess was busy earning money, the city and state's political kingmakers had been quietly taking soundings. No other politician with her kind of crowd appeal had come along in years. And Myerson was much more than a crowd pleaser. Her performance at DCA was considered one of the few solid achievements of the Lindsay administration. When the governor had commissioned a confidential poll rating various candidates, Bess Myerson had emerged at the top of the list, ahead of former Mayor Wagner, future Mayor Abraham Beame, and present Mayor Lindsay, who was last. The people of New York had given her a staggering 90 percent approval rating.

"In the mid-seventies, Bess had enormous credibility," confirms David Garth, the top-flight media adviser to politicians of every stripe. The new Democratic governor, Hugh Carey, wanted Myerson to run for the U.S. Senate in 1976. So did the powerful head of the Liberal party, Alex Rose. "It was a home run. She had everybody," says Garth. "With such backing, she would almost certainly have made it."

But Myerson's popularity with the public, and with the pols, was not echoed by everybody who actually had to work with her. A TV producer associated with her in 1972, when she returned to television on *What Every Woman Wants to Know*, has said, "From beginning to end, without change, Bess was hell to deal with. She had no regard for studio schedules or anyone but herself, and wasted thousands of dollars in overtime charges."

When the red light went on, the producer said, Myerson was well prepared but cold, with one-dimensional delivery. What's more, she had few ingratiating qualities, and she often insisted on having personal friends appear on the show even when it was unwarranted.

The veteran broadcaster Jim Jensen, who knew Bess in the same period, saw her very differently. "I liked her because I understood her," Jensen says. "I saw basically a little frightened girl from the Bronx who'd had all the trappings—beauty, success, brains, luck, money. Even power. When the trappings fell off, she always had to find ways to get new trappings.

"She was a people-pleaser, so she suffered a lot. People-pleasers always do. You've got to please yourself first, and she never did. She always saw the tall, awkward, gawky, shy girl from the Bronx.

"She would have been a darn good senator," Jensen adds. "She has a great mind. She came down almost always on the side of the angels. She was very forceful. She would have been a good politician, because politicians *have to be* what she was naturally—a manipulative person. What's more, had she been elected at that time, she would not have got into the trouble she ran into later. Because she would not have had to lean on her inner self. Bess never had an inner self; that was her problem. She would have been able to lean on her office."

Myerson made plans to capitalize on her great personal popularity and run for the Senate seat of James Buckley, who was up for reelection in 1976. Meanwhile, after four years as a public servant, she felt no hesitation in setting out after big bucks. She was frank about saying she had gone into industrial consulting work because she needed the money.

"It was not real *need*," explains Amy Green. "It was her necessity to live in style. She was always beautifully dressed, and wore the best clothes." Bess never expressed any concern that commercial consulting jobs could become an embarrassment should she return to public service. "That was typical of her," says Green. "She never looked at the negative side, never sat down quietly and weighed the pros and cons. She's a bull in a china shop. That's always her problem."

As a consultant to Bristol-Myers, one of Myerson's responsibilities was to edit a 128-page giveaway book on consumer products. The purported intention was to help consumers buy wisely, not to sell Bristol-Myers merchandise. It covered almost every segment of the company's business: nonprescription drugs, nutritional products, household products, beauty products, and what are known in the field as "personal care appliances." But it did not mention generic drugs, which are much cheaper than the brand-name varieties, and it failed to point out the common medical opinion that Americans take far too much patent medicine. Myerson said that both omissions were oversights.

She had also failed to warn against possible carcinogens in hair dyes made by Clairol, which was owned by Bristol-Myers. (Clairol was originally a family business, owned by the Gelb family, which invented and patented the hair products.) When questioned by a *Times* reporter, Myerson said the data on carcinogens was not available when she edited the book. Later that year another reporter asked, "Did you feel comfortable writing booklets for Bristol-Myers while the FDA was trying to get them to take the suspected carcinogens out of Clairol hair colorings?"

Myerson replied, "If my mother and father started a business as the Gelb mother and father did in their garage, and they tell me two of the ingredients in my fantastic business may cause cancer, I'm not going to have that warning on *my* box!"

These kinds of sudden, off-the-wall outbursts always puzzled and dismayed persons who did not know Myerson well. But her friends were aware that she had always been emotionally volatile. Several of them believed that she periodically came unstrung, and probably had had this problem for some time. She was like a double personality, they said, either "totally in" or "totally out." Others said all this was utter nonsense; the puzzlement arose from Myerson's habit of keeping the people in her life in separate compartments, like shoeboxes. People in one box, even close friends, often were totally ignorant of what was going on in the neighboring box. The only one who knew what was happening in all the boxes, if she did, was Bess. In short, she lived by choice the way secret agents and spies and guerrillas are forced to live.

Myerson worked hard, and she played hard. Carole Phillips, director of Clinique cosmetics, is an elegant blonde who, like Bess, works very hard, and has a great capacity for play. Indeed, Bess and she were at one time such good friends that they exchanged daily phone calls. "She's *fun*," Carole said, echoing every one of

Myerson's big-sister figures. To a woman, they stress that Bess is so bright, such a vivid person, and so much fun to be with that any eccentricities are tolerable, at least for a time.

On Saturdays, Bess and Carole shopped. Bess enjoyed putting on a floppy red sweater and jeans and walking down Madison Avenue, window-shopping and strolling among the populace, the Queen of the Jews in denim disguise. As the two tall and handsome women ambled along, the blonde sometimes heard the brunette muttering, "They love me! They love me!"

Bess is more than just a tightwad, said Carole. "She is one of the great moochmeisters of all time." She used to test shopkeepers' patience to the utmost, trying on endless expensive shoes, scarves, sweaters, outfits, slowly narrowing down to one favorite like a collie cutting out one sheep, then saying sweetly, "Hold it for me, will you?" and sashaying on to the next stop.

Myerson had never been reluctant to ask for special treatment and special prices. Several friends say she ate at and ordered from the Carnegie Delicatessen because they gave her free food. She wore designer dresses that she didn't have to pay for. She once gave a friend two Mary McFadden blouses that the designer had given her, then told the friend she would only charge her the wholesale price. She did the same to another friend when a manufacturer gave her a pile of cashmere sweaters. She was famous for ordering clothes from wholesale Seventh Avenue showrooms and then sometimes not paying for them. Her attitude was that when Bess Myerson wore a designer's work, she was giving him or her free advertising. On some occasions she not only shopped wholesale; she returned the outfits to the showroom when it was time to have them dry-cleaned.

Once, shopping on Canal Street, Manhattan's discount row, she admired a brooch in a little mom-and-pop store that sold cheap handmade jewelry. "How much for this one?" she asked.

"Seventy dollars."

"How much for Bess Myerson?" she countered.

It was Bella's seven-cent grapefruit over and over again.

Myerson had always hated to pay for phone calls. After she went on the board of Citibank, Walter Wriston arranged for her to have an office. At about the same time, Nelson Rockefeller gave her an office in some buildings he owned just off Fifth Avenue on Fifty-fifth Street, and asked her to consult on some Rockefeller Foundation reports. But the real importance of these offices to Bess seemed to be that she could use them for free phone calls. By then she had become famous among country weekend hostesses for sometimes making hundreds of dollars' worth of long-distance phone calls during her visits. Her usual house gift was a secondhand box of candy, or perhaps a scarf or book, something someone else had given to her that she was simply recycling. All Bess's friends knew of her pathological frugality, which they called "cheapness," and indulged.

But perhaps the supreme example of moochmeistering occurred when Bess and Carole Phillips were receiving free face treatments from the famous plastic surgeon Dr. Norman Orentreich. The doctor had developed a method of erasing frown lines with injections of liquid silicone, a highly effective though painful therapy. Because of the women's celebrity status, the treatments were given without charge. The patient sat on the examining table facing the doctor and stripped to the waist. Awaiting her turn, Carole used to gaze at Bess's "beautiful, long, straight back" and marvel that she never once flinched as the needle buzzed. "It was *free*, don't you see? For that she could stand any pain."

What Carole did not know, what Bess shared with only one or two of her closest friends, was that during this period she was severely ill. One evening, while making love, she had felt a sudden, sharp pain. Her gynecologist suspected ovarian cancer, and immediate surgery confirmed his fears. In 1974, ovarian cancer was nearly always fatal. But after a grueling nineteen months of radiation and chemotherapy, the doctors managed to pull her through. The courage and stoicism of their patient was truly indomitable. Despite the brutal side effects of treatment, which included baldness and constant nausea, she nonetheless dropped by Carole Phillips's office almost every day. "And all that time she never once mentioned what she was going through!"

In 1975, Myerson was invited by the chairman of the Hunter College political science department to join the faculty as an adjunct professor and instruct students in the new field of consumer affairs.

Hunter's best and brightest students rushed to sign up for her class. She asked for a research assistant to help carry her burden.

Some weeks later, a student complained that the research assistant was teaching the classes; Professor Myerson never showed up. The department chairman called her into his office. Bess was outraged. "How dare you question my integrity!" she huffed, and stormed out. *Huffed* may not be the *mot juste*. Myerson in a full-blown rage is a force of nature, powerful enough to reduce its object to a sniveling, groveling wimp.

But after one more class appearance, Myerson again stopped showing up. One day an entire delegation of top students came to complain to the chairman, and again he called her in. This time she was docile, and when he told her sternly that she not only had to teach the class, she also had to read her students' papers, she readily agreed to do so. For the moment, it was as if the Evil Queen had metamorphosed into Snow White. She did show up again in the classroom, but only for the final two or three sessions. And she signed off on the term papers, but she never did read them. The research assistant took care of that.

It is likely that the Hunter episode occurred during the period in which Myerson was undergoing intense chemotherapy. At any rate, fate had ordained that she spend the mid-1970s secretly fighting cancer, the crab, rather than fighting for the U.S. Senate seat that almost certainly would have been hers.

THE YEAR 1975 HAD again started out as a good one for everybody. Myerson's health appeared to be improving. Soon she and her friend Shirley Clurman would launch a joint public-relations venture, Fashion Capital of the World, designed to revitalize and lobby for the Seventh Avenue garment industry.

Andy Capasso had just bought his family their first summer home, a two-bedroom, two-bath condominium on the water at Westhampton Beach, Long Island. The following year he added a winter playground, another beachfront dwelling, in Palm Beach, Florida.

Hortense Gabel published an impassioned plea on the op-ed page of *The New York Times*. Her title, "In Darkness with Dangers Compass'd Round," was an homage to Milton's *Paradise Lost*, and her purpose was to call attention to the appalling ignorance and indifference of courts and social-service agencies to the causes of violence in children.

Sukhreet Gabel was happiest of all. She and Jan had decided to marry in June, and she was preoccupied with details of the wedding celebration—an ideal way for her to display her interest in aesthetics and her talent for design.

The festivities that took place on the afternoon of June 8, 1975, indeed showed unusual style and planning, and were a pretty showcase of the bride's taste and talents. Since the groom was a believing Catholic, and his bride a nonbelieving Jew, Sukhreet wanted a tiny, private ceremony and a big party after. She had asked her mother to ask Marietta Tree if she would give the wedding reception in her house on East Seventy-ninth Street, considered the most beautiful private residence in New York City. Two hundred guests were invited. Sukhreet planned every detail. She asked a friend who flew for KLM to bring over masses of fresh tulips and other spring flowers from the glorious Amsterdam wholesale flower market. She requested every color and as many varieties as possible, and then stayed up all night before the wedding arranging the large bouquets herself.

On the morning of the wedding, Sukhreet and her mother and her aunt Sybil sat around a table in Jan's apartment hulling a crateful of giant strawberries Sukhreet had bought at the wholesale produce market in Hunts Point the day before.

Hortense would have liked to help her daughter with the planning, but Sukhreet wanted to do everything in her own way. Her mother "can't boil water or fry an egg," she says, and if Hortense had planned the wedding, "we'd have had buffalo chicken wings and egg rolls. My mother has no taste. I have a lot.

"I made a statement. Everything was beautiful as a ballet—perfect, and exactly my way. I was a typical Virgo about it, precise to every last detail." The mission had assigned Jan to plan for a visit from a Dutch naval-training ship, so he didn't help at all. This made Sukhreet angry. "I did all the unpacking, the thanking, the returning, and entertaining his father during the day."

Her parents had given Sukhreet $5,000 as a wedding gift. She used about $2,000 of it to pay for the wedding and reception and spent the rest on furniture. Later she said she was "shocked" that her parents did not pay for her wedding and also give her a separate gift. She added that her father thought she should have put the $3,000 in a savings bank rather than spend it on furniture. She told him that since the gifts from the wedding guests were worth about $2,000, she felt they had "broken even."

Sukhreet was twenty-five. She wore a simple, size-six white dress with daisies pinned to the sleeves, and she looked shy and lovely. The wedding announcement in *The New York Times* described the groom as an alumnus of St. Canisius College in Nijmegen, with a law degree from the Catholic University of Nijmegen. He had served as a lieutenant in the Royal Dutch army, and was scheduled to join the Dutch mission to Suriname, which was to achieve independence at the end of the year. The couple planned to live in Paramaribo, the capital.

The wedding ceremony took place in St. Monica's Roman Catholic Church on East Seventy-ninth Street, with only the immediate families in attendance. Sukhreet had asked an old friend of hers, a missionary priest in Belize who was in town on church business, to perform the ceremony. He decided to leave out Catholic prayers, and said a few Old Testament prayers instead, and a few words about children. There were no wedding rings; neither bride nor groom wanted one.

After the ceremony, Sukhreet and Jan decided to walk the few blocks to Marietta Tree's house, and to steal a moment alone together upstairs before greeting their guests. They sat on a loveseat, and Sukhreet had a sudden vision of Jan as a sixty-five-year-old ambassador wearing a sash, medals, and striped pants, and she knew for certain that she would not be married to him then. But she vowed to make her marriage good for as long as it lasted and, taking a firm grip on his hand, the smiling bride and her groom descended the staircase.

IT WAS A couple of months after the Gabel-Revis wedding, at a hastily called meeting of civic leaders to save beautiful old Grand

Central Station from the wrecker's ball, that Bess Myerson was pleased to run into her old friend Ed Koch, now a congressman representing the people of Greenwich Village. After the meeting the two of them repaired to Grand Central's Oyster Bar for a bite, and then they took a long stroll together down Park Avenue. Somewhere between the Oyster Bar and Union Square, the politician and the beauty queen formed a new political alliance that would prove more powerful than anything New Yorkers had seen since the demise of Tammany Hall.

8

SUCCESS

AT A PRICE

By 1977, THE ROT IN CERTAIN PARTS OF THE APPLE could no longer be ignored. New York City had not yet been dubbed the Calcutta of the West—that honor was still ten years off—but signs of decay were visible in the schools, in the streets, in the parks and hospitals, the police department, the municipal treasury, the blocks of burned-out houses in the Bronx and Brooklyn, and probably in the mop closets of City Hall. The election contest that made Ed Koch mayor of New York City that year was wilder than most people remember. Seven candidates were listed on the ballot in the Democratic primary, more than in any other election in the city's history. When the dust settled, Koch, an unknown outsider, had nosed out five of his six rivals, each of whom was more familiar to voters than he. Then he beat Mario Cuomo in the runoff.

By common consent of all involved, the one person who did more than any other to make this miracle happen was Bess Myerson. The "genius"

(Koch's term) who put the winning campaign together was David Garth, but the person who first brought Garth and Koch together had been Myerson, and she also gave the first fund-raising party, that all-important moment when the political triage experts begin to separate would-be candidates into the living and the dead. To Garth, Koch looked like a live one, though barely; he rated his chances at 20–1.

Garth took Bess aside and told her, "We need you for chairperson of the campaign." Garth knew she was still recovering from her illness and receiving chemotherapy, but he had to have her. "Number one, she had an impeccable name. Two, she was 'a good balance' for Koch." Translation: People think Koch is gay; if I package the two of them together, maybe I can dispel the rumors. "It was basically done to give him credibility. And visibility. In 1977, *I* was better known than Ed Koch!"

Far more important, in a January poll of likely mayoral candidates taken by the Democratic State Committee, not only was Koch's name at the bottom of the list, but Bess Myerson's name was at the very top. Hence her decision to support Koch, rather than attempt to run against him, must be viewed as an act of great political loyalty and generosity. It also reflected a couple of other things: her pervasive sense that down deep she was still Olive Oyl, and the fact that she still suffered from the well-known but seldom-mentioned female complaint, the Disease to Please. Further, a woman of her generation, no matter how accomplished or "liberated," was more comfortable playing the role of number two, the role of wife. She was apt to become obscurely uneasy at the notion of playing number one.

When the Koch campaign got under way, New Yorkers used to ask one another, "Who's the guy with Bess Myerson?" But every poster showed Ed and Bess together, two big smiling heads. On TV, they appeared hand in hand. Garth tried not to call on her more than necessary, but throughout the campaign, whenever she was needed, she turned up. She was never a no-show, never late. "She just said, 'When you need me, call.' There was never any bullshit with her," Garth says. Edward Costikyan, a lawyer and former Manhattan Democratic county chairman, was in fact co-chair of the campaign with Myerson, but Costikyan's face was not on any posters.

Garth had more or less admired Myerson since she was named Miss America when he was a fifteen-year-old kid growing up in the Bronx, and nothing that occurred in 1977, or since, has caused him to change his mind. When they met, Myerson was on several major boards of directors, and Garth figured, "They may want a token woman, but they don't want a goddamn fool."

He saw her as "basically a wise guy, a free spirit. She did what she goddamn pleased. She was always a spunky gal. *Gallant* was my word for her." He thought her "a Jewish Hepburn," though lacking the same charm. "You saw the Bronx in her. She was a street fighter, but she was vulnerable too. I felt she wasn't as resilient as she looked. She was gorgeous. She had legs from here to eternity. But I felt there was more tension in her than showed at first glance." She always seemed to be on her own, and Garth felt a little sorry for her.

"Another thing: Bess had a certain lack of touching earth. I think she could be very childlike in a love situation. She's had too much public exposure," says the media whiz. "At the same time, there's been too much lack of reality in her life. I think there's one thing that is real to her—the reality of love."

IN 1977 SUKHREET GABEL REVIS was discovering the reality of marriage. Life as a minor diplomat's wife in the colonial backwater of Paramaribo was often excruciatingly boring. Although she was highly educated and a gifted linguist, fluent in French, Italian, and Spanish as well as Dutch, government policy forbade her to hold a job. She was not getting on well with Jan, who held the conventional foreign-service view that 50 percent of a diplomat's job is the responsibility of his wife.

Jan Revis was "a nice guy, a stolid, sturdy Dutchman. I married my father," Sukhreet said much later. Sukhreet was then twenty-eight, and Jan thirty-two, "but he was emotionally much older." He wanted a family, but Sukhreet was not interested in children. To test this conviction, she raised a litter of puppies and found the task uncongenial. As she often said, even when she was nearing forty, "I want to give birth to *me* first."

After Suriname, the Revises were posted to Brussels, and later Beirut. But eighteen months into their marriage, in late 1976, Sukhreet began a pattern of spending three months of each year at the University of Chicago, working toward her master's degree in sociology, and bringing study projects home. The subject of her dissertation was to be race relations in Holland since 1975, the year Suriname became independent.

Jan disapproved of Sukhreet's academic schedule. "He thought I had no right to be away three months. My duty was to be at his table, in his bed, mother of his child, hostess of his parties. In short, he wanted a *wife*, or at least someone wearing a wife suit."

NANCY CAPASSO IN 1977 wore her wife suit seven days a week. Now a prosperous suburban mother of children aged seventeen, fifteen, thirteen, five, and three, she spent the year driving kids to birthday parties, doctors, dancing school, and so on, and bringing various family pets to the vet. Shopping was still her passion, and she was invariably tastefully, expensively dressed. Andy worked like a beast at making ever more money. His goal was to top Nanco's 1976 record twenty-five-man payroll and $1 million annual sales, and of course he did. But when he was with his family, he was, as Nancy said, "all there." In late summer, Nancy and Andy and another couple went on a two-week holiday, shopping in Paris and sunning in the south of France.

HORTENSE GABEL HAD been elected a justice of the New York State supreme court in November 1975, endorsed by both the Democratic and Liberal parties, and by an editorial in *The New York Times*. Now, starting the second year of her fourteen-year term, she was presiding over a suit brought by Frank Sinatra against a woman he accused of posing as his daughter. A lower court had given the woman permission to use the name Sinatra, and thereafter she had been sending Sinatra's lawyers daily letters signed "Lil' Blue Eyes." Big Blue Eyes wanted that order revoked.

THE NEW YORK CITY mayoral sweepstakes started on a chilly day in January when Percy E. Sutton became the first Democrat to announce that he was a candidate. He spent a bundle on radio, thinking the primary would be in June. Then Governor Hugh Carey vetoed a primary bill, thereby ensuring that the primary would be held in September and would give Carey's candidate—whomever he might decide to back—time to build against the incumbent, Mayor Abe Beame.

By primary day, September 8, city Democrats could choose among seven candidates: four Jews, a black, a Roman Catholic, and a Puerto Rican, who ended up getting the Jewish, black, Catholic, and Puerto Rican votes respectively.

The early front-runners were Beame, who liked to say he was New York City's first Jewish mayor (forgetting that LaGuardia had been a hybrid Jewish Protestant), and Bella Abzug, a Jewish butcher's daughter and three-term Manhattan congresswoman. The other Jews running were Joel Harnett, a businessman who had never before run for office, and Ed Koch, the popular, liberal Manhattan congressman. Candidate Herman Badillo, a Puerto Rican, was a four-term Bronx congressman often described as the "most intelligent" of the candidates. Mario Cuomo, the Catholic, was secretary of state and Governor Carey's choice. Sutton, a Harlem leader whose father had been born into slavery, was Manhattan borough president.

Koch and Cuomo shared the middle ground on fiscal issues. Each considered the other his most formidable opponent and hoped to oppose Beame or Abzug in the runoff. Neither man was well known. Polls taken during the winter showed Koch with 6 percent voter recognition, and Cuomo with 2 percent.

Dave Garth had run two winning mayoral campaigns for Lindsay, had brought Brooklyn congressman Hugh Carey from obscurity to Albany, had handled winning campaigns for Governor Brendan Byrne of New Jersey and Mayor Tom Bradley of Los

Angeles. From this he made a good living, easily $250,000 a year.

A year after Koch and Bess's visit to the Oyster Bar and stroll down Park Avenue, Koch had asked Bess to invite Garth and himself to dinner at her apartment. Koch wanted to meet the genius in an informal setting, and see how their chemistry worked. Evidently it worked well, for Koch then invited Garth to lunch in more public circumstances, told him he was thinking about running for mayor, and wanted to hire him. Bess, too, called Garth and urged him to take on Koch, and she offered to do whatever she could. For starters, she would put Koch, a man normally uncomfortable with the rich, in touch with big contributors. Koch had $250,000 in the bank when he announced. By the end of the election campaign, he had collected more than $500,000.

Garth's first move, as with any new candidate, was to order up new polling. He found that Koch was not simply unknown outside of Manhattan; those few who did know who he was couldn't stand him. In Queens and Brooklyn, people saw Koch as a liberal, a lawyer, and soft on crime. This last flaw was easiest to fix. Garth and his candidate began reminding people that Koch was in favor of restoring the death penalty, and had been since 1970.

When Garth took a poll for Koch in September 1976, he found that only 6 percent of the voters would support him, and fewer than 30 percent even knew his name, while virtually all the Democrats knew Abzug and Beame, and some 85 percent recognized Sutton and Badillo.

"The only two people who thought I could win were my father and me," Koch told a reporter. "By the time Mario Cuomo came in [in April 1977], I still had my father and me, and I had Bess and Garth, and I had my record."

Garth saw Bess as a lifesaver for Koch; she would improve both his recognition factor and his masculinity quotient. "I sell image," Bess had always said. Now, to help sell the Koch image, she was prepared to sell her female soul and fake a relationship that didn't exist. Koch and Bess flirted and coquetted and smarmed, and dodged when asked if they were planning to marry. They were photographed holding hands on Rosh Hashanah. But Bess dusted off her old no-comment self, and simply said she didn't talk about her private life. Koch went so far as to say that marriage "could not be ruled out. It is always a possibility, but I don't want to talk about it. She's an incredible person—a warm human being that I really adore."

It was all hokum. Garth called the pair the Smith Brothers, because each was a beard for the other. But Garth's image-changing strategy worked. It switched the question in the public mind from "Is Koch gay?" to "Are they lovers?" and "Will they marry?"

No one on the campaign staff saw the slightest sign of romantic attraction between them. Indeed, close to the wire, a definite chill seemed to set in. Though Myerson would refuse comment on her personal relationship with the new mayor, she did advise someone to whom Koch had just offered a job in his administration, "Just remember, he's a man always alone. He's so alone he never even walks a dog."

Garth took a hard look at Abzug. After six years in the House, and a vigorous run in 1976 for the same Senate seat that Myerson had once had her eye on, and that she lost to Moynihan by a heartbreaking fraction of 1 percent, everybody in New York knew Bella. But only 30 percent of them liked her. Most Democrats didn't like Beame either. Cuomo was the problem, because he was Catholic, and the Catholics were the city's most dependable voting bloc after the Jews. Carey's fund-raising would enable Cuomo to outspend Koch during the primary campaign and the runoff. Carey also made Cuomo the Liberal party nominee, promising to back him on that line even if he were not to be the Democratic nominee. Cuomo's image was being burnished by his own media whiz kids, Pat Caddell and Gerald Rafshoon, the team that had guided their man Jimmy Carter right to the White House the year before. By the end of the runoff Koch had spent $1.25 million and Cuomo about $1.45 million. Both had devoted half or more of their funds to public relations and radio and TV time.

By early August, Abzug still led all the opinion polls, followed by Beame. Then the mayor's chances were dashed when the SEC published a report damning his performance as deceptive and inept. Some experts now predicted that Abzug, the most liberal and passionate of the candidates, would finish at or close to the top if turnout was typical. But in that wild election, nothing was typical. Instead of the expected 30 percent, a record 48 percent of 1.9

million eligible Democrats went to the polls on September 8, making hash of the pollsters' predictions. Badillo and Sutton both took districts that Abzug was expected to carry. The record turnout was especially surprising because pundits believed the voters had been confused and bored by the multiplicity of candidates. Perhaps the fiscal crisis helped bring people out, as well as the new options of voting for a black, a Hispanic, or a woman.

Koch won the primary narrowly with 20 percent of the vote over Cuomo's 19 percent, Beame's 18 percent, and Abzug's 17 percent. Jewish districts went overwhelmingly for Koch, Catholic districts for Cuomo. On the Republican side, Manhattan state senator Roy Goodman won the nomination over former WOR talk-show host Barry Farber, who would run in the general election as a Conservative. Both were Jewish.

The next race for Koch was a runoff against Cuomo on September 19, eleven days hence. On September 11, Badillo, Sutton, and Abzug had declared they would stand together and only endorse a runoff candidate who agreed to a policy supporting poor New Yorkers. But this coalition lasted less than a day. Badillo failed to show up for a meeting of the group in Garth's office. He sent word of his endorsement of Koch instead, and Koch immediately put him on his campaign team.

Koch also got endorsements from Beame (even though Koch had been his most vigorous critic), and one of the black leaders who had backed Sutton, Manhattan representative Charles Rangel, whom Koch also promptly brought into the fold. Two days before the runoff, Abzug declared for Cuomo.

Turnout for the runoff was 40 percent, lower than the record 48 percent that had rejected Bella, but still high. Koch won by 55 percent to 45 percent, capturing every borough but Staten Island. He even got Queens by a narrow margin. As Garth put it, "He started dead even ten days ago and ended ten points ahead. That's a helluva race." But ethnic demographics may have determined the result more than anything else. Blacks and Hispanics, having no candidate of their own this time, stayed home. Jews, as usual, turned out in larger numbers than any other group, and three fourths of them chose Koch. Cuomo got two thirds of the Catholics and four fifths of the Italians.

Both Koch and Cuomo had relied heavily on TV between the primary and the runoff. Astute observers understood that both candidates had emerged from obscurity not by virtue of their policies but because of their packaging by hired experts. After the primary, the image war had heated up and Cuomo released a couple of nasty anti-Koch spots. One showed Koch's head whirling like a weather vane, and another, which the Cuomo forces referred to as "the Dorian Gray spot," showed his head dissolving into a portrait of the hated Lindsay.

Later the Cuomo people disavowed these spots, blaming pressure from Rafshoon and major contributors, and even acknowledged that they had had a negative rebound against Cuomo, not Koch. But at the time, they looked devastating. Garth counterattacked with a pair of hitherto-unrecognized secret weapons, two enormously effective spots by Bess Myerson. In one she said dolefully, "We expected more from you, Mario." In the other she asked, "Whatever happened to character, Mario? We thought your campaign would be better than that."

"No one can do TV spots better than Bess Myerson," said Maureen Connolly, then Garth's research director, later Mayor Koch's press secretary, and since 1985 in the media business for herself. "It's so hard to deal with a negative spot. You have to figure out some way to deflect and answer it without sounding defensive. Bess made a couple of killers."

Garth simply said he didn't think he could have beaten Cuomo without her.

Koch started acting mayorlike the day after the runoff, September 20, announcing that his "transition team" as mayor would include lawyer Costikyan as first deputy, plus the Puerto Rican Badillo and Charles Rangel, the black congressman. Bess Myerson was not mentioned.

As a congressman, Koch had taken very progressive positions, and was rated by Americans for Democratic Action, the liberal watchdog group, at 91–100 from 1969 through 1976. This would never go down with middle-class voters in Brooklyn and Queens, however, so Koch toughened up. He made hard-nosed TV spots denouncing the Board of Education as a lard barrel of waste, charged that teachers' salaries were exorbitant, and said there ought to be more cops on the streets. He hammered on his pro–death-penalty stance. Nonetheless, Koch declined steadily in the polls in the seven weeks between the September runoff and the general election in November, when he would again have to face Cuomo, on the Liberal party line, as well as the Republican candidate, Roy Goodman.

The weekend before the vote his lead was down to four points. It was only speculation, but many people believed the homosexuality issue was quietly doing him in. Quietly indeed. The issue was considered so sensitive that it had been mentioned by the media only twice: once in a *New York Times* profile, and once in a TV interview. The oft-whispered slur "Vote for Cuomo, not the homo" was widespread but sub rosa, except in some sections of Queens, where it was openly said and chalked on fences.

A few days before the election, Joyce Purnick of the *Post* was interviewing Bess in Bess's limo when she saw the co-chairperson suddenly blow her cool, get furious, and go public with the gay issue. "I don't care anymore!" she almost shouted, seeming close to losing control. She savagely denounced Cuomo and other Koch enemies. She took a call from Garth on the car phone, then yelled back, "I don't care what impact it has! It's about time we raised this, talked about it . . . It just had to be said."

The authors of *I, Koch*, Arthur Browne, Dan Collins, and Michael Goodwin, say this incident "could have been the worst blunder of the campaign." But it could also be seen as a masterstroke, a refreshing plea for honesty and straight talk that no one else could, or would, have made. At any rate, nothing came of it. Myerson's comments were so blunt the *Post* decided not to print them until after the election, in which Koch defeated Cuomo by 50 percent to 42 percent.

A priority for the mayor-elect was to find a top-notch person for the city's Office of Economic Development. He wanted to raise its budget from its current $7.5 million, and to set up regional OED offices in each borough. Bess Myerson wanted the job so badly that she offered to take it on for $1 a year. But Koch wanted Costikyan. Then, after the election, the two men had a public falling-out.

As for Myerson, Koch made her no job offers of any kind. She held the Bible for him at his swearing-in, but later found herself completely frozen out. Some gossiped that the husband of one of her sisters was "politically sensitive." Others said Koch was just reverting to type: During the election, he had needed her; now he didn't. Still others said that by letting herself be linked romantically with Koch, she had unwittingly dissolved her own political capital. She had peddled her womanhood to no avail, and had inadvertently let her new image as the mayor's sweetheart blot out her real achievements as commissioner of consumer affairs.

Myerson told her friend Amy Green that Koch didn't hire her because he didn't think he was powerful enough to put a woman in an important spot. Tom Behr, a knowing attorney and Koch crony who was asked by the mayor to give Bess political guidance, had another explanation. "I think she had a big business going. I know she was making a lot of money. She was on the board of directors of Warner Communications, with Steve Ross. She was very highly paid. I doubt she wanted a city job."

This may be, but it was also true that, politically speaking, Myerson appeared to have shot herself in the foot. Her agreement to play the role of Koch's "mate" had been a Faustian bargain; she had unwittingly sabotaged her own image as a tough, canny consumer advocate, and made people think of her instead as a mere love object, a political lightweight. It was a stigma she was never after able wholly to erase. The press stopped writing about her, and for a while she seemed virtually to disappear. By the time Koch got around to publishing his own account of his first election, *Mayor*, in 1984, Bess Myerson was nowhere even mentioned, save in a picture caption.

More than a decade later, looking back at these events, Robert A. Caro, the distinguished biographer of Robert Moses and of Lyndon Johnson, found strong words to describe the phony Koch-Myerson romance. It was, he said, "one of the single most cynical acts I have ever seen in American politics."

9

....

FISSURES

Bess Myerson could be seen as a woman with several distinct personalities. One was the Jewish-American Princess, born beautiful and Jewish, and making the most of both. Another was the successful businessperson. For Myerson was always a very American Miss America. She had American values. Above all, she worshiped the bitch-goddess Success. And she incarnated her. Third, she was the classic mad Russian, a larger-than-life, manic figure out of a nineteenth-century Russian novel, someone so driven by demons invisible to others as sometimes to seem quite crazy indeed.

It was difficult to pinpoint when this third persona first appeared. Was it during her harsh childhood? Or did it happen when she banged into the wall of anti-Semitism during her Miss America tour? During the breakup of her first marriage, perhaps, when she said she was forced to give up all her hard-earned money in return for uncontested custody of her only child? Or the prolonged stress of her second marital shipwreck, which lasted from 1965 to 1971 and encompassed her first known episode of shoplifting, the arrest in Harrods in 1970?

What caused that? One can only speculate. Profound, lengthy physical stress can seriously damage mind as well as body. The complications of severe emotional and physical trauma are unpredictable. There may have been several severe illnesses in Myerson's life in addition to the deadly ovarian cancer. There had been the mysterious pills for intestinal surgery while she was commissioner of consumer affairs. There had been a possible episode of childhood polio, hushed up according to the superstition of the times, which left her with one knee that sometimes buckled or ached when she was overtired.

Bess had been fifty when her cancer was diagnosed. In the next nineteen months, the persona of Bess the survivor formed and hardened. This invincible Teflon Bess now joined the other incarnations to form the remarkable amalgam that is the mature Bess Myerson. For she is not merely the JAP and the success figure and the Russian-novel character plus, of course, the former Miss America. Bess is many people: the unloved daughter, the Jewish mother, the Medusa, the moochmeister, and Queen of the Jews. She has also been called a *Machashaifeh* (a Yiddish witch), an Israel lobbyist, a femme fatale, a woman scorned, a brave Amazon, a fairy godmother, a Lady Bountiful, and a petty thief.

Bess Myerson's history of shoplifting had been fairly well hushed up, though her daughter, Barra, told people that Bess had taken hotel linens and small furnishings "for years." Psychiatry classifies kleptomania as a form of compulsive behavior, an "impulse disorder" that strikes people who feel impoverished. The sufferer's inability to reconcile the loss of a loved one, or some other loss, leads to unconscious acting-out in order to obtain symbolic compensation. It becomes a way to get something when you feel you have no power. Successful theft brings a sense of restitution, a feeling of being more "in control."

Still another way to see Bess Myerson is as a person mortally wounded by betrayal. There were many. The first was her harsh, ever-critical Russian mother, that fierce woman who never said one good word about her daughter except behind her back. She was betrayed again by the Miss America contest, which promised a throne and a golden coach, and gave only a rancid pumpkin. After that came all the betrayals by men, and the meaningless "career," not as a concert pianist but as a regular on TV game shows. Then even the magnificent body failed her. That which had brought her the crown then brought her down, when at fifty she fought the crab.

But the fatal betrayal may have been the one by Ed Koch. Every savvy New Yorker knew it: *She* got him elected. He campaigned always with Bess by his side, the pair of them walking the streets, riding the subways, he so bald and gawky, she so lovely. "Like Beauty and the Beast," people said. After the Beast won, and did not embrace Beauty, but in fact turned away, when he offered her nothing for her troubles, that was the real betrayal. In retrospect, that infidelity stands out as the one from which she could never recover.

But we are dealing here with a professional survivor, and a woman still dazzlingly attractive at fifty-three. Once Koch moved into City Hall, Bess saw him only after hours, for dinners and movies, and it may tell us something about her sense of politics and dependency and power that although exiled from Koch's political life, Myerson was willing to remain part of his personal entourage.

On her own, Bess was enjoying an increasingly luxuriant private life. After her divorce from Grant there had always been a man in her life, and this was the period in which she had many love affairs with important, well-heeled, usually younger men, and was named co-respondent in a divorce or two.

The following year Bess Myerson made a critical decision. She had by then recovered her health, and vastly improved her wealth, reporting 1979 earnings of $493,000, and, by 1980, a rather astonishing net worth of $4 million. She was as close-mouthed about the source of her riches as she was tight-fisted in their disbursal. But close friends knew that among her lovers had been several extremely wealthy individuals, men whom they presumed had given her shrewd investment advice, especially in regard to choice Manhattan real estate.

Now she wanted power. She was ready to cash in on her phenomenal 1973 90 percent approval rating, and run for the United

States Senate. She called David Garth and told him she wanted to enter the September 1980 Democratic primary. After twenty-three years' service in the Senate, Jacob Javits was weary and ill, and Myerson, with the support of Senator Moynihan, was ready to challenge him for the seat. It would have been the glorious culmination of her career in public service, and earned a plenitude of *koved*. But it was not to be.

Garth asked Myerson to come down to his office. What he had to tell her was so serious that he arranged for Ed Koch to be sitting there when Bess arrived, in hopes the mayor's presence would underscore the importance of Garth's message.

"Bess," he said, "there is no way you can win this. The figures don't add up right."

"What do you mean, 'no way'?"

"You are certain to lose in the primary to Plain Pipe Rack."

Plain Pipe Rack was Garth's designation for Elizabeth Holtzman, the intelligent Brooklyn congresswoman who was angling for the Javits seat as well. (John Lindsay and Queens DA John Santucci were also in the race.) Holtzperson, as the Myerson team began to call her, was New York's latest political Jewish girl but, gender and religion aside, she and Bess had nothing in common but ambition. Holtzman had vastly more legislative experience—eight years in Congress, including months of national media exposure as a member of the House Judiciary Committee investigating the Watergate scandal. The two women had entirely different backgrounds. The Holtzman family of Brooklyn was a lot like the Wittsteins of the Bronx: intellectual, liberal, and upper middle class. Liz was an aloof lawyer with a no-nonsense manner and an excellent command of facts and figures who fiercely guarded her personal privacy. She was severe and intellectual, Radcliffe-educated, thirty-eight years old to Myerson's fifty-five. They would be competing directly for the selfsame voters, and the demographics were all in Holtzman's favor.

"I don't want you to spend the money and not know this," Garth said.

"How much would it cost me to run?" Bess replied.

Garth said it would take about $1 million, and the money would be hard to raise. People would not readily contribute to her campaign because they knew she was rich. But again the moochmeister did not flinch. Indeed, she was so confident and avid that she was prepared for once to pay her own way. "It's an investment in myself," she said.

Garth said later that he took her on for no fee. "My attitude was: I'm doing this because Bess is a friend. She helped us. I'm gonna help her."

Maureen Connolly, now a top adviser to Myerson, said Garth was paid. "But it's a favor" anyhow to take on a loser, and this "was the worst of all possible situations because the perception at that time was that she *couldn't* lose." Pundits had labeled her the front-runner. Only the insiders knew that she didn't have a chance.

On May 7, 1980, Myerson announced her candidacy in the Tri-anon Room of the New York Hilton Hotel as a chorus burst into "Look for the Silver Lining." Seated beside her was her ninety-year-old father, Louis. Her mother, Bella, could not be present. She had been a resident of the Jewish Home and Hospital for the Aged in the Bronx for some time.

Chicly costumed and sporting a serious-looking pair of horn-rims, Myerson gazed out over the throng of cameras and well-wishers and said gravely, "To my three careers—journalist, consumer advocate, businesswoman—I seek to add a fourth, for which all these have prepared me." But her words were at variance with her experience. Although she had the support of Governor Carey, Senator Moynihan, Mayor Koch, the Brooklyn boss Meade Esposito, and Sol Chaikin of the International Ladies Garment Workers Union, and called herself "the candidate of the heavy hitters," she knew, and they knew, that the odds were all but hopeless. Such was the cynicism of New York City politics a mere decade ago.

Myerson's cynicism matched theirs. The day before her official announcement, she and her father had returned to Sholem Aleichem, trailed by a horde of press people. No one was left at the project who had known the Myersons, but Bess threw her arms around the nearest old lady while the cameras whirred. She knew instinctively how to get "ink." What she didn't seem to understand at all was that, to old-time Jewish socialists especially, Holtzman was the natural candidate.

Said Maureen Connolly, "When you analyzed the numbers, it just didn't look possible that she could win. You'd think Bess would do best with Jewish voters, who turn out in large numbers in a primary. But in fact Bess's real base was the Catholic ethnic vote— Italians, Irish, and Polish, moderate to conservative. Liz was stronger with Jews."

Between 1977 and 1980 New York had changed, and so had Bess. Throughout the 1970s she had been a tireless speaker and fund-raiser for Another Mother for Peace, largest and oldest of the antinuclear organizations. In 1980, without resigning from AMFP, she popped up on the board of directors of the pro-nuke Committee for the Present Danger, right alongside Dr. Edward Teller, General Curtis LeMay, and Jeane Kirkpatrick. "Winds change. Times are different," she told a reporter, again sounding blatantly cynical.

But issues had never been her strong point. Instead, she traded on her personal saga of rags-to-riches, at times adding creative embellishments. Arnold Grant "was great around the track but awful in the stable," she confided to a *Daily News* reporter. "When I left him, I left with only my clothes. I refused to fight him in court. It frightened me."

She readily gave interviews at home while getting dressed, or undressed. (One key campaign aide, a young woman, quit because of Bess's habit of holding strategy meetings in her bathroom while she bathed and changed clothes.) Sometimes she became suddenly, uncomfortably frank about her private life. At a fund-raising luncheon she mentioned that her ex-husband, Arnold Grant, now had Alzheimer's disease. She described him "in his straitjacket," and said that, had she known he was ill, she would never have left him. "That's the type of person I am." In fact, she had not seen him in many years and did not visit him at the hospital, where he died November 17, 1980.

"I'd never seen Bess so crazed, never seen her want something so bad as she did that election," says a woman who recalls attending a Myerson lunch with forty or fifty other well-heeled matrons. Before starting to speak, Bess walked around the room and embraced each guest, murmuring into each of forty or fifty bejeweled ears: "Thank you for coming. It is so important to me that *you* be here. You mean so much to me."

Myerson's TV ads proclaiming "She knows how to get things done for New York" got started two months ahead of Holtzman's, and by the end of summer Bess had pulled ahead of her rival with every major religious, ethnic, racial, and ideological group except for blacks, who favored Lindsay for his principled stand on education and scatter-site housing. She was splitting the liberal vote with Holtzman, while holding on to the moderates and conservatives through her support of higher defense spending. Because she had *no* prior political track record, she could take positions all over the map. Although she supported government funding of abortions and the Equal Rights Amendment, for example, she had never been identified as a feminist, so people with opposite views on women's issues still felt able to support her.

But then Holtzman's own ads began appearing, and the balance shifted. Viewers saw Holtzman hard at work in Washington as a U.S. congresswoman. One ad criticized Myerson's position on oil-price decontrols, pointing out that she "owns more than a quarter of a million dollars of oil stocks."

Plain Pipe Rack had succeeded in turning Miss America's wealth into a negative campaign issue; Bess's financial report did not fit well with her populist image. A Holtzman radio commercial in late summer did more damage with its focus on Myerson's personal involvement with the Consumer Credit Counseling Service, a private bill-collecting agency accused by Bess's own Consumer Affairs department of deceiving customers.

With his onetime protégé now competing with him for the same job, John Lindsay felt bitterly betrayed, and by September he had joined Holtzman in attacking Myerson's corporate activities. In one debate he peered over his granny glasses at Myerson seated beside him and said, "When I retired as mayor, I deliberately went into international law. I'm sure I could have made a lot of money representing firms doing business with the city," a reference to Myerson's affiliation not just with CCCS but with Bristol-Myers, Clairol, Warner Communications, and Citibank. The previous year, Bristol-Myers had been accused by the Federal Trade Commission of deceptive advertising in claiming that Bufferin and Excedrin were gentler and more effective than aspirin. Holtzman repeatedly attacked Myerson for continuing "to collect her paycheck" from Citibank while it bowed to the Arab boycott of Israel.

In politics, Myerson knew the simple, basic moves. She returned critical shafts the way Chris Evert returned a tennis serve. On the Citibank matter, her comeback was "I don't quit. I stay and I work from the inside." Once again, she knew what to say, and did what she wanted to do.

In the last days before the primary, Myerson's ads abruptly shifted focus and began attacking Holtzman's votes to cut defense spending, as Moynihan had been urging her to do all along. But it did no good, and Myerson lost the September 9 primary by 87,760 votes, with Holtzman garnering 367,724 votes to her 279,964. Lindsay got 145,540, and Santucci brought up the rear with 109,456. "Add Santucci's vote to Myerson's and she would have won," said Connolly. "His votes came from her hide.

"It was an unusual race," she added. "She was running against Jack Javits, whom she was friendly with, and against Lindsay, who had been her patron."

But Bess had freed herself from all business and political obligations, "and she didn't want to go back. Her attitude was: 'Anytime I've gone backwards in my life it's been a failure. I've got to go forward no matter the outcome.' She's very determined; when she makes her mind up, she's going to do it. She thinks things through."

Bess's friend Amy Green said precisely the opposite, that Bess doesn't think first, that she "just jumps in." But this was scarcely surprising in so multiple a personality as Bess Myerson had by then taught herself to be. All her old personalities—the Lady in Mink, the figure in a Russian novel, the moochmeister, and the Queen of the Jews—were more or less variations of Dr. Jekyll. But now a hitherto unexpressed part of her personality, a female Mr. Hyde, was about to make a scary appearance. That Myerson was able to carry on as Mr. Hyde at night, yet behave like a U.S. Senate candidate by day, was the strangest part of all.

10

ALL HER LIFE BESS MYERSON HAS HAD ONE
female "best friend," a big-sister surrogate who out-
ranks all the other girlfriends until the big blowup
comes and she is cast into outer darkness and replaced by the next big sister. At least half a dozen
women have played this role. The confidante who
lasted longest was Marilyn Funt (ex-wife of Alan
Funt, the *Candid Camera* man), a sometime writer
who lived in a triplex apartment overlooking Central Park. In 1979 Marilyn gave Bess a big surprise
birthday party there and, oddly enough, many of
the guests did not seem to know one another. It was
as if, for this party only, the contents of all the shoeboxes had been dumped into one large pile. Shirley
Clurman arrived with the dress designer Mollie Parnis, and met Bess's daughter, Barra Grant, for the
first time. She recalls a young woman "so beautiful!" She had long brown hair, tanned skin, a perfect form and face, and was "very healthy-looking."

Then Shirley noticed Bess dancing with a new

man. He looked a few years younger than she, and was tall and tan with crinkly, graying hair. He was John Jakobson, a wealthy investor who seemed to have two interests in life, making money and making women, and he had done much of both. Bess had met him a few weeks earlier at a dinner party. Jakobson, divorced from his first wife and living in the Hotel Carlyle, had come to the dinner with his longtime girlfriend Joan Rea, former wife of *New Yorker* cartoonist Oliver Rea. They intended to marry, a plan that Myerson would effectively derail.

"You should meet my daughter!" Myerson had told Jakobson at the dinner. Barra was then in the midst of a long love affair with a married man, and her mother was forever looking for ways to break it up.

"I thought he really would be right for Barra," Bess later confided to Marilyn Funt. "Who'd ever have thought he'd choose *me*!"

Marilyn's party marked the start of Bess's own passionate, stormy, and ultimately devastating affair with Jakobson. When Mollie Parnis saw him and Bess dancing past cheek-to-cheek, she said, "Happy birthday, Bess."

"Not just birthday," Myerson cooed. "Happy the rest of my life!"

Jakobson, like Bess, worshiped physical fitness, and at the beginning of their romance they would run together in Central Park. When John gave Bess a pair of diamond earrings, she vowed never to take them off, and soon friends reported seeing the lovers jogging together, both in gray sweats, Bess's diamond earrings flashing in the sunlight.

Myerson's love affair with Jakobson was more turbulent than most. Younger, Jewish, handsome, and rich, he fulfilled all her requirements save two: loyalty and fidelity. After six or eight torrid, on-and-off months, he ended the affair for good and went back to Joan Rea, whom he later married.

In late 1979, shortly after the couple reunited, Joan began receiving anonymous phone calls and letters. These continued, escalating in number and obscenity, for more than six months.

Jakobson got letters and calls too, as did his ex-wife and several of his former girlfriends. But Joan was the chief target. A friend to whom she showed the letters says, "Some were limericks, some were written in iambic pentameter, and they were fairly organized. They talked about who is a great fuck and cunt and prick, and are really vulgar." Many letters, though not all, were signed with a child's stamp of a cat holding a plumed pen. "To me this was important. They were not saying 'Help me . . . find me. . . .' They were saying, 'I'm a cat. Fuck you!' "

The first place Joan turned for help was the annoyance bureau of the phone company. By then she was receiving up to forty hang-ups a day. The phone company discovered that the calls were coming from two public phone booths, one on Seventy-first Street and Fifth Avenue (across the street from Myerson's apartment), the other on East End Avenue (in front of her speech writer's apart-ment, and within sight of Gracie Mansion).

Next Joan heard directly from Bess, who told Joan that she too was being plagued by phone calls and letters. She read some of her "anon-ymous" letters to Joan. "That Joan Rea is out to ruin your campaign," said one. "She's calling up people and saying not to vote for you. She says you're a lesbian, and that's why your divorce papers are sealed."

Soon Bess was making nightly calls to Joan to discuss their mutual problem. Bess spoke always in very intimate terms, as if they were best friends, which seemed odd to Joan since they barely knew one another. In fact, they had met just once, at the party where the ill-starred romance had begun. Now Bess addressed Joan as "dear" and "darling," and always phoned her late at night. "After the amenities, she'd lower her voice and say confidentially, 'Wait till I get a cigarette. I've *got* to talk to you. I've gotten more of these perfectly dreadful phone calls, and another letter. . . .' " For a time, Joan believed her.

One day Joan called Bess's apartment and a secretary answered. Joan left her name, and the secretary said, "Oh, I've just sent off a letter to you."

That evening, when Bess called her back, Joan said, "Your sec-retary said you'd just sent me a letter. Why on earth would you be writing to me?"

"Oh, probably inviting you to visit a day-care center or some-thing," said Myerson.

Two days later, Joan received another anonymous letter, "a hor-rible one." And on the following day, she received an invitation from Bess to visit a day-care center. This episode is what first made Joan suspect that Bess herself was the author of the anonymous letters. Yet she told herself: The caller *couldn't be* Bess Myerson.

She's running for the Senate! How would she have the time to place forty calls a day?

Many of the letters began with a list of women's names: Gladys Rachmill, Polly Bergen, Jane Singer. "They were set up like a chain letter, and you got a sense if you didn't pass the letter along, ill luck would follow." Sometimes the names were followed by lines like "These are the women he screwed and left."

Joan Rea, a lissome blonde, was then in her early thirties. One letter called her a "stupid, anorexic, bleached blonde *shiksa*," adding, "Dark roots look cheap."

The harassment had a childlike quality, as if the perpetrator were a naughty schoolgirl. Perhaps in response, Joan and a friend began behaving like characters in a Nancy Drew mystery. The calls were now coming in such torrents that the two women decided that the caller must have an assistant helping her place them, and that the callers probably first had to go to banks for rolls of dimes. Joan and her friend started shadowing Bess, their prime suspect, and staking out banks. Once they believe they saw Bess riding the subways wearing John's pajamas concealed under her trench coat.

Joan began to receive calls from persons claiming to be gossip columnists, who asked her, "Is it true John Jakobson is planning to marry you?"

"I'm sure Bess was listening on the other phone," Joan said later. "It was like when we were in seventh grade."

Joan said she was certain these calls were phony after they continued coming in during the New York City newspaper strike, when no columns were being published.

Four or five years later, Bess's assistant was finally identified. Or at least the Jakobsons found a woman, a former best friend and "big sister" of Myerson, who admitted to having hand-delivered some of the letters.

"Would you tell that to the police?"

"No. And don't subpoena me or I'll deny it."

What most amazed Joan and her friend at the time was that Myerson could be such a high-profile public figure by day, "and then after five o'clock it all fell apart. She was two people! How *fascinating* that she could handle both!"

Slowly the letters were turning uglier. John's first wife, Barbara, got one saying that John was the real father of Joan's daughter. Joan's next letter said, "Your husband left you without a sou. You didn't care because you had your Jew."

The anti-Semitism stunned Joan. The writer *"couldn't* be Bess. I mean, she called herself Queen of the Jews!"

At last Joan told Bess she was going to call the police. "Please don't do that, darling," Bess beseeched her. "The publicity would ruin my campaign. Send your letters over to me and I'll take care of it. I have a friend who's a lawyer. He knows how to handle this thing, for both of us, and do it very, very quietly."

After Joan sent the letters, Bess stopped calling her, and stopped accepting her calls. It took Joan several months to get her letters back. Meanwhile Bess had begun calling John to complain, "Get your girlfriend off my back! I can't stand her."

The costly Hotel Carlyle functions among other ways as a kind of protected game preserve for well-heeled Manhattan bachelors. During the same period as the letters and calls, Joan said that Bess "was constantly breaking into the Carlyle and searching Johnny's apartment." She had a key to the apartment made, and often snooped through John's things when he was away on a business trip. She would telephone the hotel doorman to find out when John was out of town. "Bess gets in anywhere," said Joan, adding that she used her celebrity status to get her way, and was skilled in the techniques of intimidation, as well as seduction.

One time John returned from a trip and found a yellow Post-it sticker on the door of his hotel suite: "For all the women you've laid and left, you'll pay."

Once John bought Joan a beautiful antique cameo ring. But she was holding out for marriage, and "I would not take it, except for the right reason. So Johnny put it on a shelf in his Carlyle closet. Then he was going to make a plane trip—just the D.C. shuttle, I think. But he put a note on the ring box: 'Should anything happen to me, this ring belongs to Joan Rea.' A few months later, he looked in the box, and the ring was gone. We figured Bess got it."

At four o'clock one morning when John was sleeping at Joan's apartment the phone rang. Joan picked it up, and a female caller said she was "Elizabeth Rubin," calling from Miami, and wanted to "talk to Johnny."

"What about?"

"One of his children."

Joan handed the phone to John. He listened briefly, then got dressed, returned to the Carlyle, and phoned Bess from there. Later he told Joan that Bess had said she was in a hospital in Miami, about to have emergency surgery for lung cancer. She said she was already on the gurney, and somewhat sedated, and wanted him to come down there right away. She wasn't making much sense. She was having the surgery in Miami, she said, because she wouldn't be recognized in Florida as she would in New York City.

The next morning Jakobson called Theodore Rubin, Bess's close friend and her onetime psychiatrist, to ask his advice on whether or not to go to Miami.

"Don't go," Dr. Rubin advised. "That would only give her false hope."

Later John and Joan learned that Myerson had really gone to the Miami hospital for plastic surgery, this time a tummy tuck. But most significant, they felt, was that Bess had registered under the name of Elizabeth Rubin. Some of the letters also had been signed "Elizabeth Rubin."

One evening at a dinner party Joan and John were talking about the scourge of letters and calls. Another guest, Betty Prashker, then a senior book editor at Doubleday, suggested, "Why don't you deal with it by writing about it?" Eventually Joan wrote about 250 pages, which she described as "a sort of *roman à clef* on Barbara Jakobson, Bess, and me." But she stopped because the language of the actual letters was "so dirty."*

"Have you heard the latest on Bess?" her friends had begun asking one another in the daily round of morning phone calls by which fashionable women catch up on what's happened in Gotham in the previous twenty-four hours. "It's so sad. She sits for hours in the lobby of the Carlyle, waiting for him to come in."

At another point in all this, Bess assigned someone to tail Joan and John. Joan is not sure if the man was a friend, a private detec-

* Several years later, in the summer of 1984, when the Jakobsons rented a house in England, Joan left her working manuscript, plus her stack of letters, on the desk in the study of their Manhattan apartment. When she returned, they were gone. She has never been able to find them, though copies of the letters are in New York Police Department files.

tive, or a taxi driver. He made tapes logging his route as he followed the couple around town, and the tapes were left outside the door of John's hotel suite. A man's voice would say: "We know where you've been," and tick off the various stops.

Once the couple went to Washington, D.C. They stayed at the Madison Hotel, and invited Joan's parents to lunch. Joan's mother is a small-town librarian in Virginia. The next tape at the Carlyle described the Washington trip and Joan and John dining with "an older, unidentified couple that lives in Virginia."

Soon Joan's mother, the genteel librarian, was also getting anonymous letters, six in all. One said,

> Your son must not marry the jew-girl.
> But it's all right if your daughter marries the jew-boy.
> The money . . . the money . . . the money . . .

These grew increasingly obscene, and one said, "His Jewish nose has been in more cunts than . . ."

"It was *relentless!*" said Joan. One day in the mail Joan's mother received a color poster of two gross hippopotamuses rolling in mud, with some comment about this being her daughter and John.

After many months, by which time the Senate primary was over, and Bess had lost, Joan was finally able to get Bess to return her letters. She turned them over to a private detective, who undertook to dust them for fingerprints.

Then a plastic Baggie of human excrement was left in a Bonwit-Teller shopping bag on the doormat outside Jakobson's suite at the Carlyle. It happened again, and this time the container was stenciled JOHN BAG. It looked like something bought at a shop that sells cute bathroom accessories.

At this point the detective advised Joan to call the police. Jakobson was reluctant to turn in his former, obviously sick girlfriend. He phoned her and said, "Look, Bess. I know you're the one who's doing this."

Her answer was odd, Joan thought. She did not deny it. Instead, she replied, in sarcastic tones, "Oh sure, Johnny . . ."

Jakobson told Bess, "I don't care what you say. Your campaign is over now, and I'm going to the police."

When Jakobson called the cops, however, he found that Bess had already called them herself. She had rung up former fellow city official Police Commissioner Robert J. McGuire, complained of anonymous calls and letters, and demanded an investigation. McGuire assigned Detective Gloria O'Meara, who worked in the special projects section of the police department's intelligence division, to look into the matter.

O'Meara did a thorough job. She interviewed Bess, Joan, John, and Barbara Jakobson individually and privately. She asked each one if he or she was willing to take a lie-detector test. Bess was the only one who refused. Instead, she called the NYPD and protested haughtily, "Look—I *instigated* this investigation!" Later, when the cops began questioning the other recipients of calls and letters, she complained again. "Look, this is *my* investigation. *I* am the person being harassed by anonymous letters. You're not supposed to talk to all these other people. . . ."

The police advised Joan and John that sending obscene materials through the mails, or hand-delivering them, was a Class B misdemeanor. However, since they had no physical evidence or other positive proof that the sender was Myerson, they could not press charges. Later the Jakobsons came to believe that the NYPD was simply reluctant to file charges against Mayor Koch's dear friend.

Koch received a confidential police report on the matter in late 1980. He made no public comment until the summer of 1987, by which time Myerson had been forced to resign from city government. Judge Gabel had stepped down from the bench, Andy Capasso was in prison on tax charges, and the press was chasing the story at full gallop. When a story about the Jakobsons' 1980 harassment appeared on the front page of *The New York Times*, Koch acknowledged he knew of the incident, but he dismissed it as "a lovers' quarrel." Only at that point did "police sources" openly acknowledge that they knew the sender was Bess.

"Bess is *without scruples*," Joan said sometime after that. But she insisted she still felt sorry for her. "I cried for her sometimes, for the tragedy of being all alone at four A.M. with no one to call. It was too sad; I wept."

Joan was much impressed by the big, red-haired, bright cop, Gloria O'Meara, who headed the confidential investigation. "She was right out of *Cagney and Lacey*," Joan said. But, she added rue-fully, "I don't think Gloria played it entirely straight." Although the detective had originally told the Jakobsons that, personally, she thought Myerson was the perpetrator, she also deliberately misad-vised them, they came to believe, by saying, "You can't do any-thing; you can't press charges." The overriding police concern, it appeared to the Jakobsons, was to head off needless potential scan-dal involving Mayor Koch.

Some thirty-five years before, when Bess had toured the nation as a speaker for the Anti-Defamation League, she had told audi-ences, "You can't be beautiful and hate, because hate is a corroding disease and affects the way you look." Did the plumed cat recall these lines, one wonders, as she penned her anonymous filth?

There is a postscript to the story. A few years after the letters episode, Joan Jakobson arranged a lunch for four women, all of whom had reason to dislike Myerson. Besides herself, there were her old Nancy Drew friend and Nancy Capasso, whose husband by then had left her for Bess. The fourth woman was to have been Marilyn Funt, but at the last minute she canceled out, later con-fessing that Myerson's great friend Dr. Rubin had agreed to write the foreword to her book. (Rubin is a prolific lay writer who has frequently used his caseload for inspiration. One of his books, about a pair of schizophrenic teenagers, was made into the movie *David and Lisa*.) Marilyn feared that if she spoke out against Bess, she would not get her foreword. She went so far as to call Dr. Rubin to assure him personally that she intended to remain loyal to Bess. Then she added, as a quid pro quo, "But I just want to know one thing, Ted. *Did* Bess write those letters?"

"Yes," said Rubin.

"How did she get into Johnny's apartment?"

"She had a key made."

Dr. Rubin categorically denies Marilyn's story. "Absolutely not," he says. "I knew they went out together; that's *all* I knew. That's the God's honest truth."

11

LOVE AND

SORROW

NOT ONE OF MYERSON'S POLITICAL AIDES HAD THE slightest suspicion of the bizarre double life the candidate was leading during the campaign. Her staff knew only that the campaign was not quite working. Speeches on issues tended to dissolve into inappropriately personal reminiscences. Reporters said that Myerson often seemed unprepared.

"Bess tried very hard, and worked very hard," said the loyal Maureen Connolly. "But there comes a certain point where you are comfortable with the information, and I never saw that. If you look at tapes of her debates you will see someone struggling to remember, more like a student taking an oral exam than a candidate convincing an electorate.

"When she'd wade into audiences live, especially older people, they'd go crazy." But on television, the normally self-confident Bess "was not there." She did not come across in interviews, debates, or even in the kind of spots she'd once done so well for Koch. "I don't know why. Some candidates blossom under adverse circumstances. Nothing clicked for Bess."

Myerson lost to Liz Holtzman amid floods of tears. She acknowledged defeat in a hotel ballroom, tossing a bunch of long-stemmed American beauty roses one by one to the crowd. She felt bitter and proud. Asked why she lost, she said, "I was too tall, too beautiful, and too rich."

A rare word of consolation came from her ninety-year-old father. "You didn't lose, Besseleh," he told her. "You just got fewer votes." But a few months later, Louis Myerson was dead, leaving Bess feeling more alone than she had ever been in her life.

Holtzman's short-lived victory (she would lose the general election to Alphonse D'Amato) left Bess in great disarray. All at once she was a failed pol, a washed-up beauty queen, an insanely jealous woman, and $1 million of her own bucks in the hole. What's more, after a lifetime of iron discipline, she had allowed herself to become forty-two pounds overweight. The cause, she said, was a prolonged diet of political banquet food. Always dutiful, Bess for six months had hit every single stop on the rubber-chicken circuit.

On one such evening near the start of her campaign in early spring, she had found herself at Antun's, a polyester-draped catering hall in Queens Village, where a routine Democratic party dinner and fund-raiser was in progress. The host and ringmaster was Queens borough president and Democratic leader Donald Manes. Queens was by now home to the largest concentration of Democrats in the United States, which had helped make Manes the Apple's number two politician, second only to Koch in the New York City power structure. Indeed, Manes was the mayor's personal choice to succeed himself in office—providing he could persuade himself to step down. No wonder the chubby, canny pol had begun to refer to himself as the King of Queens.

After the dinner and speeches, a flashy-looking couple came up to the dais to embrace Manes, and he in turn introduced them to Bess. They were the wealthy Capassos. Their company was now New York City's largest sewer contractor, and they were both enjoying the high life. A couple of weeks before they had bought themselves a $3 million apartment on Fifth Avenue, and hired award-winning architect Robert A. M. Stern to remodel it for an additional $3 million.

Nancy, now forty, was proud that she still looked good enough to model bikinis in charity fashion shows. Once her children were all in school, she had put her sharp shopper's eye to excellent use and studied real estate. As a broker at Sotheby's International Realty, perhaps the Apple's toniest firm, she dealt in the highest-priced residential real estate market in the world, and averaged about $50,000 a year selling apartments and houses on commission.

Andy was thirty-five and still a ferocious hard worker with vague political connections and possible mob links through his friendship with Matty "The Horse" Ianniello, and his blood relationship to his mother's brother, the late Tony "The Sheik" Corillo.

Manes always sent the Capassos free tickets to his political dinners, and Andy always made a generous pledge to the Queens Democrats.

After tonight, however, his interest in politics broadened, and Capasso began contributing large sums directly to Bess Myerson's Senate campaign. Soon he was soliciting additional contributions from his friends in construction work. As spring faded into summer he gave her something more precious than money, the full-time use of a Nanco-owned chauffeured limousine. Then he offered her a spacious office at Nanco headquarters in Long Island City. He positively begged her to make use of Nanco's phones and secretaries and mailroom. He invited her to work out with him in the company gym.

After Myerson's defeat in early September, Capasso's generosity increased. He personally helped her move her office files to Nanco. He made available Nanco accountants to tally her massive campaign debts, and he personally solicited funds to help pay them off. At around this time, he began saying that Nanco had been named for Naples, birthplace of his grandparents.

Andy was gentle and kind and concerned and fatherly/motherly with Bess, just as he was with his children, and this was as important to her as any of the tangible gifts. As Nancy said, "When Andy was there he was all there. You always got a hundred percent of whatever he had to give."

Andy now offered Bess himself, a kind and vigorous and much younger Italian male who declared himself madly in love with her, and acted the part. Her stinging defeat had caught her off guard and knocked her flat. She had lost about $1 million. She did not know what to do, how to function. She was "a woman of a certain age," and at her most vulnerable, when she met a nice young man eager to help, and filthy rich. What woman could resist?

Andy "literally picked her up off the mat," her friends said. "Whatever you need, Bess—it's yours," he told her . . . the loveliest words a woman in her condition could possibly hear.

This new relationship was quite different from the one she had enjoyed with Arnold Grant. Then, Grant had been her Professor Higgins. This time she played that role to Andy's Eliza. At first she seemed a bit ashamed of her new man. When she had theater tickets, she often invited a woman friend to accompany her. Afterward Andy would pick them both up in his limo and take them to dinner. Though sometimes a heavy drinker, he did not drink much around Bess, and always seemed to be on his best behavior.

These women liked Bess's new boyfriend. "Andy makes you feel that if you have any problems, Andy will help you out."

"I am certain Bess was not in love with Andy. But he was *comfortable*. Oh yes, he was ga-ga for *her*. That *he* could interest a Miss America! That she was really in love with *him*! He couldn't believe it."

Thus the gods had brought matters full circle, and the vibrant creature who once made Koch a man had now found a man who made her feel like a woman for the first time in many years. October blazed and dimmed and sputtered into November. Now Bess's friends scarcely saw her. But they knew she was with a new man, and that he was making her happy.

Everybody knew but one. The wife. Always the last to know, they say. But this wife went the old cliché one better. This wife fought not to know; she refused to know. She could bear any humiliation but the humiliation of reality. Rather than that, she preferred to become the all-time, world-class duped wife. Thus she managed to postpone the inevitable for more than a year. In a way she was buying herself time, letting herself down gradually, but the pain was great. It might have been easier to cut her throat and get it over with.

Nancy had no words to describe her experience of losing her husband, the breakup of her marriage, her growing, incredulous sense of betrayal, the pulverizing of her own foolish trust, her sense of naked, public humiliation, the slide from very rich wife to very reduced, self-supporting ex-wife; from a $6 million palace on Fifth Avenue to a high-rise rental on Lex. She felt she was re-experiencing Ingrid Bergman's role in *Gaslight*, though Andy the sexy Brooklyn roughneck was no Charles Boyer.

Always Nancy was bewildered; sometimes she was furious. "So many times, I wanted to kill him. Really *kill* him! Then I'd say to myself, over and over: Jean Harris, Jean Harris. It became my mantra."

Nancy came to believe that she almost had a nervous breakdown, but somehow did not, quite. "But I was crashing . . . I was 'gas-lighting' . . ."

The gaslighting had begun in mid-1980 when two women, one a friend, the other a co-worker, called Nancy the same morning with the same story. Both had been at a party the night before and had heard a friend of Bess's, art dealer Phyllis Goldman, openly gloating: "Nancy thinks Andy's off playing tennis. But he's with Bess. He's so nuts about her, he bought her a forty-two-thousand-dollar Mercedes."

When Nancy heard the story, "It was almost a relief! I'd thought *I* was nuts." Andy's strange behavior, she said, had been driving her out of her mind. He didn't come home. She didn't know where he was. He wouldn't permit her to ask. When she tried, he would stonewall and refuse to answer. She had wild fantasies: Maybe he was meeting hoods in bars; maybe he was lending money at exorbitant rates. She had let herself become so tormented and upset, she had begun to wonder if Andy was deliberately trying to make her crazy.

"Once I *knew*, I was a hundred percent better right away. I confronted him. He denied it. He said they were just friends. He said he loved me. I said, 'You have to give her up.' He promised. But he couldn't do it. She ran him like a puppet. She was so much smarter, older, more sophisticated. Andy has great street smarts. But she *really* knew her way around."

Nancy credited her "good Jewish parents" for giving her a solid upbringing that kept her from cracking up under all the pressure. But she also lamented that her upbringing did not in any way prepare her, or warn her, that such things could happen to a marriage. Very likely her parents didn't know. When Nancy first mentioned her suspicions to her equally unworldly mother, "Mom said: 'Don't be ridiculous! He doesn't even *like* women.' "

So Nancy told her some hard facts. "Listen, Mom, the first time he didn't come home at night was three days after our wedding. He just said, 'I'm going out with the guys.' That's all he ever says."

An Italian mother might have counseled: "Say nothing, do nothing. You have the children. You have the home. You have your pride. You don't want to spend every night with him anyway. Who knows, maybe he'll come back. Take my advice and he's *sure* to come back, though it may take him twenty, thirty years."

But even if she had been offered this sort of advice, a spirited woman like Nancy could not have accepted it.

To keep her mind focused on something concrete, rather than letting it drift toward speculation and shipwreck, Nancy decided to check out the Mercedes story. It would not be difficult. There were three Mercedes-Benz dealers in the metropolitan area, and the Capassos, who between them owned four Mercedeses, had already dealt with two of them. "So I marched into the only dealer we *hadn't* dealt with—you know me, playing Polly Polyester—and said I wanted to see a car like my friend Bess Myerson's. Sure enough, they'd sold her a blue two-seater convertible. Later, when it was stolen, Andy bought her another one."

When the time came for the family to move from Old Westbury to their new $6 million apartment in Manhattan, the three younger children, Debbie, Michael, and Andrea, now ages sixteen, eight, and six, would have to change schools. Steven and Helene were already in college. Over the summer of 1980, Nancy and her children visited several schools and settled on Horace Mann and Dwight. By this time the gaslighting had driven Nancy to overeating and chain-smoking. She was now smoking literally all night long, and quit in 1981 when she realized she was going through four packs a day. She went to Smokenders, and told herself, "Everything in my life is so bad, I must be in control of *something*." When Nancy stopped, Andy also stopped, but only temporarily.

Architect Stern's remodeling of course took longer than he had predicted, and school was starting soon. The kids could scarcely be expected to commute from Old Westbury, so Andy arranged to move his wife and children after Labor Day to the Hyde Park Hotel, on Seventy-seventh Street and Madison Avenue, across the street from and far more modest than the Carlyle. It was not far from the new apartment, and after Nancy put the children on their school buses, she could walk over and check the workmen's progress and try to spur them on. Weekends, everybody could come home to Old Westbury.

The hotel suite was small, with two bedrooms. It had no kitchen and no help save for the regular hotel maid service. Breakfast was cold cereal or toast. The limo brought Nancy and her three youngest children home to Old Westbury on weekends, but the rest of the time they played games in the clean but drably furnished hotel living room. They lived on takeout food from nearby restaurants, and everybody felt trapped and miserable.

Andy was rarely around. "He was disappearing. Sunday nights after we got back to the hotel from Old Westbury, he'd just vanish," said Nancy. Once she followed Andy out the door and into the elevator and down into the lobby wearing only her nightgown, crying and begging, "Where are you going?" He pulled away, said he had an appointment, and walked off.

A further note on geography: Bess Myerson for some years had occupied a modern two-bedroom apartment just off Fifth Avenue at Seventy-first Street. The color scheme was Arizona desert, and there were Etruscan vases, Byzantine mosaic fragments, archaeological finds from Israel, and a few nice antiques. A grand piano sat in an alcove with a wall removed, where the dining room was meant to be. It was perpetually piled high with stacks of clothing and an ironing board was permanently set up alongside. Thus her quondam music room, symbolic of her teenage hopes, had become a TV star's dressing room, representing the adult reality. Myerson's bedroom was what one visitor called "conventional Scarsdale," with king-size bed and floral chintz. The second bedroom was set up as an office.

In one of those coincidences that so delight the gods, Andy Capasso had invested $6 million in a regal new abode for himself and his family at the precise moment he had fallen madly in love with another woman who lived a few blocks away.

By Christmas people had been telling Nancy for six months that her husband was having an affair with Bess Myerson. She still refused to accept it. She couldn't. "If she'd been an airline stewardess, that would not have been so surprising. But *Bess Myerson*! She was Miss America the year he was born!"

A few days after Christmas, at about noon, an ambulance pulled up to the emergency entrance of Lenox Hill Hospital on Park Avenue, followed by a Nanco limousine. A frantic Andy jumped out and followed the medics, who were taking an obviously stricken woman inside. Myerson was registered under an assumed name. The chauffeur knew only that she had collapsed earlier that morning in her Nanco office.

Rumors swirled through the city. Bess Myerson was in intensive care. She had had a stroke, had made a suicide attempt, had suffered a nervous breakdown. Some people were told she had fallen off a ladder, others that she'd hit her head on a cabinet.

When she was able, Bess telephoned several of her close friends and told each one the same thing: "I'm in Lenox Hill and I've had a slight stroke. I'm just telling the people I care *most about*. I want *only* my nearest and dearest around."

The first woman to rush over found Senator Daniel Patrick Moynihan at Myerson's bedside, "a man she barely knew!"

But the friend was wrong, a consequence of Myerson's habit of keeping people in separate shoeboxes. Moynihan had endorsed Bess for the Senate. She could have known him quite well.

The cause of her collapse turned out to have been a brain aneurysm. "A bubble in my brain burst," she explained.

The normally fit and disciplined Myerson had put on her forty-two extra pounds in only a few months. Doctors said her rapid weight gain during the campaign probably caused the aneurysm. Such compulsive eating could be related to her loss of John Jakobson, or could perhaps be the consequence of campaign stress and overwork, or might even reflect the strain of carrying on a torrid love affair with a married man devoted to his children over the Thanksgiving and Christmas holidays.

Andy Capasso visited Bess's hospital room every day. Lenox Hill was only a few blocks from the Capassos' new apartment, and one day as Nancy was going to inspect the workmen's progress, she saw her husband's limousine and driver parked across the street from the hospital. "Tony! What are you doing *here?*"

"Waiting for Mr. Capasso," the driver stammered. But Nancy still managed to see nothing.

Before Bess's illness, she and Capasso had kept pretty much to themselves. Many of Bess's friends met her new lover for the first time in her hospital room. One of these was Bess's old friend at City Hall, the mayor's special assistant Herbert Rickman. When Rickman saw the lovelorn Capasso hovering outside the intensive care ward, he murmured to another visitor, "Dear lord, we've just gone through John Jakobson—and now we have to put up with *this*!"

Visiting Myerson in her hospital room after she got out of intensive care, Rickman was alarmed. "I saw a sudden loss of control. Her speech was erratic. Barra was scared."

Others noted that Bess had trouble walking for a while. She had a slight speech problem too, seemed fragile and vulnerable, and had difficulty remembering things.

Once Myerson was discharged from the hospital and began to recover, people noted a distinct change in her personality. She seemed to have become "more mellow," they said, though perhaps it was just that she talked more slowly. The super-cheap behavior, however, became more pronounced. She not only cadged phone calls, and offered to sell to friends clothes that had been given to her, but other curious habits took hold. Bess had wealthy friends who made a yearly trip to Israel. After she got out of the hospital, she took to inhabiting their vast and grandiose apartment when they were out of town, wandering through the empty, carpeted rooms, past heavy furniture shrouded in dustcovers, under darkened chandeliers wrapped in cheesecloth, making free phone calls.

Possibly the stress of the political campaign had been responsible for the seeming Jekyll/Hyde split in her personality. People who knew the private Bess gossiped about other freakish episodes, some dating back many years. For example, the morning after the writer Gail Sheehy published an interview that Myerson did not care for, Bess telephoned her. "Gail, I'm calling you from my gynecologist's office. In fact, I'm lying on the table. My feet are up in the stirrups right now! But I consider it *that* important that I speak to you."

Sheehy sensed an implied threat in this grotesque statement. "It felt like her technique was to try to embarrass, and to intimidate, by being bold."

Bess worked hard to recover her faculties, and she went on a strict diet. She looked around for a collaborator on a book about her recent experience. The result was *The I Love New York Diet*, written with Bill Adler and published in January 1982. Alas, the book was instantly denounced by the New York City Department of Nutrition as a dangerous crash diet, and a misrepresentation of the ideas of Norman Jolliffe, M.D., the city's beloved and much-respected former director of the Bureau of Nutrition. The diet was too rigid, the daily allotment of calories was much too small, and portion sizes were not defined. Nonetheless, the book lasted twenty-two weeks on the *Publishers Weekly* best-seller list, and the royalties helped pay Myerson's hospital bill.

Please Make Me Happy was a 1981 cable-TV psychology talk show that Myerson co-hosted with her friend Dr. Rubin. The producer came to believe that Bess did the show in order to work out her own problems. She had "mellowed" a bit in comparison to the old days on the consumer show, but she was still cold and difficult, and still came across on camera like a "robot." The show's agent said he had to take her to court to get paid his commission.

In April, however, ABC-TV made Bess a six-figure offer to host a morning talk show. She turned down the network executives in person, saying she wasn't interested "at *this* moment." For now, at least, money was no longer a problem for her.

Herbert Rickman soon changed his mind about Capasso. He grew to like Andy almost as much as he did Bess, and wound up as the unlikely Mercutio to this improbable pair of star-crossed lovers. When Barbaralee Diamonstein and her husband, Carl Spielvogel, held a grand dinner in honor of the sculptor Louise Nevelson, Bess brought Andy, and Rickman would recall later that Capasso was the hit of the party. "He was *brilliant*! The cleverest s.o.b. I've encountered. The deeze, dem, and doze accent is a pose, an affectation. People adored him. He was the catch of the season! And it went on for three years. I was enchanted."

For some years Herb Rickman had also been a close personal friend of Hortense Gabel, an admirer of her quiet wisdom and political savvy. "Horty was another one of my heroines," Rickman has said. He had served as personal assistant to Ed Koch "since day one." During that first year in City Hall, he felt he was foundering. He had no government experience, except for a few early years in the U.S. attorney's office, where he had specialized in immigration matters. So Rickman had sought out eight or nine people to consult with regularly and give him counsel. Judge Gabel was one of the most important, and every six weeks or so he took her to lunch at a Chinese restaurant near her courthouse. "I knew she hated Ed Koch, but it didn't matter; I loved her responses."

THE CAPASSOS MOVED into their new duplex pleasure dome early in 1981, even though sections of the apartment were still under construction. Situated just across Fifth Avenue from the south end of the Metropolitan Museum of Art, the corner apartment, one of only six in the narrow, elegant building, had breathtaking views south and west across Central Park, which in spring was ablaze with azaleas and flowering fruit trees. The apartment formerly had been owned by Peter and Patricia Kennedy Lawford as well as the Marshall Fields, and it was considered one of the loveliest in Manhattan.

In the beautiful space allotted to him architect Stern had created a kind of dazzling, Hollywood-style Roman villa floating in the sky. The impression stepping off the elevator and directly into the apartment was of a lyrical sky colonnade in bisque plaster floored with acres of white marble. The columns were interrupted at regular intervals by exquisite, balconied floor-to-ceiling windows, and the entire space hung and seemed to pivot on a broad white marble floating stair with handrails of beaten brass. The sublime staircase led up to the private family quarters, which, like the living space below, were accessible directly from the elevator. Students of conspicuous consumption in the late twentieth century could study the apartment on the cover and ten inside color pages of the April 1983 issue of *Architectural Digest*.

Despite the family's lavish new circumstances, Andy was home less and less. His behavior did not seem normal in any respect. He was beginning to drink heavily, and Nancy thought he was "acting cuckoo." That spring he began saying that the family needed to spend more time at the beach, and in May he spent $1.975 million on a several-acre beachfront estate with pool and guest house in Westhampton Beach.

Nancy was still in such an extreme state of denial that one day in early summer she suggested to her husband that they have Bess out for a weekend at the new house. "If you want," Andy said, and Nancy made the invitation. Even when Myerson arrived for the weekend driving her blue Mercedes-Benz, Nancy refused to become suspicious. How the plumed cat must have purred with pleasure as she drove along the Long Island Expressway.

In June Bess hosted a benefit for veterans that took place on a boat ride around Manhattan island. On board were cocktails, a buffet, and twelve-piece jazz band, and a fireboat saluted the revelers with sprays of red, white, and blue water. Among the guests were Barra Grant with a new boyfriend, Brian Reilly, a bartender with aspirations to become a playwright. Glancing in his direction, Bess told a friend, "Looks like that's my new son-in-law."

In the midst of the hectic summer of 1981, Andy asked Nancy to sign some papers. Andy's company had to be bonded to become eligible to bid on city contracts, and that year Nanco had just switched to a new bonding company, Aetna Insurance. As Andy's wife, Nancy was required to co-sign the documents. There also were several real estate matters to be dealt with. Nancy noticed that her husband had put the Westhampton Beach estate in his name only, but she said nothing.

IN THE SAME years that Bess and Andy were rediscovering the joys of love, Sukhreet Gabel was forgetting what it was like. She felt like a damp rag, and knew she was sliding into one of the deep pits of depression that had plagued her since childhood. The first had occurred when she was only five; another bad one came at eighteen. They did not necessarily relate to what was going on in her life at the time. All through her childhood and adolescence her parents had dragged her from doctor to doctor, seeking a cure for whatever was wrong with her, something besides the underactive thyroid that, until diagnosed and treated, had made her feel so listless and sluggish.

Mental illness in the young is hard to classify, and Sukhreet was in her early twenties before she found out what the trouble was, and in her thirties before she learned that it could be treated more or less satisfactorily with certain drugs. Since 1986, three daily capsules of Prozac, one of the newest antidepressants, plus three capsules of lithium, and her regular thyroid tablet, kept her on an even keel. Other medications could upset the delicate balance, however, and she was scrupulous in her avoidance of alcohol, tobacco, and recreational drugs.

The proper term for Sukhreet's illness was unipolar depression complicated by severe anxiety, an unusual combination, she said. Without medication, the depression made her feel she was inside a perpetual gray cloud, or behind a gray scrim. Combined with anxiety, it felt like "two stereos playing at once in neighboring rooms." In her room, she heard a radio full of "nervous annoying nasty static." The static was the sense of anxiety. Audible on the other radio were pounding bass notes—"you know how, when somebody is playing rock and roll in the next apartment, you hear only this pounding bass coming through the wall?"—which told her, "You are ugly; you are stupid; you are fat; you are crazy." This was not to say that she *heard* voices; it was her metaphor to describe the way she used to *feel*. With the Prozac and lithium, however, she said she felt fine—better than ever before in her life.

Sukhreet said depression is genetic, that her mother also took medication for depression, and that mother and daughter had openly discussed their experiences. It was the depression that made Hortense say, as she often did, "I feel so guilty about Sukhreet," and that made her worry constantly that her daughter might commit suicide, a tragedy Hortense would then see as "all my own fault." But according to Sukhreet, she was not, and had never been seriously suicidal.

Her mother dealt with her problem by burying herself in her work, Sukhreet believed, and sometimes felt that Sukhreet was foundering because she was insufficiently focused on work, and too much of a gadabout.

By mid-1980, Sukhreet and Jan had broken up for good. He was preparing to marry his former secretary, and Sukhreet was living in Chicago full-time. Her mother had helped her out financially, and emotionally, by buying her a condominium apartment near the university. It cost $47,500 and Sukhreet referred to it as "a handyman special." She helped herself out by taking in Tony Babineck, a computer expert who became her handyman, roommate, and lover, and paid half of the $625 due each month to Hortense Gabel, who owned the mortgage and title.

Babineck, the son of a librarian and a cop, was from the "mill rat" neighborhoods around the steel mills of East Chicago, and he knew more sociology than Sukhreet did. Sukhreet felt she and Tony had two things in common: their interest in sociology and "our marginality." She thought of herself as "a misfit, like Alice at the tea party."

She loved the intellectual challenge of academic life, but found it ugly in contrast to the "elegant and beautiful" world of diplomacy. "Chicago was frumpy cords, Indian cotton skirts, and fuzzy legs."

Sukhreet and Jan Revis had split their savings and possessions equally, she taking half their bank account, $9,000, and half their savings, $15,000, which she put into an account at Merrill Lynch. This would give her enough to live on for the three years it would take to get her sociology M.A. and Ph.D., if she earned extra money through part-time work. (Sukhreet had secured approval to work toward the Ph.D. even though she had not completed her M.A. thesis.)

At different times in her three years of study Sukhreet held as many as five part-time jobs. She interviewed lawyers for the American Bar Association; she coached prelaw students; she taught sociology at Chicago State; she worked as a teacher for Amity Testing Services. One of her jobs ended when her boss came to her apartment and tried to seduce her. When she rebuffed him, she was fired.

In the fall she got another job grading essays and teaching sections of a lecture course in English writing and research given by University of Chicago English professor Joseph Williams. In the spring he wrote her a letter of reference, mentioning that she was a "very patient" teacher. "I was amazed by Sukhreet's thoroughness," he wrote. "She is better than a couple of graduates from the English department with far more teaching experience. She is hardworking and very intelligent." What's more, his students said that

Sukhreet gave them the best assignments they had ever had. She told them to pick any U.S. holiday, for example, and explain it to a visiting student from any foreign country.

BY 1982, NANCY CAPASSO's life was going from bad to worse. One night in January she went to a Chinese restaurant, the Fortune Garden, in the old days a favorite spot for the Capassos, "and there he was, at *our* table, having dinner with *her*." Nancy didn't know which part hurt the most.

Nonetheless, another eight months passed before she first went to see a lawyer. Why did she wait? "I listened to his bullshit and I wanted to believe it. That was the gaslighting."

In this painful period, two events stood out in Nancy's memory: the Ragamuffin Parade, and Barra's wedding. The parade was a yearly civic festival designed for young children and sponsored by the merchants of Bay Ridge, Brooklyn. The streets were closed, and there were marching bands, food, costumed comic-strip characters, amusement-park rides, and free gifts for children. Local dignitaries turned up, and the mayor traditionally made a speech to the kids. That year Bess was marching, and Andy thought it would be great to bring Michael and Andrea, then ten and eight. It was early morning when Andy's limo picked up Nancy and Andy and the children first, then headed for Bess's building.

"Oh, good morning, Mr. Capasso!" said Bess's doorman with a yard-wide smile. Nancy felt sick, and then Bess slid in beside her.

Barra's wedding was worse. "The shabby wedding," she called it, and she hated every moment. Andy was unusually nasty and short-tempered that morning as the couple were getting dressed in their thirty-foot white marble bathroom. It was raining, and Andy screamed at the driver as their limo stopped to pick up Arthur and Sissy Fischer, a shopping-mall developer and his wife, who were unknown to Nancy but good friends of Bess's. (Later Nancy would learn that Bess stayed at the Fischers' lodge in Aspen whenever Andy took the children there on skiing trips.)

The Fischers and Andy were acting odd, Nancy thought, and Andy stayed cranky. The wedding service at Harkness House, a rentable East Side mansion, was "a *schlocky* budget wedding,"

Nancy thought. "Bess wore yellow polyester. You know, she dresses terribly. She has no taste, and she won't spend any money. She's so cheap she squeaks. It's her 'statement': 'I'm so wonderful I don't have to be dressed. I don't have to wear any makeup.'"

The party afterward in a midtown restaurant was worse yet. Most guests couldn't understand why Bess had invited the Capassos at all. "It was such a terrible idea—it put everybody off," said one. Several guests recall hearing Andy say, "Bessie, you look beautiful," and were astonished at her response.

"Not as beautiful as at *my* last wedding," she snapped.

Nancy thought "Andy followed Bess around like a puppy dog," and he seemed to know all the guests. Nancy knew hardly anybody. She felt like crying. At one point she got up and left, but came back when she couldn't find the limo driver in the rain. She thought people were staring at her.

She would have felt even worse had she known what Bess was whispering to her other guests: "Go over and talk to poor Nancy. I feel so sorry for her. She doesn't know a soul here."

12

FOLIE

À DEUX

ANDY CAPASSO'S LIAISON WITH BESS MYERSON swiftly made him New York's most charismatic sewer man since Art Carney played Ed Norton on *The Honeymooners*. But though Capasso's name and mug and large bankroll soon became familiar to the ranks of headwaiters, hostesses, and gossip columnists who are the true calibrators of Apple society, almost nothing else was known about him, which was fine with Capasso.

He was born Carlantonio Capasso, the third child of Josephine Corillo and Michael Capasso. His grandparents were Neapolitan, his parents American-born. The family fortunes were erratic. Mike Capasso sometimes had a sewer business, and was sometimes unemployed.

As a boy, Andy shined shoes, delivered papers, stacked goods in a supermarket, and did whatever else he could to earn the $50 weekly household money he gave his mom. After graduating in 1963 from Wheatley High School in East Williston, Long

Island, he went to work for his father digging ditches. Andy took great pride in his work, and refers to himself in his divorce papers as a third-generation sewer entrepreneur.

Many people besides his girlfriend and his wife appreciated Andy's Flintstone charm and sweetness. He was a warm Italian, generous, and generally a very nice guy. Men liked him as much as women did; children adored him. Enid Nemy, the chic and savvy *New York Times* style writer, once arrived for a lunch date with Bess at Il Valletto, and found Bess with Andy in tow. "I thought he was very nice, though I must say his class was a surprise. I know Bess also comes from a working-class background, but she transcended that long ago. Some people never do. Others, and I suspect Capasso may be one of those, never try and don't care." Nemy also observed that Bess was motherly and protective toward Capasso, as well as seeming sexually turned on. "She corrected his English at the same time that she was showing him her great political clout and power—which must have been quite a turn-on for *him*."

Nemy did not know it, but Bess was already working to improve Andy on several levels, urging him to dress better, lose weight, become more of a gentleman, and cut down on his drinking.

Charlotte Schiff-Jones, a stunning and successful Manhattan businesswoman who has known Myerson for many years, sees her friend as a highly sensual woman "who really likes sex. And Andy struck me as a very sexy guy, primitive, but funny and warm. Bess has always been attracted to dangerous men, and Andy to me was somehow frightening. There was something behind his eyes. No, not Mafia connections. Something in him."

At first Charlotte thought Bess was somewhat ashamed to be seen with him, as if she were wondering, "What am I doing with this guy? He doesn't even read *The New York Times*." But later, "she began to teach him, and behave rather maternally toward him. As for Andy, he was utterly enchanted by her position in the power corridors of the city."

When their affair first began, Bess introduced Andy by saying, "I want you to meet Andy Capasso. His wife is my friend." But within weeks she had given up this pretense. Each of the lovers was defiantly proud of the other. Their love affair was open, even flagrant; at dinner parties they talked about how great the sex was.

Andy was public *only* about his private life, and not all of that; he also had a *private* private life. About his business life he was totally close-mouthed, a clam. Bess was his equal both in braggadocio and in discretion. Eventually, she would take the Fifth Amendment—that is, she would commit professional hara-kiri—rather than testify without immunity to a grand jury that was looking into Capasso's financial irregularities and possible organized-crime connections. Eventually, Capasso would enter a sudden, surprise guilty plea and accept a four-year prison term and a fine of $500,000 rather than undergo a trial in which he might be forced to testify not only about his private life with Bess, but about his business affairs.

Andy was what his lawyer called "a stand-up guy." In the best wiseguy tradition, he spoke in code. Asked to talk, he stonewalled. His lip was permanently buttoned. Questioned by federal prosecutors, he did not even *know* Matty "The Horse," who had been his family friend/patron/goombah for a quarter-century. In the same mode, he told Nancy that he scarcely knew Bess Myerson, that they had only a formal business relationship. And such was Nancy's need to believe him, so absurd was it, and so painful, to lose one's husband to a woman old enough to be his mother, old enough even to be her mother, that believe him Nancy did for more than two long, miserable years.

Capasso was one of those charmed people who make you think they need you. And they do, of course, though not perhaps for what you think. Judy Yaeger, Nancy's chum, saw Andy as "upwardly mobile with a vengeance." Indeed, Capasso and Myerson were both climbers, skilled social and professional Alpinists, and when they met, each used the other as ladder, or trellis. Bess had the power and status; Andy had the dough.

A sewer man, a rich, happy, and unabashed sewer man, was something new on the Manhattan party circuit, and for six months or so Bess and Andy were the hottest couple in town. Hostesses sparred over their presence at dinner parties. Some said, "We can't stand *her*. But he's so refreshing!" He was particularly popular with museum directors and other Manhattan taste-makers who did not ordinarily get to know sewer magnates.

Much as people liked Andy, they felt Bess was embarrassed by him. She seemed to think he didn't "look right" because he was so much younger. They had frequent fights. The underlying issues never changed. Her fallback position was her age; one day he would leave her for a younger woman. He countered with "You're ashamed of me because I'm a guinea, and I don't talk right."

Capasso was troubled about rumors that his beloved also had, or had had, female lovers, and he spoke to Rickman of his concern. "Andy *hated* Bess's gay women friends. He didn't mind my gayness at all. He would joke about it, and openly kiss me in public."

Capasso's complicated domestic life had resulted in sudden, explosive expansion of his domestic turf. Within a year he had become the owner of two elaborate pleasure domes: the Fifth Avenue duplex, and the Gatsby-like estate in Westhampton Beach. There was also the original Westhampton Beach condominium and the two apartments in Palm Beach, and the automobile count was up to nine.

One midsummer's day at Richard and Shirley Clurman's country house in Quiogue, Bess drove up unannounced in what Shirley called "a perfectly gorgeous blue Mercedes convertible. She said her new and very generous boyfriend had given it to her, and 'If we ever break up, I'm giving back everything but *this*!' " Then she said, "I would *so* like you and Dick to meet Andy."

In early September Bess invited the Clurmans to come over to Capasso's new Westhampton Beach estate and watch the Miss America contest on TV. Although they were specifically invited after dinner, they found an elaborate buffet laid out on a sideboard. Except for this oddity, Shirley thought it "a quite marvelous house, beautifully decorated, in excellent taste." Bess's deficiencies as a hostess did not matter because "everything was done right, and very lavishly, by the servants, a very proper English couple."

The butler served drinks, and the four people sat down to watch the show on TV. Bess chattered and nattered, offering caustic comments about each contestant. One oft-repeated refrain was "Have you ever *seen* such ugly thighs!"

Andy finally said indulgently, but meaning it: "Bessie, would you mind keeping quiet for a moment? I want to watch the show."

Silently, the hostess rose and left the room. She came back carrying a large scrapbook. "You want to see thighs? I'll show you beautiful thighs!"

"And she was right," said Shirley. As Miss New York, 1945, contestant Myerson had absolutely gorgeous thighs, and thanks to the very strict regimen of diet and exercise she normally lives by, she had them in her fifties, and probably has them still.

Shirley invited Bess and Andy to dinner a few weeks later. Dick Clurman is an aggressive questioner, a habit he picked up from Henry Luce back when Clurman was chief of correspondents for Time-Life news bureaus around the world. Over the soup, he said to Andy, "Tell me about the construction business."

Clurman was enchanted by the directness of Capasso's reply. "It's a pay-off business. You gotta pay off everybody. There are blacks; we gotta pay off the blacks. There are women; we gotta pay off the women. . . ."

During this recital, Myerson sat quietly. Then she mentioned that she and Andy were expecting Ed Koch and Herb Rickman as their lunch guests over Fourth of July weekend.

ALL THREE GABELS were quietly prospering. In the fall of 1981, Sukhreet was in Chicago working toward her master's degree in sociology, and had begun writing a thesis entitled "Therapeutic Approaches to Conflict Resolution in Divided Societies." In New York City, Milton Gabel was much enjoying his retirement, and the pleasure of taking daylong trips to the Catskills with his hiking club after so many years standing on his feet practicing dentistry.

Also in 1981, Hortense Gabel made one of her rare appearances in the newspapers. Brinks, Inc., had a contract with the city to collect the money from municipal parking meters, and authorities had broken a small-time thievery ring of six Brinks guards. Together, they appeared to have stolen a total of about $5,000 from city meters. One of the guards, James Gargiulo, twenty-eight, of Queens, pleaded guilty to stealing $730, the amount found on him when he was arrested. In late March Judge Gabel sentenced him to four months of weekends in jail, thirty-two days in all. One first-time felony count could have gotten him up to four years in prison.

District Attorney Robert Morgenthau had asked for one to three years.

Seeing a ready-made opportunity to portray himself as tough on crime, Mayor Koch denounced Judge Gabel's sentence as "unduly lenient. Crimes involving official corruptions such as this should not be taken lightly," he solemnly intoned.

Joining in the chorus of righteousness, State Commissioner of Investigation Stanley Lupkin called the sentence "absurd." A nine-month inquiry by his department showed that the guards had stolen at least $1.2 million from the city. He even had videotapes of the thieves loading heavy bags into their cars each day after work. Alas, sometimes the luck runs not with the hounds but with the fox. On the day of the arrests, the men had only $5,000 in their possession, sufficient to charge one Class E felony only, not larceny.

Koch said the additional evidence against them should have been the basis for a higher sentence.

Judge Gabel countered, "How could anybody who respects the law expect me to sentence based on allegations that haven't been proved in a court of law?" She also told *The New York Times*, "What I did I think is enough to in a way tragically hurt him the rest of his life. I want to give him a chance to support his family. But he ends up a convicted felon, on probation for five years, with a real four months' taste of what jail is like and with the prayer that he can support his family as a truck driver. His future, to put it mildly, is limited." She contended that Koch's remarks were "very dangerous" because they could intimidate judges.

That same week, Justice Irving Lang gave the identical sentence to another guard. "The charges before us were for stealing a specific amount of money," he said. "Neither Justice Gabel nor myself are naïve enough to assume that the only time these people did this was when they were caught. But we still can't take that quantum leap to say they're responsible for two million dollars in thefts from parking meters."

NANCY CAPASSO'S OLD friend Judy Yaeger was now an attorney, specializing in matrimonial matters, and practicing law in New

York City. One evening in the summer of 1981, Nancy arranged to meet her for a drink at the Stanhope hotel, across from the Metropolitan Museum of Art, and hard by the Capassos' new duplex.

"I hadn't seen Nancy in a long time," Judy recalled later. "She said she was desperate. Over the drink she said, 'Something is very, very wrong in my life.

" 'Andy is never home,' she told me. 'I don't know what's happening. I can't make plans to meet anybody on the weekends. I can't have guests or plan parties, because I never know if Andy will show up.' "

"Where do you think he is?"

"I don't know. I think he may be meeting men in bars at night. He may be in the money-lending business."

"She was *very* upset," says Judy. "She thought he was doing some kind of dirty business. But she never said anything about another woman, let alone Bess Myerson. And frankly it never dawned on me either."

BESS'S DAUGHTER, BARRA GRANT REILLY, and her husband were both working as Hollywood scriptwriters, and parenthood was definitely not in their plans. Early in 1982, Barra learned that unhappily she was pregnant.

"Give me the baby and let me raise it," Bess begged. Barra and Brian consented, and Myerson set up a nursery in her apartment and ordered the layette. Her granddaughter, Samantha, was born that November. The Reillys soon asked for their baby back, and Bess of course agreed. But for the next several years Samantha and her parents made frequent trips east from California, and often stayed in Capasso's beach house. The Jewish grandmother has all the pleasure and none of the *tsuris* of the Jewish mother, and friends agree that Samantha's visits were unmistakably the happiest moments in Bess's life.

IN THE FALL of 1982, Nancy Capasso finally bit the bullet and paid a call on Matty "The Horse" Ianniello. Matty had been Andy's most frequent excuse for going out at night, probably one of the beard. "I gotta go see Matty," Andy usually said before taking off.

Matty was a man of honor, and Nancy knew she could count on him to give her a straight answer to a straight question. "What's with Andy and Bess Myerson?" she asked.

"I could tell he didn't approve of what Andy was doing," Nancy said later. "He didn't like Bess, and he thought Andy was being used. So he was trying to show me the handwriting on the wall without being a rat to Andy."

A man like Matty the Horse prefers not to speak directly, even when speaking the truth. "Nancy honey," he told her gently, "you know nobody sees Matty every night."

She understood, and she went to see the noted divorce lawyer Raoul Lionel Felder the very next day. He laid out for her the rules and customs of the high-stakes divorce game, and told her to come back and see him whenever she was ready to put the ball in play.

One Friday night in early November, Nancy Capasso invited Judy Yaeger to dinner at 990 Fifth, saying she didn't know whether Andy would be home or not.

"Well, Andy did come home," Judy said later. "The two little kids were there, plus Helene, the oldest. Andy and Andrea were in the kitchen cooking pasta and chicken." Judy went into the kitchen to talk privately to Andy. "Because Andy had once tried to help *me* out, when *my* marriage was on the rocks, I really made an effort. But he was not responsive. He was drinking steadily. . . .

"I'd say, 'Andy, what is going on?' He wouldn't answer. Instead he'd complain, 'My wife is telling the whole world I'm having an affair with Bess Myerson. She's slandering me!' And he would have another drink. And he would deny it again. '*Nothing* is going on. We are *just . . . good . . . friends.*'

" 'Just friends!' " said Judy. " 'Andy, you don't come home at night.'

" 'We are just friends,' he'd repeat. He wouldn't respond. In part because he was angry, in part because he was drunk.

"Then Nancy and Andy went upstairs to put the little children to bed. I heard a commotion and screaming and I ran up. Nancy was on the floor. Andy was kicking her with his heavy boots. Helene was trying to break it up. Everybody was screaming. I think Michael was watching. Andrea was in her room.

"The next thing I remember, Andy was sitting on Andrea's bed, and she was cowering. Andy was raging: 'She told my *daughter* that I was going out to see my girlfriend!'

"He was working himself up. He went into another bedroom, and started yelling again. I said, 'Nancy, I am calling the police.' She said, 'No. Call the doorman.' "

When the doorman rang the bell at the bedroom level, Nancy sent him away; she didn't want him to see what was going on. Judy returned to the living room and in a short time "Nancy came down, shaken. Andy had left the apartment. He was truly out of control. Andy is a smart guy, but he was irrational. Not focusing."

Judy and Nancy sat on one of the new $25,000 couches and leafed through old photograph albums, talking about the good old days when they were neighbors and their children went to camp together. About 11:30 P.M. Andy came back, talked briefly with Nancy, then left again. Judy went home.

The next day Nancy photographed her abrasions and contusions, took the pictures with her to family court, and readily obtained a temporary court order barring Capasso from approaching his wife in or out of the apartment.

"And that made him nuts!" says Judy.

One does not throw a husband like Andy out of his castle, not when he has worked like crazy to get together the money for a $6 million apartment for himself and his family, *and* a $1.9 million beach house for his mistress. Not unless one is prepared for the consequences. An Italian wife might have known better, or taken a less dangerous tack. Unknowingly, or uncaringly, the irate Nancy had unleashed the full wrath of her Neapolitan mate.

Andy moved to the Westbury Hotel, just down Madison Avenue from the Carlyle, and around the corner from Myerson's apartment, and on December 20 he filed for divorce. Nancy filed a counterclaim charging cruel and inhuman treatment and adultery, and hired detectives. Her complaint identified Myerson only as "B.M." Her lawyer also filed a motion seeking exclusive occupancy of the apartment at 990 Fifth Avenue for herself and her children.

In retrospect, it was apparent that Capasso never really wanted a divorce; he loved his family too much. He wanted to have his life with his family *and* his life with Bess. Such an arrangement would have seemed quite natural to him. His own parents had lived that way ever since he could remember.

But when Andy got angry, you got 100 percent of his fury; he held nothing back. He had no use for the proverb "Revenge is a dish best served cold." So when his wife threw him out of his own house, he vowed instant vengeance, and he exacted it continuously thereafter, ever figuring out new ways to punish Nancy—a game in which Bess Myerson swiftly became his enthusiastic and innovative partner.

They painted Nancy as grasping, vulgar, sluttish, greedy, and a bitch on wheels. They said the Capasso marriage was effectively over long before Andy and Bess had met. They said that from the beginning of the marriage, Nancy made Andy feel small, that she mocked him and called him a guinea. They added that she was a terrible hostess, a beast, a slattern, and a rotten mother. Nonetheless, they said, Andy, like a good Italian family man, did not want a divorce, because of the children. It was Nancy's neglectful behavior as a mother that had finally forced his hand.

As Andy and Bess worked on this scenario, each of the lovers fed upon and escalated the fury of the other until their mutual passion became a shared obsession, a *folie à deux*. Their friends said they spoke of little else, and the Capasso servants, who loathed Bess for her rudeness and hauteur, observed it all. In each of the three investigations that eventually were held—a secret personal investigation commissioned by Mayor Koch; a formal inquiry by the New York State Commission on Judicial Conduct; and the federal grand-jury proceedings that resulted in indictment and trial—Capasso's weekend guests, his house servants, and his chauffeurs would describe a beach house littered with legal papers, and would testify that Andy and Bess spent hours together poring over divorce documents, reading Nancy's briefs aloud, and devising responses. They spoke of little else, the witnesses said. Working together, they searched for ever more ingenious ways to punish evil Nancy for all time.

Andy was not a man afraid to admit guilt. In his original affidavit on the fracas at 990 Fifth Avenue, he acknowledged that he struck "the defendant back . . . as a result of the aforesaid provocations." The central "provocation" was eight-year-old Andrea piping up, as she watched her father knot his black tie, "Where are you going, Daddy? Out with your girlfriend?"

The affidavit asserted that after attacking his wife in front of the children, Capasso "became seriously depressed, anxious, embarrassed and upset . . . As a result of the provocations of the defendant, the plaintiff was required to consult a psychiatrist . . . because of the trauma he underwent after striking the defendant."

Which psychiatrist? Not surprisingly, the healer in question was Theodore Isaac Rubin, M.D., director of the Karen Horney Clinic. Later, Capasso became the institution's newest trustee.

Still later, in 1987, by which time his patient was divorced from Nancy and facing yet another purgatory, namely a four-year prison term for income tax evasion, Dr. Rubin again tried to smooth his way. In a presentencing letter to Capasso's probation and parole officer, Rubin wrote, "Andy Capasso has consistently demonstrated an unusual capacity for empathy, generosity, compassion, and sensitivity to the needs of others . . . I would like to believe that I played some small role in his recent self-development, because after thirty years of analytic work I have never witnessed so much growth by an incredibly curious human mind in so short a time."

Room for growth in empathy, generosity, compassion, and sensitivity to the needs of others had been readily apparent in each of the Capassos from the start of the couple's marital warfare. In February came a ten-day school holiday, and Andy took all five children on a ski trip to Aspen, Colorado. Bess stayed nearby with Arthur and Sissy Fischer. While they were gone, Nancy's motion requesting exclusive occupancy of the Fifth Avenue duplex was granted.

The morning it was time to leave Aspen, Bess and Andy and the kids arrived at the overcrowded airport to find that their tickets were worthless. "I'm sorry, Mr. Capasso, but yesterday all your reservations were canceled," said the clerk.

"Impossible!"

"No. It shows it right here. Mrs. Capasso called from New York and said you wouldn't be needing them."

Capasso arrived back in New York in a towering rage, and delivered the children to the lobby of the building to which he was no longer permitted access. Later that evening, court orders be damned, he came charging into the duplex to collect some clothes and belongings. His fury so impressed Nancy that she thought it prudent to lock her daughter Helene and herself in the marble bathroom while the rampage was at its height. But before Andy left, her courage returned, and she emerged from the bathroom shouting, "You get the hell out of here! I'm older than you are. And I'm *taller!*"

13

FOLIE

À TROIS

THE DEPARTMENT OF SOCIOLOGY AT THE UNIVERsity of Chicago, where Sukhreet Gabel thrived as a graduate student from the fall of 1979 to early 1982, was considered the finest in the nation. In her time there her grade-point average rose from B- to B to B+. By early 1982, nonetheless, Sukhreet had made a crucial career decision. Rather than write her doctoral dissertation on Surinamers and race relations in the Netherlands, she would abandon her plan to become a Ph.D. and settle instead for an A.B.D., "all but dissertation." At thirty-three, after seven years of part-time or full-time graduate school, she felt she had "academic dishpan hands" and was "entitled to join the real world." In this choice one sees an important aspect of Sukhreet's nature: Although bright, creative, and highly innovative, she is quickly bored and easily distracted.

Her newest plan: Free at last from both matrimonial and academic obligations, she would forsake the ivory tower, return to the Apple, and find her-

self a solid commercial job, something leading to a reasonably lucrative career in international affairs, foundation work, or financial
or management consulting—the fields in which she believed herself
qualified.

Her parents entirely approved. Her mother, now nearly seventy,
was still on the bench. As a New York Supreme Court justice, she
earned $82,000 a year. At retirement she would be entitled to an
annual pension of as much as $41,000. Despite her steadily eroding
health, Judge Gabel would be recertified later that year for a two-
year term, and again in 1984 for the term beginning January 1,
1985.

Horty's salary was in fact the major support of the family. Milton, seventy-five, had closed his dental practice five years earlier,
and his income came from $400,000 worth of municipal bonds,
which yielded roughly $35,000 a year tax free. Both parents were
concerned about their daughter's future livelihood. She was thirty-
three, and had never been self-supporting. Who would look after
her when they were gone?

The circumstances of Sukhreet's return to Gotham were just as
optimistic, though less gala, than her departure as a bride seven
years before. She arrived with a nest egg of $12,000 still intact, and
an extensive wardrobe of colorful, unique outfits and accessories,
most of which she had designed and made herself. But because of
her limited funds, she elected for the first six months to bunk on the
living-room couch in the Central Park South apartment of her aunt
Sybil Phillips. Then, no job yet having materialized, she moved to
her parents' living-room Hide-a-Bed on East Sixty-eighth Street.

The arrangement was not ideal. Sukhreet longed for privacy.
She found the atmosphere in the little apartment smothering. As
she put it, "I really didn't want to live on top of them and to be . . .
the child returning home at age thirty-three." Her parents, or at
least her father, who did the cooking, found his daughter's easy-
going personal habits intensely irritating. She despised his cuisine
and went out to eat every single night.

Hortense Gabel knew a great many influential people in New
York City, and she had begun making calls and writing letters on
her daughter's behalf even before Sukhreet hit town. When Sukhreet learned of this she became resentful, and demanded that in

future her mother consult with her before contacting people Sukhreet didn't know. Nonetheless, the moment she got to New York, she headed straight down to her mother's office to enlist her help.

Over the next year Hortense made as many as two hundred phone calls to persons of influence whom she knew, asking if they could find time to talk to her daughter. Almost always, Judge Gabel sent out letters following up on the calls. Though marked "personal and unofficial," the letters were typed on her official Supreme Court stationery and signed, "Hortense Gabel, J.S.C." In addition to these requests for interviews, mother and daughter sent out three hundred résumés and form letters blind to three hundred heads of companies, summarizing Sukhreet's experience, credentials, and interests.

The response to the personal calls and letters was excellent; almost everyone said yes. The response to the three hundred résumés was disastrous. Few companies even replied, and nobody offered a job. It was Sukhreet's luck to have hit the job market at a time when it was glutted with Ph.D.'s and A.B.D.'s in all the social sciences and liberal arts. An advanced degree was not just useless, it could be a hindrance. Harvard Ph.D.'s took their degrees off their résumés.

Dr. Steven Buff, director of professional development at the American Sociological Association, said later that 1982–83 "was the absolute pits for social scientists." The Reagan-induced recession had hit social scientists especially hard. "Lots of academicians spend more than a year looking for a job. The world is not friendly. Businesspeople are often provincial and narrow. They don't think of getting a highly intelligent, qualified person and putting him in a more broadly defined job."

Dr. Buff spoke with authority. His association was the nation's largest organization of sociologists, and he was director of a department created specifically because of the difficulty sociologists were encountering in finding jobs outside of academia. "It's entirely understandable," he said, "that a brilliant academic who spent a lot of time at the University of Chicago, and who is bright and amiable, might still not be able to get a job. And there would be nothing wrong with that person. Just someone in the wrong place at the wrong time."

Unfortunately, none of the Gabels ever met Dr. Buff. All three were entirely ignorant of the formidable odds against them. Hortense worked intensively with Sukhreet to devise a standard pitch to make at each interview, and Milton lent his wife and daughter maximum moral support. Although he had nothing to contribute directly to the job hunt, there is no doubt that mother, father, and daughter were united and single-minded in their quest.

Sukhreet thought of their standard pitch as "a marketing strategy for myself." First Hortense would comb her files for a likely name, call the person up, exchange a few pleasantries, and then say something like "My brilliant daughter, my very *interesting* daughter, has just returned to Manhattan after some years living abroad." She would sketch in a bit of Sukhreet's background, then say, "She's looking to switch to a nonacademic career. Could you find fifteen minutes to sit down with her and give her some advice as to what you think she might do well at?" Put in this gentle manner, by a much loved and respected judge, it would have been unusual to receive a negative answer, and so far as is known she never did.

"It was not asking for a job," Sukhreet later pointed out. "It was subtle enough so I could then go visit and say, 'Would you mind looking at my résumé? Do you have any suggestions that you think might improve it? If you were me, to whom would you show this résumé?' "

In this way, the Gabels built up a network of contacts, kindly persons then willing to look through their address books and come up with four or five more names of people Sukhreet might go to see.

Sukhreet has explained that she and her parents devised this approach "as the most effective way of not putting anyone on the spot. So we worked together on this script, as it were, and we thought it was an effective one, because we thought I could get the most information with the least pain for me, and for the poor subject who was being interviewed."

In retrospect the pitch seems to have been a mite too polite. A question so carefully designed not to elicit a "no" answer was unlikely to elicit a "yes," and it did not. Sukhreet's dream of hearing someone say to her, "Oh, boy! You're just the person we've been looking for!" never materialized, and the overweight, well-behaved, and charming young supplicant seems to have been handed along from one person to the next without anyone really coming to grips with her problem.

At the start of her quest, Sukhreet had as many as four appointments a day, and in the first year of her search she had actual interviews with 150 to 200 people. They included the writer and *Daily News* columnist Jimmy Breslin and, separately, his wife, Ronnie Eldridge, then director of the New York State Women's Bureau; Nathan Leventhal, chairman of Lincoln Center; Barbara Cohen of National Public Radio; lawyer and politico Edward Costikyan; Bronx borough president David Dinkins; Judah Gribetz, partner in Mudge, Rose and counsel to Governor Hugh Carey; Neal Hardy, Hortense Gabel's former assistant at the New York City Rent and Rehabilitation Administration; New York City deputy commissioner of economic development Larry Kieves; Sister Colette Mahoney, president of Marymount Manhattan College; Manfred Ohrenstein, majority leader in the New York State Senate; Herbert Rickman; Fabian G. Palomino, special counselor to Governor Mario Cuomo; Brendan Sexton, New York City's commissioner of sanitation; Donna Shalala, president of Hunter College; Manhattan state assemblyman Mark Alan Siegel; and former Mayor Robert F. Wagner.

One of the most cordial people she spoke to was Rickman, who invited her to lunch at the Delegates' Lounge of the United Nations. After looking over her résumé, he said, "Well, I can't see you working in sanitation . . . and you are not right for the fire department. . . . Let's try the New York City Commission for the United Nations, or Larry Kieves at Economic Development."

Sukhreet had sufficient smarts to "jump at Economic Development, and yawn at the Commission for the U.N. I wasn't particularly interested in worrying about diplomats' parking tickets."

But she lacked the savvy to recognize the cruel game that was being played. For example, Rickman sent Sukhreet's résumé to Henry Stern, who by then was New York City's parks commissioner, and sent a copy of his covering letter to Stern to Judge Gabel. But he was merely creating a paper trail. Stern says that Rickman also telephoned him and told him confidentially, "She's got problems." (As a longtime family friend, Rickman was aware of Sukhreet's emotional history.) The parks commissioner made only a *pro forma* response to Judge Gabel's letter, and he did not call Sukhreet.

As the year went on, Sukhreet had fewer and fewer interviews. She had run through most of their contacts, even the friends of friends. But Hortense and Milton remained unflaggingly optimistic, and sometimes they, rather than their daughter, seemed to be the major source of energy behind the search. Whenever Horty attended a lunch or dinner or civic event she never passed up an opportunity to make a pitch for her "interesting daughter." At the monthly meetings of the Women's Forum, an association of high-powered career women set up for the purpose of providing its members with the same "networking" opportunities already available to men, members grew accustomed to Horty's regular appeal: "Can any one of you suggest a career path, or a job opportunity, or an interview for my daughter?"

As Sukhreet worked her way through her A-list of contacts, and then through her B-list and C-list, she found the names were becoming "redundant." When someone gave her a list of new names to contact, she would already have spoken to three out of five. Her job hunt had begun to resemble the activity of a rat in a maze. Over twelve months this intense search had produced only two solid offers. One was a secretarial post at an obscure foundation having something to do with Africa, unsuitable because Sukhreet was a poor typist. The other was a pork-barrel offer from one of her mother's former assistants, a $14,000 city job as resident superintendent of a municipal housing project in Harlem.

The Gabels several times offered to send their daughter to law school, a proposition Sukhreet firmly rejected. She despised lawyers as much as she did politicians, she told her mother. For the same reason, she had vetoed the suggestion of a paralegal's job at Shea & Gould, the prestigious law firm that represented her mother.

In the same twelve-month period, Sukhreet's résumé went through nine or ten rewrites as she and Hortense, singly and together, and sometimes with Milton's help, struggled to assemble her oddly assorted cornucopia of credentials into the most impressive possible package. Sukhreet would bring twenty copies at a time of each revision to her mother's office, and Judge Gabel "handed them out like movie fliers." The judge's faithful secretary did the same. "In other words," Sukhreet said later, "virtually anyone who walked into that office was handed a copy of the judge's daughter's résumé. This is my loving mother, please understand."

As the search dragged on, Sukhreet took temporary jobs tutoring students in subjects such as formal logic and reading comprehension for the LSAT and GMAT tests. The senior Gabels grew increasingly bewildered, and insistent. Why should it be so difficult for their talented, cultivated, interesting daughter to find a job? Each time they spoke, one parent or the other would say, "I just can't understand why you're having all this difficulty." Sukhreet had no answer. Nonetheless her retired father asked her the same questions every single day for a year, she said. "Have you found a job today? Did you talk to so-and-so? Is there anything new?"

The pressure Sukhreet felt must have been immense. Later a psychiatrist and psychoanalyst familiar with details of the family job search would characterize the obsessive behavior of the three Gabels as "a classic *folie à trois*."

By the time Sukhreet went to lunch with Rickman in the early spring of 1983, "I was very, very upset. I was depressed, frightened, scared, confused. I just couldn't figure out what had happened, what had gone wrong and why I was in this dreadful pickle, and I was becoming increasingly panicky." She felt she "had no home," and ached to return to her "home" in Chicago, and to "be comforted" by her old boyfriend Tony. "I wanted a security blanket," she explained. "And then I vowed to come back to New York for a while to go through the torture of showing that résumé for the nine hundredth time."

In March 1983, the one-year anniversary of her ordeal, Sukhreet got in her old Toyota and headed back to Chicago. Watching the oncoming traffic, she thought, *I have only to cross the white line and my miseries will be over.*

Before moving to New York she had had a discussion with Tony about bringing other women to their apartment. She told him she would understand if he did this, and not object, providing he was truthful about it and did not attempt to deceive her. When she returned home unexpectedly and found unmistakable evidence that Tony had failed to keep his promise, it seemed to her the last straw.

The one friend on whom she felt she could depend had turned out to be undependable after all. She crawled into the bed and stayed there two whole weeks, crying almost nonstop.

She knew she had now slid deeper into a genuine clinical depression and would need professional help to climb out. She returned to New York and checked herself into a psychiatric hospital, the Payne Whitney clinic. The doctors said she needed supervision and intensive psychotherapy, and she remained in their care for two months. After a week, she notified her parents of her whereabouts. Her grief-stricken and doubtless guilt-ridden mother visited daily, or as often as her daughter would allow, bringing flowers, a delectable snack, a card, a pretty nightgown, a fascinating book. Milton also visited, though not quite as often.

When Sukhreet was able to go home, doctors said it would be essential to her mental health that she have her own apartment. Once again, Supermom rode to the rescue. As the city's former rent administrator, Hortense Gabel knew a great many landlords, and a small apartment was soon found on East Eighty-ninth Street. The Gabels paid the $500 rent. Sukhreet prepared to resume her job search, but first she and Tony Babineck arranged to spend the last of her savings on an eighteen-day holiday in Europe.

Not long after her return Sukhreet was able to move to a better, larger apartment just around the block from the Gabels' own. The building belonged to their own landlord, their longtime friend Sol Goldman, the real estate tycoon.

DURING THE PERIOD just prior to Sukhreet Gabel's crack-up, several important events had occurred. Both Capassos had filed for divorce; and Nancy's lawyer had asked the court to grant her exclusive occupancy of the family apartment. On February 15, 1983, while Andy and the kids were still away in Colorado, Nancy's motion had been granted. It was the first of seventeen pretrial motions that would have to be decided in the case of *Capasso* v. *Capasso* before it could go to trial.

Word of the favorable decision was leaked to the *New York Post*, and on March 7 the paper ran a story about Nancy's victory with a banner head, IRATE WIFE EVICTS BESS MYERSON'S ESCORT. The

March 11 *Post* ran another item: NO WEDDING BELLS, SAYS BESS'S
BEAU. The story quoted both Andy and Nancy snarling at one
another, and again mentioned that "Andy is barred [from the marital apartment] by a court order . . ."

In those days (the law was changed on January 6, 1986) every
matrimonial motion filed in the New York Supreme Court, County
of New York, was returnable in the same court, known as Special
Term, Part Five, or as the lawyers call it, Special, Five. The sole
judge then assigned to Special, Five was Hortense W. Gabel.

It is important to understand that Justice Gabel was the motions
judge, not the trial judge, in the case. She made rulings on various
matters that had to be settled before a trial could get under way.
She never saw any plaintiff or defendant in her courtroom, only
their lawyers, and she issued rulings on their various written motions. She also on occasion heard the lawyers in oral argument.

Like every judge, Justice Gabel operated with the assistance of a
"law secretary"—in reality a lawyer, not a secretary, selected by
the judge as her personal assistant—and, in Special, Five, a second
lawyer/helper, her "law assistant." Together, these aides did the
considerable preliminary work necessary in deciding matrimonial
motions. This included keeping up with current trends in the divorce marketplace, and recommending the appropriate dollar
amounts for the judge to award for temporary maintenance, child
support, and other items, as opposed to the often wildly inflated
amounts requested by the lawyer for the dependent spouse. The
general idea is to enable that spouse—almost always the wife—and
the children to live in the style to which they are accustomed during
the often lengthy interim period between filing for a divorce and
obtaining the decree.

It was uncommon, but by no means unheard of, for Justice
Gabel, like any other judge, to change the dollar amount suggested
by her law secretary. Normally he handed her the rulings with his
suggested dollar figures already typed in, and she signed the order.
If she disagreed, she scratched out the typed figure, wrote in another one, and initialed the change.

Justice Gabel was thought not to have the stamina to oversee an
entire trial. That is why she was assigned to Special, Five, which
met only on Tuesday and Thursday. But her workload was mon-

umental nonetheless, and she dealt with up to 120 motions per day. Her law secretary, Howard Leventhal, habitually referred to Special, Five as "the Russian front" of the state court system. In her two-year hitch there, Judge Gabel was required to read and rule on a staggering 3,704 motions, including the 17 concerning *Capasso* v. *Capasso*.

ON FEBRUARY 22, 1983, the same day that Andy Capasso and the children returned from their ski trip to Colorado, a tumultuous public City Council hearing was in progress on a gay-rights bill supported by Mayor Koch. An Orthodox rabbi from Brooklyn threw the meeting into an uproar by insinuating that Koch was homosexual. "This evil man, Edward I. Koch," he said, did not need legal permission to join a certain male city official "in his Greenwich Village apartment."

Speaking in favor of the bill, Rabbi Balfour Brickner of the liberal Stephen Wise Free Synagogue denounced the first rabbi, and later termed him an "ugly, crude, poor excuse for a human being." Members of the right-wing Orthodox rabbinate, particularly Hasidim, were present in full force, jamming the balcony and jeering, booing, and hissing at the bill's supporters. Brickner interrupted his own testimony to say, "Every circus has its clowns, and these are *its* clowns." The right-wingers yelled back, and the bailiff threw them out. The City Council rejected the bill after fourteen hours of testimony marked by outbursts from both sides. The next morning, three council members who voted nay found the words GAY RIGHTS NOW carved into their desks.

Later that day, Koch called a press conference to say he was "distressed" by the tone of the opponents' charges. Standing at his side was—of all people—Bess Myerson, "in a familiar diversionary role—or so it appeared," wrote *The New Yorker*'s astute City Hall watcher Andy Logan.

Then Koch announced with pride that he had chosen his old friend Bess to become the city's newest commissioner of cultural affairs. Unmentioned was the fact that Koch had had an unusually difficult time filling the post. Before he turned to Bess, thirty people had been approached, including Beverly Sills and Jacqueline Onassis.

Ms. Myerson beamed and pledged to bring more culture to the boroughs outside of Manhattan. "Keeping the arts in business is everybody's business," she said, and Koch kissed her on the mouth.

A few days later the new commissioner and Andy Capasso took off for a vacation at Caneel Bay in the Virgin Islands. While they were away, Andy's men constructed the tennis court Bess had asked for at Westhampton Beach, and they made a few other improvements. Earlier, they had installed a $5,000 fireplace in Myerson's apartment, and paneled a bathroom with smoky mirror. Later in the year, Capasso bought an apartment at 563 Park Avenue, presumably for Myerson and himself, and paid $1.6 million, all cash.

Cost was no problem; Nanco was doing better than ever. In 1983, the company's fortunes made a quantum leap upward. In March the city awarded Nanco a $5.5 million contract to do some track work and reconstruction on the Brooklyn railroad yards. In April it won a whopping $53.6 million contract to rebuild part of the Owl's Head sewage treatment plant in Bay Ridge, Brooklyn. Until now, Nanco's biggest contract had been $5 million. The Owl's Head job, located on a twenty-two-acre landfill that juts into Upper New York Bay, was not only ten times larger but maybe fifty times more complicated than the simple water mains, sanitary sewers, and paving jobs Nanco had heretofore undertaken.

Nanco was one of twenty prime contractors signed to work on rehabilitating the plant to make it conform to EPA standards under the Clean Water Act. The work was not expected to be completed until 1995. A $10 million emergency program was launched concurrently with the new construction in order to keep the plant in operation while repairs were under way.

Nanco's task was to demolish the existing sludge-processing portion of the plant and replace it. Andy Capasso initially estimated a final profit of $6–$8 million. By December 1986, cost estimates were up to $57 million, and Capasso's profit estimate was down to $4.5 million. The work was supposed to be done by June 1986. By the time it was actually completed in November 1988 under the supervision of HHN Inc., a company operated by Capasso's nephew and Nanco general manager "Flash" Corillo, both Capasso and Nanco were in ruins, at least for the time being. Andy was simultaneously serving a four-year prison term on tax-evasion charges and standing trial with Bess and Justice Gabel for conspiracy. Nanco was the subject of unusually complex and expensive litigation, and utterly nonfunctional.

But the slowdown at Owl's Head was not Nanco's doing. Serious problems arose with Nanco subcontractors responsible for supplying steel and concrete, and the city kept changing its design plans. As of December 9, 1986, there had been a total of sixty-nine change-orders (documents requiring changes in the original order), and each change-order could involve many revisions. One, for instance, called for fifty-seven changes.

Owl's Head aside, however, Nanco by 1984 would have "a virtual monopoly on city sewer contracts," according to Koch-watcher Jack Newfield, author with Wayne Barrett of *City for Sale*, a fascinating, meticulous, true whodunit tracing and mapping the extent of corruption in the Koch administration. But Capasso's virtual monopoly had nothing to do with corruption. Nanco was simply one of a very few companies capable of handling the largest jobs.

Furthermore, in 1983 Capasso was positioning himself to branch out into even bigger, more difficult kinds of construction work, and perhaps build his own cement plant as well. If that happened, the thirty-eight-year-old former ditchdigger would be able to crown himself construction czar of New York City.

Earlier that year Bella Myerson died. Bess drove to the funeral in a Nanco limousine. Afterward she instructed the chauffeur to bring her directly home and skip the trip to the cemetery. "That won't look too good," the driver said, and he persuaded her to change her mind.

Herbert Rickman had not seen a great deal of his friend Bess since her release from the hospital in January 1981. The day she called him and crowed, "Guess what? The mayor's just tapped me for Cultural Affairs!" Rickman shuddered. He had not been consulted, and he had a fleeting sense of impending disaster at the thought of his emotionally volatile friend occupying a highly visible city post. "I felt as if someone had just stepped on my grave," he said later. "But by then, it was a *fait accompli*."

On April 25, Bess Myerson was sworn in. The post carried an $83,000 salary, and perks included a city chauffeur and limousine. On May 25, Mayor Koch planned to honor his newest commissioner with a reception and cocktail party at Gracie Mansion. Myerson asked Koch's secretary to add two names to the guest list: Justice Hortense Gabel and Carlantonio Capasso. Justice Gabel was thrilled to be invited back to Gracie Mansion. She had not been inside since serving in the Wagner administration eighteen years before.

The day before the party, Nancy Capasso's lawyer filed his first motion with Justice Gabel regarding temporary alimony and child support. Raoul Lionel Felder, divorce lawyer for such clients as Robin Givens, David Merrick, and Ethel Scull, is known throughout the world of matrimonial litigation as "a bomber," someone unashamed to ask for the moon, and his motion bore out his reputation. He told the court that his client needed $6,000 a week for herself and $2,000 for the children to maintain everybody in the style to which they had become accustomed.

On the same day Andy Capasso's lawyer filed a voluntary pledge that his client intended to pay the children's third-party expenses: school, camp, medical fees, and the like.

The following day Commissioner Myerson thoughtfully sent her car and driver to pick up the judge and bring her to the reception, and later to drive her home. Capasso arrived in his own limousine, and so far as is known was not introduced to other guests, at least not by Bess. He was present to watch the anointment of his beloved because that's the way she wanted it, and so did he.

Another guest at the party was Herbert Rickman. Much later, in his testimony at the 1988 BessMess trial, Rickman would tell the jury that at the party Judge Gabel had asked him, " 'Is what's-his-name here?'

"I said, 'You mean Andy Capasso?' She said, 'Yes.' . . .

"I looked around . . . I couldn't spot him at that moment. I told her so. I knew she was legally blind . . . and then I left."*

....

* Under cross-examination by Gabel's lawyer, Rickman admitted that on the eighteen prior occasions over the two and a half years that he had spoken about these matters to government and law-enforcement officials, he had never before recollected nor mentioned such a con-

The following day Bess again sent her limousine to the Gabels' apartment to bring the nearly blind judge to the opening of an art show at City Gallery, lodged in DCA headquarters in the old Huntington Hartford Museum on Columbus Circle.

BY LATE MAY Sukhreet Gabel was back from Europe and again looking for a job. For some years Hortense and Milton Gabel had been in the habit of giving modest, family-style dinner parties in their apartment every six weeks or so. Milton cooked, and the twelve or fourteen guests served themselves buffet style and balanced their plates on their laps. Invitations were much prized because the guests were certain to include interesting people involved in city affairs. The Gabels always invited Sukhreet, although she did not always attend.

One June day Hortense told her daughter on the phone that Bess Myerson was coming to dinner. The judge had run into her old friend Herbie Rickman at a political cocktail party, she explained, and had invited him to the next Gabel dinner party, Friday night, June 17. Bess Myerson, standing near Rickman, had overheard, and asked if she could come too. Hortense hoped that the prospect of meeting so glamorous a guest would please her daughter.

"Really, Mother," said Sukhreet. "Aren't we coming up in the world!"

·······································

versation on May 25, at Gracie Mansion. He had variously mentioned a similar conversation at a Chinese lunch with Justice Gabel in September 1983, or possibly at some time during 1984. On re-cross, Rickman said that what had triggered his new recollection was sitting on a garden bench at another Gracie Mansion party in the early spring or summer of 1988. This led one of the defense lawyers to suggest in summation that never before had he heard of a witness "who had his recollection refreshed through the seat of his pants."

14

CULTURAL

AFFAIRS

SUKHREET WAS FLATTERED WHEN BESS MYERSON came and curled up on the floor beside her at the Gabels' dinner party, and the two women chatted amiably throughout the evening. Sukhreet didn't mention to Myerson that she was looking for a job. "The simple reason was pride," she said later. "I didn't want to be seen as a beggar . . . didn't want to look bad in her eyes. I wanted to be seen as a person, if you will, and not as someone with a problem."

A few days later Bess telephoned Sukhreet's apartment. "Hi, babe! Joe Papp's putting on *Richard the Second* in Central Park. Want to come to opening night?" She instructed Sukhreet to wait at the West Sixty-seventh Street entrance to the park, and she would come by in her limousine.

When the car pulled up, Bess told Sukhreet to sit in the jump seat. In the back seat, beside Bess, was a large woman who looked eerily like her twin sister. Bess introduced her good friend Sandy Stern.

Mrs. Stern, the wife of a stockbroker, said their friendship had begun years ago when she had won a Bess Myerson look-alike contest. After the play, Bess said Sukhreet could come along with her and Sandy to the cast party at Tavern on the Green.

Richard II had long been a particular favorite of Sukhreet's, and she had a trick memory that enabled her to swallow large chunks of Shakespeare, among other poets, and spit them back letter-perfect. As she got to know Myerson better, certain of the king's lines—"O that I were as great as is my grief, or lesser than my name! Or that I could forget what I have been! Or not remember what I must be now!" —began to reverberate in her mind in relation to the former beauty queen, whom she eventually would come to see as a kind of female King Richard.

A day or two after going to the play, Bess invited Sukhreet to dinner at Foo Chow's, on Third Avenue. They talked about the arts, and Sukhreet's interest in cultural events and museums, and Myerson's new job at Cultural Affairs. She mentioned casually that Sukhreet sounded like just the sort of cultivated person who could be happy, and useful, at Cultural Affairs. It might be a good idea, she said, if Sukhreet came to work for her, and in the evenings attended Fordham Law School, which was nearby. "I can fix it," she said.

Sukhreet was surprised at the suggestion. She had never discussed law school with anyone except her mother. But she said she thought it sounded like a nice life, and would be very happy studying law under those circumstances.

A chunky man in a dark suit appeared behind Bess and leaned down to whisper in her ear, something about people waiting for them next door, at Abe's Steak House. Bess said sorry, she preferred having dinner with Sukhreet Gabel, and the man left without being introduced.

Bess telephoned Sukhreet a number of times in the next few weeks, always with a spur-of-the-moment suggestion. Sometimes they took long evening walks, or went to a movie, once with her old friend Herb Rickman, still Koch's assistant. Sometimes they ate lunch or dinner, usually takeout from the Carnegie Deli, where Bess had an account. On other occasions Sukhreet was just invited over to Myerson's apartment, where she usually reclined on Bess's bed watching TV while Bess balanced her checkbook or talked on the phone. She much enjoyed all the attention from the smart, witty, and beautiful older woman. She told her mother she and Bess Myerson were becoming good friends.

"That's nice, dear," Hortense said.

On another June evening Bess invited Hortense and Milton Gabel out to dinner at an Italian restaurant. Bess's escort was Herb Rickman.

Around this time Sukhreet told her mother she was pretty sure that Bess had a boyfriend. Their long walks often ended abruptly, at about eleven o'clock, at the entrance to the Westbury Hotel on Madison. Bess suddenly would say, "G'night, babes," grin, and disappear inside.

When Hortense acted surprised, Sukhreet bristled and said, "Mother, why ever shouldn't she?"

On weekends Bess led a rather different life. Each Friday morning, and sometimes on Thursday, she and Andy, often accompanied by Rickman, boarded a chartered seaplane to Westhampton Beach for a long weekend. Rickman loved playing tennis, and by late spring had become a regular visitor at the beach house. He was there every weekend but one that summer of 1983, until August 15, when he took a two-week trip to Eastern Europe. The other tennis regulars were Donald Manes, who had his own beach house nearby, and Stanley Friedman, the powerful Bronx borough president, who was a friend of both Manes and Capasso.

Rickman took pains to be an unusually generous and considerate guest. He always brought his hosts an expensive gift, often a side of Nova Scotia smoked salmon. He cleaned his own room. When the servants allowed him, he even did the cooking.

Bess had always found something endearing in Rickman. He was from the same background, had the same yen for Chinese food, was a useful escort, knew all the jokes, and they could converse entirely in Yiddish. The Park Avenue apartment Rickman had lived in for years was furnished as if a shrine to his Bronx origins. It actually looked like a thirties Bronx working-class apartment, down to its linoleum floor. "You think you're in an Odets play," said Rickman's old friend Nick Pileggi, who always called his pal Herbie Linoleum.

Some of their weekend guests said that being with Bess and Andy could be difficult, "a very unsettling relationship to be around. There were constant fights," exacerbated because "he's a drinker." Bess drank too, but "she drinks well."

Making matters worse was the way Myerson treated the servants, Shirley and Raymond Harrod. Her behavior toward them was imperious and nasty, so ugly that Andy once walked out.

At first Bess and Andy appeared very much in love. But as the summer wore on, guests began to notice what one called "a Svengali-Trilby relationship. She was Svengali, he was Trilby, and she was making him crazy. She absolutely *hated* his kids. She hated his mother, his sister. She hated his nephew Flash. But she abided by all of it because there was this financial arrangement between them. He stayed with Bess and took all her abuse for the same reason."* In ugly sum, greed once more won out over love.

JUNE 29, TWELVE DAYS after the Gabels' dinner party at which Sukhreet met Bess, Justice Gabel made an important and controversial ruling in the Capasso case. After reading Felder's "bomber" motion that his client required $6,000 a week in temporary maintenance and $2,000 in child support, the judge's two law clerks had carefully analyzed the court's financial data on the Capassos. Howard Leventhal, Gabel's chief aide, then recommended that Andy be ordered to pay $2,000 a week temporary alimony, and $350 child support, in addition to the $6,000 monthly maintenance and the utility bills on 990 Fifth Avenue *pendente lite* (pending the outcome of the litigation).

On the twenty-ninth, Justice Gabel looked over her staff's typed-up pages, scratched out the $2,000 alimony and wrote in $1,500,

·······································

* The reference was to evidence presented to the grand jury, but not used at trial: 1) allegations that Andy Capasso personally paid off Myerson's million-dollar campaign debts; 2) testimony by a former DCA chauffeur that in the early 1980s he twice took Myerson from Nanco's Long Island City headquarters to a Manhattan branch of Dean Witter to deliver large envelopes of cash; 3) testimony by a Nanco chauffeur that he had overheard Bess boast to Andy that "I can take care of anything in this town," and had heard Andy yell at Nancy during a fight, "I can fix any judge in this city."

and signed the order granting Nancy a total of $1,850. All was strictly routine.*

Despite Judge Gabel's reputation as an ardent feminist, her June 29 order was the largest matrimonial award she had ever made, and it drew a howl of protest from Andy's lawyer, Sam Fredman, who was not known as a bomber. Rather, Fredman was frequently identified as "the dean of the matrimonial bar," a position so august that it eventually led him to bill Capasso $500,000 for legal services.

Early in July, three important things happened. Fredman had immediately filed an order to show cause criticizing Justice Gabel's award at length, and asking her to grant oral reargument. His protest was so swift, and its language so strong, that it gave Justice Gabel pause. "I think perhaps we were a little too generous with Mr. Capasso's money, Howie," she said when she read it.

On July 5, after listening to Fredman's plea, she dropped the temporary maintenance award from $1,500 to $750, and the child support from $350 to $250, "pending hearing and determination" of the motion. There she would let the matter rest until September 14.

Also on July 5, Andy Capasso offered Nancy a $2 million settlement on what he said was a $15 million estate. She refused it. She felt entitled to keep the $6 million Fifth Avenue apartment on which she had lavished such care and love, and money, free and clear for herself and the children.

A third event, on July 7, was brought out more than five years later, in the prosecutor's opening statement to the jury at the Myerson/Gabel/Capasso trial. "Two days after the judge cut Mrs.

---

* The full order contained a number of other preliminary rulings *pendente lite:* Gabel denied Nancy's request for counsel fees without prejudice to renewal before the trial court. Gabel awarded Nancy interim accountant's fees of $5,000. Gabel ordered Andy to pay all mortgages, maintenance, and utilities on all marital residences, i.e. the Westhampton Beach estate, the condo, the two Palm Beach condos, as well as 990 Fifth Avenue. Gabel ordered Andy to maintain in full force all present life insurance and medical and dental insurance benefiting Nancy and the children. Gabel directed both parties not to transfer or dispose of marital assets. Gabel granted Nancy's custody motion "to the extent of placing it on the part 5 calendar for July 13." Gabel denied Nancy's motion for exclusive occupancy of the Westhampton Beach estate. Gabel directed that Nancy and Andy work out an alternating schedule for its exclusive use, and further directed that Andy either deliver to Nancy or allow her agents to collect certain personal items in that home.

Capasso's support payments in half, the judge . . . telephoned Bess Myerson. Judge Gabel left a message for Ms. Myerson to call her at home, and for the remainder of the summer . . . Judge Gabel delayed making that final decision on the issue of how much money Mr. Capasso would have to pay . . . The possibility that the maintenance payments might be further reduced stayed an open question."

During the crucial period between meeting Sukhreet on June 17 and hiring her on August 24, Myerson frequently telephoned Judge Gabel's chambers on her private line. (No other callers used the private line, save for Dr. Gabel.) When Gabel was on the bench and unavailable, Bess always left the imperious message "Tell her the commissioner called."

Leventhal, playing his own game, always said, "Which commissioner?" even though everyone in Judge Gabel's office recognized Myerson's voice.

Bess then started saying, "Tell her Mrs. Robinson called." This happened a couple of dozen times. Sometimes she used the name Mrs. Goodman.

Leventhal one day asked his boss, "Who is this Mrs. Robinson or Mrs. Goodman that keeps calling?"

"Oh, that's Bess Myerson," said the judge offhandedly. "She's just being Byzantine."

On July 12, Bess invited Sukhreet to another gala evening of Shakespeare-in-the-park. The next day Bess and Andy flew off for a few days' holiday in Europe and ran into Nancy at Cap d'Antibes.

In early August, Bess suggested Sukhreet come to work as a full-time volunteer at the Department of Cultural Affairs while awaiting a budget "line" that would permit the department to put her on the city payroll. "Mother thought it was a superb idea," Sukhreet said later.

Cultural Ladies Bountiful were something of a tradition in the department. Others who contributed their services that season were Bess's friends Jane Safer and Ellen Liman, the wives of Morley Safer, the TV reporter, and Arthur L. Liman, a prominent lawyer who later distinguished himself as chief counsel to the congressional committee holding the Iran/contra hearings. The department's new press secretary was Judith Gray, former wife of Barry Gray, a popular radio talk-show host. The unusual number of new faces reflected the agency's recent stormy history. The staff unhappiness at DCA was well known.

As a volunteer there, Sukhreet attended senior staff meetings and read up on DCA history. Bess told her she wanted her staff to get to know Sukhreet and have a sense of her qualifications. She did not tell her that several senior staff members despised their new boss and, behind her back, called her Lady MacBess. Her senior deputy commissioner, Randy Bourscheidt, had in fact been promised the top job, and then was unaccountably passed over.

After office hours, Sukhreet's duties changed. She was made a kind of "escort," and accompanied the commissioner to events like the opening of the New York Philharmonic summer concerts in Central Park; a meeting at the Henry Street Settlement House; an opening at the Jamaica Arts Center; and a conference with the top public relations men in the Japanese government.

But it was not all work. Bess told Sukhreet she enjoyed very relaxing summer weekends at a friend's home in Westhampton Beach, and she invited the young woman to come out and join them on the first weekend in August. She supplied driving directions, and when Sukhreet arrived Saturday morning a housekeeper opened the door and led her through the expensively decorated house to a poolside patio, where she found Myerson sunning herself and reading a spec sheet for earth-moving equipment.

Bess guided her visitor to the best upstairs guest room. "We call this Herbie's room, he's been here so often," she said. But since he was out of town, this weekend the room would be Sukhreet's. She showed Sukhreet three other upstairs bedrooms, and took her on a tour of the rest of the house. The visitor noted that there were a lot of "beautiful flowers, and good crystal, but nothing personal. It was like a hotel, pristine and untouched. The furniture all came with the house, and there were lots of very expensive antique duck decoys."

At one point, Myerson paused to open a hallway drawer full of bikinis. "My friend's ex-wife's," she said. "I wear them now."

Back on the patio, they saw a man standing in the garden. Bess introduced Capasso, and Sukhreet recognized him as the man from the Chinese restaurant. Bess said that later on they were invited to a cocktail party at the home of Dr. Rubin and his wife, Ellie, in nearby Quogue. When Sukhreet and Bess were alone, she confided, "I don't know if I should bring you or not. Andy's not in favor of it, but . . . by the way, what was your married name?"

Sukhreet said "Revis," and Bess instructed her to use Revis, not Gabel, at the Rubins' party. But no one at the party ever asked her her name.

Sometime that weekend, Bess said she would like to see a copy of Sukhreet's résumé, and offered to have her secretary type a new draft that she would ask her DCA speech writer to compose. Sukhreet accepted the offer. That same weekend Sukhreet also met Barra and her husband and baby, who were living in a rented cottage next door, and for dinner Andy and Bess brought her to a seafood restaurant. Over their lobsters Sukhreet told her hosts about the partition of India and Pakistan. On Sunday afternoon she drove back to Manhattan.

Later Sukhreet was asked her impression of Capasso. "Andy's a *schlemiel*, a *schlimazel*. A *hasenpfeffer*. Andy don't talk much. He's good with kids. He's good with girls, they say. I wouldn't know." Andy kept himself very reserved around her. She surmised that Andy felt Bess could become angry if he "paid any attention whatsoever to a woman so much younger than his girlfriend. So he didn't."

During the week, Sukhreet brought a copy of her résumé to the DCA offices and, as promised, Walter Kanter, the staff speech writer, revised it, and Bess's secretary retyped it. Sukhreet thought the slick rewrite made her sound like some sort of toothpaste or canned soup. "I didn't want myself to be new, bright, and shiny. I wanted to describe myself as a professional," she said later, and when she got home she chucked the revision in the trash.

The following weekend, Sukhreet drove her parents out to the home of judges Sybil Kooper and Willie Thompson in Mattituck, on the North Fork of Long Island, an hour's drive from Westhampton Beach. Kooper and Thompson were away and had lent their house for two weeks to the Gabels, who had never owned a summer cottage, or even an automobile. Sukhreet did not want her elderly parents to have to make the journey by bus.

Bess invited Sukhreet back to the Capasso estate for the third

August weekend. She found Barra and her husband playing doubles with Bess and Andy when she arrived late Saturday morning. Bess stumbled and fell, and Sukhreet used her nursing skills to patch up a bad scrape on her cheek.

Capasso's nine-year-old-daughter, Andrea, was another guest. The child was to occupy one of the bedrooms in the big house, Sukhreet was told, whereas Sukhreet was shown to a tiny sleeping loft in the guest house that was furnished with two children's bunk beds.

The next morning, the housekeeper noted that Bess had rumpled up the bed in one of the unoccupied bedrooms to make it appear, presumably for Andrea's benefit, that she had slept there and not with Mr. Capasso.

On Saturday afternoon Bess said to Sukhreet, "I'm bored. Want to go for a drive?" She picked up her eight-month-old granddaughter and got behind the wheel of a large blue Mercedes-Benz. A brass nameplate BESS MYERSON was affixed to the dashboard. Sukhreet took the passenger seat, and held the baby on her lap.

"Andy's so generous and good to me," Bess said. "He lets me use anything on this property."

They drove to look at a village fair in Westhampton Beach, and Bess pointed out a house she had rented there years ago. "By the way," she said, "isn't your mother on Long Island? Why don't we go there?"

Sukhreet did not remember having told Bess her parents were nearby. Bess drove to the house at Mattituck, and they visited for about an hour. Justices Kooper and Thompson had returned home, and everyone admired the baby. Then they drove back to Capasso's.

Sometime that weekend, on the drive to Mattituck, perhaps, or during a beach walk, Sukhreet could not remember just when, she told Bess that she had recently been in the hospital. In retrospect, it was odd that Bess, the champion Jewish mother, a woman who was continually telling friends, "You must go to see *my* doctor . . . *my* lawyer . . ." did not ask Sukhreet where she had been hospitalized, nor why. Unless, of course, she already knew.

The following morning, Sunday, Sukhreet wandered into the kitchen at about nine-thirty. The others were still asleep. Shirley

Harrod, the housekeeper/cook, was peeling vegetables. She asked Sukhreet if she would like some orange juice. She said yes, and when nice Mrs. Harrod served her the juice, the grateful young woman stuck out her hand and said, "By the way, my name is Sukhreet Gabel."

"Gabel? Gabel!" Mrs. Harrod exclaimed. "Gabel is a very familiar name . . . isn't there a Judge Gabel? Isn't Judge Gabel presiding over Mr. Capasso's divorce?"

"I don't know," said Sukhreet, and changed the subject fast.

That evening as soon as she got home she dialed her parents in Mattituck. Milton Gabel answered.

"Hi, Dad," she said, and after a few pleasantries she repeated the conversation with the housekeeper. Then, in an angry voice, she demanded, "What the *hell* is going on?"

"Never mind. Don't get involved," Milton said. "Your mother knows all about this . . . keep your nose clean . . . just don't get involved."

At some later point Sukhreet asked her mother directly what was going on: "What's happening? Somebody give me a clue." But she got a similar answer: "It really isn't important. Don't worry. Don't get involved."

She did not recall the date of this conversation, nor whether it took place in person or by telephone.

At the office, Myerson never spoke to her directly of the possibility of a paid job at Cultural Affairs, and Sukhreet was much too polite to bring the matter up, or perhaps too bemused by the heady air of culture into which she found herself suddenly plunged. One day Myerson told her to go downstairs to the personnel office and fill out some forms so that all would be in readiness when a budget line did become available. A few days later the personnel people arranged to get her fingerprinted and photographed for the criminal-records check required of all city employees.

On August 24, Sukhreet's thirty-fourth birthday, Bess Myerson summoned her to her private office. "Happy birthday, and congratulations!" she said. "You're going on the payroll, salary twenty-four thousand dollars. How do you like the title 'special assistant to the commissioner'?"

Sukhreet stammered her thanks and struggled not to cry. She

rushed to call her mother, who congratulated her and said it was "just wonderful." Sukhreet noticed that her mother's voice "was very happy and light. She was delighted!"

The three Gabels had planned to hold a birthday dinner a few days later, when Tony Babineck could join them from Chicago. Bess asked to come too, so they could all celebrate Sukhreet's new job together, as well as her birthday. Bess suggested the Fortune Garden (where Nancy had caught her with Andy eighteen months before), and when they all met, many toasts were drunk to Sukhreet's good fortune. Afterward, Myerson insisted on taking the check. She paid it with an American Express card belonging to Andy Capasso, and signed his name.

When Sukhreet reported for work on Monday, her salary turned out to be not $24,000 but $19,000. She didn't ask why, and Myerson volunteered no explanation. "Go down to the personnel office and say you need business cards," Bess told her. Then she was assigned a desk in the large open space outside the door of the commissioner's private office.

The same day Sukhreet came to work, August 29, Judge Gabel heard the second set of oral arguments by the Capassos' lawyers regarding her interim July 5 reduction of Nancy's maintenance and support payments to $750 and $250. Again she reserved her final decision.

Sukhreet's DCA duties included making public appearances with the commissioner, attending staff meetings with the commissioner, doing writing and research for the commissioner, preparing budget reports, and distributing excess Carnegie Hall tickets to city agencies. The latter activity formed the bulk of her work. In a deal worked out in 1960 to save Carnegie Hall from the wrecker's ball, New York City had become the de facto owner of Carnegie Hall, and in partial payment of its rent the Carnegie Hall Corporation gave the city 12,000 free tickets per year to pass out to the elderly, the needy, and the handicapped. The contract with the city also called for the Carnegie Hall Corporation to pay the salary of the person handling the distribution, specified as $19,000. Hence Sukhreet Gabel spent a fair amount of her time walking the three or four blocks to Carnegie Hall, personally picking up and signing for the excess tickets for performances by child prodigies and *lieder* singers and gamelan players that nobody wanted to pay to hear, and distributing them around the five boroughs to in effect paper the house that Andrew Carnegie built.

But even with her Carnegie Hall ticket assignment, she did not have enough work to fill an eight-hour day, 10 A.M. to 6 P.M. She made up assignments for herself. She read everything she could find on how her agency worked. She pored over the annual report, and studied the budgets and charts. She read the musty old personnel manuals. At the suggestion of one friendly senior staff member, she wrote up a building-cleaning contract to be submitted for bids. She did it by pretending to be a housewife, then walking around the curious modern building, originally built to house the Huntington Hartford Museum, and jotting down the varieties of cleaning services required.

She wrote a second contract, this one for a new phone system. She wrote a paper on student groups in the arts. She wrote a brilliantly imaginative proposal for how to turn the *Intrepid*, a rusting aircraft carrier anchored in the Hudson River, into a valuable cultural resource for the children of New York City. She prepared a list of one hundred city cultural institutions to be incorporated into a map, and another list of one hundred cultural birthdays. "I did whatever I could pester, cajole, or beg anyone into letting me do," she said later.

Bureaucracy finds ways of making work bloat to fill the time available, and Richard Bruno, the assistant commissioner and part-time speech writer at DCA, decided the department should regularly scan the city's newspapers for items of cultural interest. He assigned Judith Gray, the press officer, to read and clip the *Times*, the departmental chauffeur to monitor the *News*, and Sukhreet to check the *Post*.

"Happy to cooperate!" she memoed back, and reached for her shears.

Next Sukhreet was assigned to deal with job applicants who walked in off the street, people who knew nobody and had no "pull," people who were just interested in "culture." In this endeavor, Sukhreet was told to follow strict departmental policy: Encourage them generally, but discourage them specifically from expecting to find any sort of work at DCA.

Except for the dearth of things to do, Sukhreet had few complaints. She continued to see her boss out of the office, accompanying her to the many civic activities at which Bess had to make an appearance. "Culture" included everything from holding a press conference on the theft of costumes from the Dance Theatre of Harlem (at which Bess forbade Sukhreet to be seen on camera) to attending the dedication of a new whale tank at the aquarium.

From time to time her boss asked her to come to her apartment and watch while she dressed to go out. Once Bess asked Sukhreet to fetch her pearls, and she was astonished to discover that Myerson stored her jewelry in a standard metal hardware-store toolbox.

The Jewish holiday of Rosh Hashanah fell on September 8 that year, and when Bess learned that Sukhreet had no plans for the evening, she turned instantly into her Jewish-mother persona and insisted she come along with her to Sandy Stern's apartment. It would be an intimate family dinner, nobody else but Sandy's family and, of course, Andy.

Six days later the tabloid *New York Post*, which was by now doing for Bess and Andy what Hearst had done for the Lindberghs, printed a large photograph of the lovers nuzzling one another on its front page. Hortense Gabel would later tell investigators that this story, published September 14, was the first time she knew that Bess, her longtime acquaintance, was the Other Woman in the Capasso divorce.

When Nancy Capasso saw the picture, she said her husband looked like "a thug," and his girlfriend looked like Dustin Hoffman in *Tootsie*.

Within two weeks the media were referring to the Capassos' marital war as "the Bess Myerson case," and the tabloids were in a condition of red alert. No development was too small to overlook. When Bess later disclaimed any interest in the Capasso divorce, reporters found a Capasso chauffeur who said he had delivered legal papers to her apartment. They found another driver who said he had heard her gloating on the car phone that Justice Gabel had again reduced Andy's temporary obligations to his wife and children. The occasion for this reputed exultation seemed bewilderingly small.

After three months' delay, Justice Gabel had finally ruled on the reargument motions the same day as the *Tootsie* photo appeared. Her original temporary maintenance award of $1,500, cut back in July to $750, had now become $500. The original $350 child support, reduced in July to $250, was now set at $180.

What was going on? It couldn't be the principle, and was surely not the principal. Capasso's income, after all, was more than $1 million a year. Nancy Capasso claimed that Andy and Bess had vowed to "starve her out," and enforce a "scorched-earth policy." That sounded about right.

Judge Gabel wrote that she was trimming the child-support payments to $180 "in view of" Capasso's voluntary May 24 pledge to pay all the children's third-party expenses directly. He had pledged this in an affidavit assuring the court that he was already making direct payments to schools, doctors, dentists, orthodontists, prescription druggists, summer camps, tennis coaches, and indeed was paying voluntarily for all the children's needs, "even though I have been forbidden to reside under the same roof with them . . . Frankly, I do not need my wife, her lawyer or anyone else to remind me of my obligations toward my children . . . ," and so forth.

But pledge is different from payment, as every horseplayer knows. In fact, Andy sometimes paid the children's bills late, annoying Nancy no end, and embarrassing the children, she claimed. At other times he failed to pay altogether. Nancy had to file court papers on at least two occasions during the months and years that followed to compel Andy to pay $85,500 in back alimony and $10,000 in children's camp fees.

The *Post*'s biggest scoop, headlined SMALL WORLD, came on October 18. That day "Page Six" reporter Richard Johnson revealed for the first time anywhere that the daughter of the Capasso divorce judge was personal assistant to Myerson at DCA, and added that it was Koch aide Rickman who had gotten Sukhreet the job.

The next day Mayor Koch received a two-page letter from Commissioner Myerson (in fact, ghosted by her assistant Richard Bruno) assuring him that Sukhreet's hiring had been done by underlings, in a "routine" manner, and that in any case Judge Gabel had finished ruling on the Capasso matter by the time Sukhreet came aboard. That none of this was true seemed of no interest to anyone.

But the SMALL WORLD story turned out to be a watershed event in Sukhreet Gabel's DCA career. After the item appeared, it seemed as if a gradual ice age was descending upon her. She had less and less to do with the boss in the office, and no more little chats after hours. The party invitations dried up as well. One day Bess called Sukhreet into her private office and told her that Richard Bruno was dissatisfied with her work. But Bess said that she was on Sukhreet's side, and intended to fight for her.

In another conversation, Bess and Sukhreet discovered that they both were under treatment for depression, and had some familiarity with the new antidepressant drugs. Bess told Sukhreet she was considering switching to the same MAOIs (monamine oxidase inhibitors) that Sukhreet once used to take, but was worried about the severe dietary restrictions necessary to prevent side effects. Wine, hard cheese, pickles, avocados, and other foods could produce a terrific headache, Bess had been told. Yes, said Sukhreet, they sure could.

Bess mentioned that she was connected with a psychiatric institute, the Karen Horney Clinic. The place had "a great outpatient program" that Sukhreet should take advantage of. For only $50, a qualified psychiatrist would do a two-hour evaluation, after which the patient received a tentative diagnosis and a referral to some appropriate therapist for outpatient treatment.

"Your insurance as a city employee takes care of the outpatient care," Bess advised.

Sukhreet decided she had nothing to lose. If nothing else, "maybe I'll get a decent diagnosis." She visited the clinic, accepted the referral, and thereafter saw the recommended therapist four times a week for nine months. She quit because she believed (correctly, it would turn out) that the cause of her depression was chemical, and this particular therapist did not believe in drugs. Later, according to Sukhreet, federal agents told her that the therapist had told them he was reporting details of their private talks back to Bess Myerson.

In Sukhreet's next conversation with her boss, Bess told her, "I want you to lay low for a while." Thereafter Bess not only stopped bringing her personal assistant along to evening cultural affairs, she stopped bringing her to board meetings as well. By November she had taken away her business cards, and then dreadfully embarrassed Sukhreet in front of a visiting delegation of Russians by reaching into her jacket pocket to check whether Sukhreet still carried hidden business cards that she could hand out surreptitiously.

But the cruelest blow concerned the location of Sukhreet's desk. She had been led to expect that her desk was going to be placed closer to Myerson. Instead, shortly before Christmas, the closer desk was given to Judith Gray, and Sukhreet was banished to Siberia. Her new desk was as far away from Bess as possible, just outside the office bathroom.

It was too much. Sukhreet retreated into the bathroom and began having a good cry. Then came three loud raps on the door, and Bess barged in. The commissioner habitually left her curlers on the bathroom shelf, and rolled up her hair in them for a few hours before leaving the building for a public appearance.

Upon finding Sukhreet in tears, she told her, "You just gotta roll with the punches, kid."

In early December Bess told Sukhreet that Randy Bourscheidt wanted her fired, as did Bruno and several of the others. Only one senior staff member wanted to keep her, Bess said. "But don't worry, kid," she finished up. "I'm gonna protect you."

In an effort to improve relations, Sukhreet decided to follow the diplomatic custom of entertaining one's supervisor once a year at home. She invited Bess to a Christmas dinner party in her honor at Sukhreet's small apartment. The other guests were Dr. and Judge Gabel, Herb Rickman, and Robert Vanni, the DCA house counsel.

THE DINNER WAS under way, and Sukhreet was sitting no more than three feet away from Bess, when she heard her say to Vanni in crisp tones, "I can't *stand* Sukhreet! She makes me crazy. I don't know what I'm going to do about her."

Dreadfully upset, the hostess retreated to her tiny kitchen and began vigorously washing dishes to drown out the sound of her sobs.

By January Sukhreet was actively looking for another job. She sent out more letters, revised and reformatted her résumé, and attended a job-hunting seminar. Again her mother helped her with each aspect of the hunt, and was supportive in every way.

In late winter Hortense phoned her daughter to say she had had a talk with Bess, and Bess wanted to use Sukhreet to work with the two staff DCA lawyers to help draft some legislation for the City Council. It sounded good, but again nothing happened.

One of Judge Gabel's contacts was Dr. Marcella Maxwell, then dean of development at Medgar Evers College in Brooklyn. Dr. Maxwell was attempting to relocate to Manhattan and be appointed executive director of the city's troubled Commission on Human Rights. The mayor's annual management report had called it "one of the worst-run agencies in the city." Dr. Maxwell and Judge Gabel were old friends, and Gabel wrote to Deputy Mayor Stanley Brezenoff recommending Dr. Maxwell for the post.

In early June 1984, Dr. Maxwell learned she would get the job. Sukhreet heard Maxwell intended to fire one or two assistants, so she wrote her a long letter detailing her extensive qualifications in human rights and race relations, and proposing herself for one of the empty slots.

On June 15 Sukhreet Gabel was hired by Dr. Maxwell as deputy executive director, New York City Commission on Human Rights, at a salary of $40,000. That day she handed Commissioner Myerson a two-line letter of resignation, beginning, "I respectfully request permission to resign. It has been a pleasure and an honor to serve on your staff."

Bess was livid. She summoned Sukhreet to her private office and raged, "What is *this*? How *dare* you do this to me!" and fired Sukhreet on the spot. Then she telephoned Dr. Maxwell and threw a similar tantrum. "How dare you have the nerve to take Sukhreet away from this office!"

When the conversation ended, the astonished Dr. Maxwell reported it to Justice Gabel, who called her daughter.

"I just cannot believe the things Bess said to Marcella," said Horty. "It doesn't make any sense. Here she's been saying she wants to get rid of you. Now she says she wants to keep you! It doesn't make any sense at all!"

15

FALLOUT

Among the many mysteries in the bessmess case, the biggest is this. After the events took place in 1983 that would comprise the evidence at trial, nothing happened for almost three years. Despite the SMALL WORLD item in the *Post* making public the fact that the daughter of the judge in the Capasso divorce had been given a city job by Capasso's girlfriend, U.S. Attorney Giuliani did not look into the case, nor did Manhattan's district attorney, Robert Morgenthau, nor New York State's attorney general, Robert Abrams, nor any other city, state, or federal official. Mayor Koch had his own special, personal criminal-justice coordinator with an office in City Hall, and this man, John F. Keenan, saw nothing to investigate either.* Ironically, by the time the case finally went to trial in October 1988, Keenan had been appointed a federal judge, and it would fall to him to try the case.

* Keenan served from June 9, 1982, until October 20, 1983.

Another mystery: Why had Mayor Koch failed to act on receipt of Police Commissioner McGuire's confidential 1980 report that Myerson, while in the midst of campaigning for the Senate, was writing anonymous letters, making harassing phone calls, and delivering bags of excrement? Perhaps the mayor felt too much compassion for his obviously ill friend. But then why, three years later, did Koch appoint her to a highly visible post in his administration? More interesting: How did she get through the compulsory police background check of public employees?

Whatever the reasons, the entire BessMess story lay dormant as a hibernating possum until March 1986. What woke the possum up was the suicide of Donald Manes. For some months, Rudolph Giuliani had been digging into municipal corruption in the Koch administration, and finding plenty. By the end of that year, the zealous prosecutor would have convicted five top city officials of bribery, racketeering, and fraud.* Several other city officials would be under indictment, though not yet tried, and Rudolph Giuliani would be perfectly positioned astride his white charger to challenge Ed Koch for mayor of New York City in the next election. The city's last prosecutor with these kinds of political smarts and ambitions had been Thomas E. Dewey. Giuliani looked at least as good.

A central figure in the corruption probe was Donald Manes. Giuliani persuaded the bagman, Geoffrey Lindenauer, to plead guilty to collecting $400,000 in bribes from city contractors and splitting the money with Manes. At trial, Lindenauer would testify that any company that wanted a contract to collect parking fines had to bribe Manes with either money or stock. Lindenauer and Shafran, his boss, got a cut. In the same trial, Stanley Friedman was convicted of bribing Lindenauer and Manes on behalf of two PVB contractors, Datacom, a computer service company, and Citisource, which made hand-held computers that were supposed to facilitate the collection of fines. Shafran and Lazar also were convicted of, among other things, bribing Manes.

----

* They were Stanley Friedman, Bronx Democratic county leader; Lester Shafran, commissioner of the Parking Violations Bureau; Geoffrey Lindenauer, a onetime quack sex therapist who was deputy director, and bagman, of the Parking Violations Bureau; John McLaughlin, former chief of New York City hospitals; and Mike Lazar, former city councilman and former New York City transportation commissioner.

What helped open this can of worms was the January 17 confession by a guilt-wracked Queens lawyer, Mike Dowd, to fellow Irishman Jimmy Breslin, that he too had been paying bribes to Manes in return for PVB contracts with a debt-collection agency Dowd owned. When Breslin broke the story, Manes knew that exposure and disgrace were certain, and imminent.

Manes had attempted suicide the first time on January 9. Shortly before midnight, he drove his car to a secluded spot and slashed his ankle and left wrist, severing the artery. By the time police brought the blood-soaked figure into the hospital emergency room two hours later, he had scarcely any pulse, and was close to death. As soon as police had realized who he was, they made every effort to hide his identity from the news media and hush up talk of a suicide attempt. Manes himself had mumbled something about mysterious assailants. The hospital emergency room and trauma room was cordoned off. Marlene Manes, Mayor Koch, and one or two others were sneaked inside the building through a rear door.

But reporters soon found out that a big story was breaking. At 4:00 A.M. Friday, January 10, Koch faced the press and said that the Queens borough president had collapsed after going on a severe liquid diet.

Some days passed before anyone confirmed that the mysterious slashing had been done by Manes himself. Manes had suffered a genuine heart attack the morning after he was admitted to the hospital, which meant he had to be transferred to the coronary-care unit, a move that further isolated him from unwanted visitors.

On Tuesday, January 21, Manes admitted his knife wounds were self-inflicted. A few hours later Koch paid him a twenty-minute visit and the next day the mayor told reporters he had hugged his friend, kissed him on the forehead, and said, "Don't worry, Donnie. Everything is going to be okay."

But by the end of that week, federal investigators had traced $2 million in bribes for city contracts in the past five years, and the PVB probe had widened to incriminate at least ten city departments that used collection agencies to collect fines.

On Saturday, the same day Manes was released from the hospital, Koch asked him to resign as Queens borough president, and added that if he didn't, Governor Cuomo should begin proceedings to get rid of him. In a TV interview on Sunday Koch called Manes "a crook," which prompted Cuomo to say that Koch should at least have waited until Manes had been formally charged.

Although his wounds had been patched up and his heart stabilized, Manes remained severely depressed, and seemed disoriented. He was put under the care of a psychiatrist and readmitted to the hospital for tests. The doctor and Marlene Manes discussed committing Manes to the Payne Whitney clinic, or some other psychiatric hospital. He still seemed intermittently suicidal, and the doctor told the family to watch him carefully at home and not leave him alone.

At about ten-thirty on the evening of March 13, with his wife talking to the psychiatrist on the bedroom phone, and his daughter watching him in the kitchen, Manes picked up the kitchen phone, exchanged some words with the psychiatrist, and then, when the psychiatrist excused himself to answer his doorbell, Manes managed to grab a steak knife and thrust it into his chest. He was dead by the time help arrived.*

By that time, the widening scandal had caused four more high-ranking city officials to resign or be fired. They were PVB director Shafran; transportation commissioner Anthony Ameruso; Investigations Department director Patrick McGinley; and taxi and limousine commissioner Jay Turoff.

The day after Manes's death, Koch appeared at a St. Patrick's Day lunch given by the Queens Chamber of Commerce at Antun's, which had been one of Manes's favorite watering holes. After eulogizing the fallen leader, the mayor began making jokes and giggling. Joyce Purnick, now with *The New York Times*, wrote that Koch seemed like a man who had been "released from a vise."

When Giuliani looked into Manes's affairs, he found that between his first suicide attempt and his death, both while Manes was in the hospital and at home, he had received almost daily phone calls and visits from both Andy Capasso and their mutual friend Stanley Friedman.

---

* Interestingly, Manes's father had been a suicide. Despondent over business losses, he had gone down to the cellar, put a gun in his mouth, and fired. Donald Manes, age twenty-one, found him. Ever after, Manes refused to descend a darkened stairway. Not three years after Donald Manes's death, his twin brother, Morris, attempted suicide with a carving knife, but police were able to save him.

With Friedman already under investigation and about to be indicted, and Manes dead, Giuliani had to move swiftly. Within
days, he had subpoenaed the sealed records of the Capasso divorce,
all of Andy's business records, and anything he could find even
remotely relating to the Owl's Head job. Giuliani knew that Friedman had patronage appointees high up in the Department of Environmental Protection, where the Owl's Head contract had
originated. State officials also were investigating, and on April 9
Stanley Friedman was indicted by both state and federal authorities
and charged with attempting to bribe National Guard officials in
yet another tentacle of the PVB scam.

The hunt was in full cry, and right behind the feds and New
York State came a pack of investigative reporters led by Marcia
Kramer, the *News*'s City Hall bureau chief. Kramer is not the usual
bureau chief. She is a good-looking blonde with long red fingernails
who works off tension by running six miles a day, and most mornings she does six hundred sit-ups as well. She is in her late thirties,
aggressive, and smart. In late April, Kramer and an associate forced
their way into Justice Gabel's chambers, waving copies of her decisions twice lowering the maintenance and child-support payments
in *Capasso* v. *Capasso*, and demanding an explanation.

"Dollars to doughnuts that decision was written by some law
assistant," said the judge, not in the least flustered.

On May 8, Kramer broke the story of the federal investigation of
Capasso, of the $125 million in city construction contracts awarded
him in the past five years, of his bitter divorce and Myerson's
alleged role in it, and of his lavish entertainment of such city officials as Manes, Friedman, and Rickman. Amid all the talk of boodle
and spoils, the story of Justice Gabel's "secret bargain with Bess re
alimony slash" seemed almost an also-ran.

The federal grand jury now subpoenaed all records of the Department of Cultural Affairs since Bess had been appointed commissioner. When the DCA inspector general arrived at Myerson's
office, subpoena in hand, a considerable dustup ensued. At first,
Myerson told the woman, "You will find nothing here," and said
she always threw away her desk diaries at the end of the year.

The woman returned the following day with another subpoena,

and matters took a turn for the worse. "I don't give a fuck about any of this shit!" roared the commissioner of cultural affairs.

Soon she was out of her office, and screaming down the corridor, "I'm still commissioner around here! To hell with . . . Giuliani! I don't want anybody cooperating with those guys!" Giuliani's grand-jury investigation of her and Capasso was nothing but a "witch-hunt," she shrieked. If she was right, and considerable evidence has since accumulated that she may have been, starting with her own acquittal on all charges, then the ultimate target of the witch-hunt was not Myerson but Ed Koch.

Ten minutes after her outburst, the commissioner returned to her office and apologized. "I'm sorry," she said, "but all this happened because his wife only got two million dollars, instead of fifteen million." Then she said, "She had thrown him out before I had anything to do with him."

The missing diaries never turned up. Later, Myerson allegedly withheld a favorable employment report on her department's inspector general in retaliation for her insistence that the commissioner comply with the government subpoenas.

Giuliani's next subpoena was easier to serve. He asked New York City authorities to turn over all records of city dealings with Nanco and all other Capasso businesses, going back to January 1, 1978. That was the day Ed Koch was sworn in for the first time on the steps of City Hall. Manes, Friedman, and Rickman had been among the bigwigs in the grandstand, and Bess Myerson had held the Bible. Everybody was back in position at Koch's second inauguration, in 1982. By 1986, Myerson was the city commissioner who introduced the mayor, and her lover Capasso had joined the luxuriantly overcoated ranks of grandstand VIPs. From a high corner grandstand seat the dark figure of Rudolph Giuliani silently observed the scene.

Records turned over by the city comptroller Harrison Goldin showed that since 1982 Nanco and a couple of other small Capasso-owned construction companies had gotten over $200 million in city business.

On June 15, the *News* published another scoop. Nancy Capasso, on her lawyer's advice, had been taping Andy's telephone calls, and she had recorded him asking some injudicious and possibly incriminating questions. The tape was already in the hands of the grand jury, the *News* said, leaving not a few readers wondering what the source might be of the paper's information.

The very next evening Sukhreet Gabel got a phone call from Bess Myerson, whom she had not heard a word from in more than two years. "Hiya, babes," said Myerson, as if they had just talked last week. "I have some wonderful news to tell you. Want to take a walk around the block?"

It was about 9:00 P.M. when Myerson arrived at Sukhreet's apartment house and phoned up from the lobby. When she learned Sukhreet was with her boyfriend, she declined to come upstairs and insisted Sukhreet come down. Sukhreet found Bess waiting not in the lobby but out in the darkened street. She wore large wraparound dark glasses, a bandanna over her head, and gray sweats.

They walked round and round the block for nearly an hour while Bess grilled her former assistant about her recollections of how she had come to be hired at DCA, and how Richard Bruno had happened to compose the letter to Mayor Koch in response to SMALL WORLD. Bess repeatedly interrupted Sukhreet's narrative with exclamations such as "You *would* remember that!" and "Did you tell *that* to your lawyer?"

Bess said she had forgotten a great deal about these events, and said Sukhreet "should learn to forget more. You could be very dangerous! Do you tell your lawyer *everything*?"

Specifically, Bess asked Sukhreet to "forget about" the episode in which DCA staffers rewrote and retyped her résumé, and then she denied to Sukhreet that it had occurred.

Bess turned the discussion to the fact that two out of three assistant commissioners at DCA, and the deputy commissioner, had been dissatisfied with Sukhreet's job performance, but Myerson had "enjoyed" her work.

"Don't you see?" she added. "They were all out to get you, because they were jealous of our close relationship."

After a final question about whether Sukhreet intended to mention this conversation to anyone, her lawyer in particular, Myerson disappeared into the darkness.

When Sukhreet's roommate Kenneth Chase, himself a lawyer

with Davis Polk & Wardwell, heard what had happened, he advised Sukhreet to report the visit to her own lawyer in the morning, saying that it sounded to him like a possible attempt to suborn a witness. (The grand-jury indictment would charge Myerson, Hortense Gabel, and Capasso with conspiracy and mail fraud, plus an additional obstruction-of-justice charge against Myerson only, based upon the visit to Sukhreet.)

Sukhreet's lawyer was Philip Schaeffer, a Gabel family friend who at this point was representing both mother and daughter without fee. When Schaeffer heard about Bess's visit, he told Sukhreet to write a memorandum of as much as she could recollect of their conversation, and she filled four handwritten pages.

The Gabels and others were preparing themselves for the first official investigation regarding the divorce-fixing allegations against Justice Gabel. The New York State Commission on Judicial Conduct was due to begin taking confidential testimony in July. The CJC was a self-policing panel that had been set up in the mid-1970s in the wake of charges of statewide judicial corruption.* Subsequently, every other state, the District of Columbia, and Puerto Rico had set up similar judicial watchdog agencies.

In September, saying she was concerned for her personal safety, Bess Myerson asked the Koch administration for confidentiality on her city financial form, a document required of all city officials.

That fall, Stanley Friedman, PVB director Shafran, and three others accused of paying off Manes and friends went to trial in New Haven, Connecticut, a city adjudged remote enough from the rotting Apple to assure an unfixable jury. After a two-month trial, the Connecticut jurors returned convictions across the board. Friedman got twelve years and later an additional seven years, not concurrent, on state charges. The verdict was the greatest personal victory of Rudolph Giuliani's career; he had handled every phase of the prosecution, including heading up the courtroom team.

---

* More irony: The first New York State special prosecutor assigned to look into judicial corruption had been Maurice Nadjari. His successor was John F. Keenan, the Myerson/Gabel/Capasso trial judge, who served from June 30, 1976, until April 9, 1979, when Mayor Koch appointed him chairman and president of the New York City Off-track Betting Corporation. He remained at OTB until June 9, 1982, when he became criminal justice coordinator for the City of New York.

Three days before Christmas, 1986, the federal grand jury investigating Andy Capasso subpoenaed Bess Myerson. She refused to testify, citing her Fifth Amendment privilege. She said she was acting on the advice of both her newly retained criminal lawyer, Fred Hafetz, and her old psychiatrist buddy Ted Rubin, and she simply ignored the fact that the beleaguered mayor had ordered all city officials to cooperate with federal investigators. Bess might be a crook, but she was not a fink. She too would dummy up, Andy style.

When Koch saw on the January 10 six o'clock news that Bess had defied his orders, he said he was "distressed," but had "confidence in her . . . integrity . . ." Three days later, his confidence had ebbed sufficiently for him to order a confidential inquiry, and Myerson took a ninety-day leave of absence while the city investigated.

To head up his inquiry Koch appointed Harold "Ace" Tyler, a Republican and a former federal judge. Tyler, now back practicing law, was the longtime mentor and a former law partner of Rudolph Giuliani. They had first worked together in 1975, when both men were members of the Nixon/Ford Justice Department.

The very next day, January 14, 1987, Giuliani indicted Andy Capasso for evading $774,600 in federal and state income taxes by falsifying expense records on city projects. He faced possible imprisonment for thirty-seven years and fines up to $1.5 million.

One part of the indictment charged that Nanco filed false liability claims. Using a Cole's Directory, which lists people by address rather than by name, Capasso had allegedly selected at random the names of persons living adjacent to ongoing Nanco construction projects, and written checks to these people on the pretense that they had filed liability claims for injuries suffered at Nanco work sites. Capasso then had Nanco employees cash the checks and turn the money over to him. The checks totaled $358,323 for the period 1981–1983.

Another part of the indictment charged Capasso with avoiding taxes by billing Nanco for $1.3 million worth of renovations on his two new apartments, the family one at 990 Fifth Avenue, and the one for him and Bess on Park.

To understand what happened next, it is helpful to know something about Jay Goldberg, fifty-five, Andy's lawyer for criminal matters. (Sam Fredman was Andy's matrimonial lawyer only, and a third attorney, Alan Ross, looked after Nanco and other Capasso business affairs.) By the end of the BessMess trial, Goldberg would be rated by his peers the finest trial lawyer in town.

Tall, bald, handsome, blue-eyed, funny, and fiendishly smart, Goldberg had been a federal prosecutor on the staff of Robert Kennedy. To earn money for Harvard Law School he had worked as a stand-up comic. By the time he took on Andy Capasso, his hearty client list included all sorts of people, songbirds and jailbirds as disparate as Willie Nelson, Waylon Jennings, and Matty "The Horse" Ianniello. In 1986, Goldberg had defended "The Horse" on twenty-six counts of garbage racketeering in a complex, multi-defendant case that ended with the exquisite sound, to Goldberg and client, of a jury foreman repeating the words "not guilty" 156 times in a row. To be sure, Ianniello had earlier been convicted of skimming profits from his string of nightclubs, restaurants, and topless bars, and failing to pay taxes on the swag, and he was currently doing a six-year stretch in federal custody. But without Jay Goldberg's services, it is generally agreed in the precincts of the criminal bar that the punishment could have been more hideous by far, say twenty or thirty years.*

When Capasso was indicted, Goldberg immediately told the press that the government's charges were based on false information supplied by Capasso's embittered ex-wife. "The case had no defense," he said later, adding, "Nancy ratted him out because she was interested in punishment."

The lawyer's stinging charges goaded Nancy Capasso into speaking to the press for the first time. On January 20 she told the *News* that she was "furious and hurt . . . I never testified against him. I never turned over a record. I never threatened him, or anything." She admitted having made a tape on which Andy begged her not to turn him in, but she denied giving it to the grand jury. "I never

---

* Later in 1987, even Goldberg couldn't save Ianniello when Giuliani charged him and "Fat Tony" Salerno with rigging bids on $30 million worth of concrete work for the new Jacob K. Javits Convention Center. They were convicted May 4, 1988, and Ianniello was sentenced to thirteen years. On May 10, a New Jersey federal prosecutor announced the indictments of eight reputed Genovese family members, including Salerno and Ianniello, for extortion and racketeering stemming from the 1984 takeover of an Edgewater, New Jersey, gravel company.

even used it in my divorce case, because it was too incriminating."
Giuliani had stumbled upon the tape when he subpoenaed the
sealed records of the couple's divorce.

Goldberg's biggest fear was not that his client was guilty of tax
evasion, though he was, and would soon admit as much. "Nine out
of ten criminal defendants are guilty," Goldberg often said. He had
no illusion that he had to admire or even like a client. "I think of
myself as an emergency-room doctor," he explained. "And the
client doesn't have to be Dreyfus . . . as long as he pays."

Goldberg's big worry was that the prosecutors would convince
the judge on Capasso's tax case to hand him a very tough sentence
in order to pressure him to talk about other matters—Manes and
Friedman perhaps, or organized crime and the Mafia, or corruption
under Koch in awarding city contracts. Such things often occurred.
Judge John J. Sirica, for example, had used the same tactic in
handing out stiff sentences to the Watergate plumbers. If Capasso
went to trial, and was convicted, which was a good possibility
despite Goldberg's art, the judge might well give him twenty or
more years, intending to reduce the sentence later, after he had
obliged the government by telling it what it wanted to know.

Such a scenario would have been a genuine disaster, because
Goldberg knew his man. Andy never talked. He was "a stand-up
guy . . . who won't rat. It would take more than a tax case to make
him talk." Indeed, when Giuliani began looking into the affairs of
Nanco employees, Andy let it be known around the company that
he would personally pay the legal fees that would enable all his men
also to be "stand-up guys" in the Nanco tradition.

Eight days after Capasso was indicted, Goldberg astounded the
prosecutors by entering a guilty plea for his client on all nine counts.
His strategy: He had happened to notice that the sitting arraignment judge in the second circuit, the man whose job it was to accept
pleas and supervise the spinning of the bingolike wheel that deter-
mines which judge is assigned to which case, was Charles E. Stewart. Arraignment judges are rotated. If a defendant pleads guilty,
the arraignment judge automatically handles his case for sentencing, and never spins the wheel. Goldberg considered Judge Stewart
"remarkably fair" and, unlike certain other judges of the second
circuit, "not an arm of the prosecutor."

This being the situation, it was far better for Andy to plead guilty, which Goldberg was quick to admit he was, and take a chance on the fair-mindedness of Judge Stewart. The lawyer had no trouble convincing Andy to go along with his idea, and later said the prosecutors had come to call it "the Goldberg maneuver."

The idea had first come to him about two days after he saw Judge Stewart's name on the calendar, and he was careful to keep his intentions quiet during the ten days yet to elapse before the actual arraignment. Goldberg had never before had a client plead guilty without warning the prosecution.

During the ten days, Goldberg and some of his lawyer cronies drafted a high-minded statement for Andy to make at the time he entered his plea. As the moment drew nigh, Andy told Goldberg he wanted to show the statement to Bess, who was sitting out her ninety-day temporary leave of absence while Tyler investigated. As Goldberg later confided to a friend: "Andy, he's a moron. He shows it to Bess, the big scholar, and she says: 'Let me do something about it.' "

In fact, Myerson thought it sounded too dry and lawyerlike; it needed humanizing. So saying, the Jewish mother swung into action, and at nine-thirty the evening before Andy was to plead, the phone rang in the apartment of DCA assistant commissioner Richard Bruno. It was Myerson, saying she needed some help rewriting a statement to be released the next morning. Could she bring it over for him to look at?

Of course, said Bruno, who assumed his harried boss had decided to speak out in her own defense.

Bess was well connected in the world of public relations, and could have called on any number of high-powered professionals to revise Andy's words. But she was too smart to take such a risk. If David Lawrence, the chief prosecutor, had found out Andy was going to plead, Goldberg feared "he would take the case off the calendar and put it in front of some monster judge," instead of Judge Stewart. Hence Myerson went to a rewrite man who was also an employee, and trustworthy—someone she knew would not betray her to the federal authorities.

Bruno was surprised when Bess showed up accompanied by a stocky, dark-haired man in an expensive suit. She explained the actual circumstances, and handed Bruno the proposed Capasso statement. Bruno was acutely uncomfortable. He was a speech writer for cultural, not criminal affairs. But he agreed that the phrasing lacked a certain felicity. Switching on his word processor, he spent perhaps thirty minutes producing what all hands agreed was a more mellifluous run of words.

Andy offered to pay him, which made Bruno even more uncomfortable, and he firmly declined. As his guests were leaving, Bess drew Bruno aside and whispered that in a few years Andy would be out of prison, and would doubtless require the services of a good speech writer. Bruno gulped and said good-bye. A few moments later, he discovered a crisp new $100 bill lying on his sideboard.

The next morning Judge Stewart accepted Andy's guilty plea on all nine tax counts, and Andy read his statement admitting his tax misdeeds, denying any "improper influence, bribery, or bid-rigging" in obtaining city or state contracts, and defending his friend Bess Myerson. "She has been an extraordinarily dedicated and honest public servant. I would never jeopardize either her reputation or our relationship by any request for assistance. Bess's integrity is such that she could be counted on to reject out of hand any action which departs from what is required of a dedicated public servant."

Sentencing was due in ten weeks, leaving time for all interested parties to write to the judge. Andy's friends and family sent thirty or forty letters citing his good character and begging for a lenient sentence. The letter from Dr. Rubin calling Capasso his "most improved" patient was written at this time.

The government, as expected, requested a very stiff sentence, in view of its contention that Capasso had "ties to organized crime." A basis of this belief, prosecutor Lawrence wrote, was Andy's refusal to acknowledge he knew anything about evidence that had surfaced in another government investigation into ties between organized crime and the construction industry. One June morning in 1984, an FBI bug installed at the Palma Boy Social Club in East Harlem had picked up a conversation between "Fat Tony" Salerno and a hood named Louis DiNapoli. The rambling, sometimes incoherent chat seemed to concern payoffs in the construction industry. At one point, "Fat Tony" said, "Andy's lookin' to build a cement plant," and three times DiNapoli asked the sibylline question "Who the fuck is Andy Capasso?"

On the morning of March 30, 1987, Judge Stewart sentenced Capasso to four years in prison, and fined him $500,000. The "Goldberg maneuver" had worked. After that, the federal judiciary, Southern District of New York, made a new rule. A defendant who pleaded guilty no longer automatically got to keep the arraignment judge as his sentencing judge. Instead, the wheel was spun every time, and each defendant got whatever judge came up, no matter what his plea.

The confidential seventy-four-page Tyler Report was submitted to Mayor Koch on April 8. It was an unusual document, written in a flowing narrative style and divided like a Trollope novel into chapters with headings such as "Spring 1983: The Courtship of Justice Gabel" and "Aftermath of the *Post* Article: Justice Gabel and Ms. Myerson Conceal the Facts."

The next day Bess Myerson resigned, and the report was sealed by Mayor Koch. Nonetheless it was known that all the evidence gathered so far was circumstantial, making conviction by no means a certainty should the case go to trial.

A week later came the Jewish holiday of Passover, and the Mayor invited Bess to a seder at Gracie Mansion. Later he told *The New York Times:* "I believe there was a serious question of her stability. By that I mean, when this occurred, it was at Passover, and I thought to myself: She is alone. I worried about what she might do to herself."

Bess Myerson had been hidden from public view since January, when her temporary leave began. She remained invisible until May 16, on which day three hundred original residents of the Sholem Aleichem apartments held their sixtieth reunion at a midtown hotel. Bess Myerson turned up, flanked by both of her sisters, and vigorously plugged her new book.

Then a lot of things happened at once. Someone leaked a copy of the "sealed" Tyler Report to *The Village Voice*, which on June 10 printed it nearly in full. The article included testimony from all of the major witnesses, including all three of the Gabels, and reported conclusions that Myerson "intended to and did improperly influence the judge." It revealed that the report charged Myerson with "serious misconduct," termed Judge Gabel "unbelievable," and said a "secret understanding" had existed between her and Commissioner Myerson. It added that Myerson used city employees to do her personal errands, and it charged her with failure to disclose "lavish gifts" from Capasso—furs, jewelry, the two Mercedes-Benzes—in violation of city regulations governing the relationship between city officials and city contractors.

The weekly paper sold out overnight. The next day Koch said the report proved that Bess had deceived him, but she was "still my friend," an odd remark that could be interpreted in at least two ways. Koch might have been going easy on Bess because of her fragile mental health. On the other hand, he might have been going very easy because he feared she could have something on him that he wanted to be careful not to goad her into using. In *City for Sale*, reporters Newfield and Barrett write that "Koch seemed afraid of Myerson. She was erratic and capable of saying almost anything. She knew many potentially embarrassing secrets about him, and had already been quoted in *New York* magazine as stating, 'I'm the perfect route to the downfall of this administration.' Some of the mayor's friends read this as a veiled threat of blackmail."

The following day, Friday, June 12, a strongly worded *New York Times* editorial demanded further investigation and prosecution. "After Ms. Myerson showered attention on the judge and created a city job for her daughter, the judge reduced the award by two-thirds . . . both women concealed key facts from the public . . . Mr. Koch . . . needs to explain why . . . [he] sought to keep the Report secret . . .

"With the Report under lock and key, Mr. Koch appeared to deserve praise for sensitive handling of Ms. Myerson's case. Now he needs to say why he did not provide more information and express more outrage until now. Last year, on less incriminating evidence, the Mayor denounced the late Donald Manes of Queens as 'a crook.' "

The *Daily News* editorial said, "At long last, the Bess Myerson rock has been kicked over, and what's crawling out is sickening: arrogance, abuse of power, payroll manipulation, case-fixing, coverup . . . Yet even after [Koch] knew the Tyler Report's contents, the Mayor allowed Myerson to resign and preserve the fiction *she* was the victim, while she wallowed in the most cynical graft. Friendship is no excuse for tolerating gross corruption."

As these editorials were being written on June 11, Koch was finally blasting Bess to the press, saying, "I am aghast at what she did. It's deplorable . . . dishonorable . . . and disgraceful."

The next day, at a small press conference in his office, Koch answered all questions about Myerson with a weary "I don't know," or "I can't recall." Reporters said it was the first time they had seen the mayor lose his composure in nine years.

By Monday Justice Gabel was demanding that the mayor make public the alleged evidence against her in the Tyler Report. Koch had said he had sealed the report "lest people get killed."* But Justice Gabel in a very real sense had already been killed. All she had was her good name. The following day she temporarily stepped down from the bench, and the influential lawyer Milton Gould, whose firm represented her, charged that Harold Tyler had "suckered" Ed Koch into ordering the Tyler Report. The following day the state judicial administrative board decided to "take no action" on yanking Justice Gabel's third special waiver permitting her to serve beyond the mandatory retirement age of seventy.

On June 29, Justice Gabel gave up the ghost and retired for good. By that time Capasso had gone to prison, and Sukhreet Gabel had given her third special deposition to the grand jury and had allowed a team of U.S. attorneys and FBI men to attach a tape recorder to her home phone and instruct her in its use. Additionally, the grand jury had subpoenaed all business records of Bess Myerson, Andy Capasso, and Nanco.

In a letter to Sol Wachtler, chief judge of the State of New York Court of Appeals, Justice Gabel wrote, "Recent events have subjected me to physical and mental pressures which make it impossible for me to perform my judicial tasks in conformity with the standards I have set for myself throughout my judicial career."

It had all happened with tragic, dizzying speed. Only a few months earlier, with great fanfare, the National Association of

---

* In his presentencing memorandum on Capasso, David Lawrence had mentioned that a cooperating witness testifying before the grand jury had found on his doorstep a dead bird with a dollar bill in its beak, a traditional Mafia warning to "canaries."

Women Judges had announced its 1986 Judge of the Year. She was the Honorable Hortense Wittstein Gabel.

The next day Mayor Koch said he thought Justice Gabel had made the right decision. The Commission on Judicial Conduct soon dropped its investigation, and the judge applied for the $41,000 life pension to which she was entitled whether or not criminal charges were ever filed.

Two days after Gabel's resignation, June 30, *The New York Times* front-paged a story it had been sitting on for seven years. It disclosed the 1980 confidential police report to Mayor Koch about Bess Myerson's "obsessive behavior" in regard to John Jakobson: the anonymous phone calls, the "up to 50" anonymous letters, and the "vulgar message" Jakobson had found on his Hotel Carlyle doorstep.

Koch told the *Times* that he "still ha[d] not seen the report," and "had only sketchy knowledge of its content in 1980," when Police Commissioner McGuire visited City Hall to tell him about it. But the mayor now acknowledged that the report "could have served as an early warning of . . . what appears to be a pattern of extreme conduct surrounding her personal entanglements."

16

IN ALL, JUSTICE GABEL WOULD MAKE SEVENTEEN pretrial rulings in *Capasso* v. *Capasso*. It seemed to Nancy that nearly every one after the first one, on February 15, 1983, granting her exclusive occupancy of 990 Fifth, was favorable to her husband, some bizarrely so. For example, Gabel's September 30 order on reargument gave Nancy the city apartment *pendente lite*, and Andy the beach house. The two condos in Palm Beach also went to Andy. As for the small Westhampton Beach condo, which had been the family's original beach property, and was Nancy's favorite, Justice Gabel awarded it to husband and wife on alternate months. This meant that every other month Andy had two Long Island beach properties and Nancy had no place to take the children, and no car to do it in. (One of Justice Gabel's prior decisions had been that Andy did not have to return Nancy's Mercedes-Benz, which he had seized, because it was legally registered as the property of Nanco—as was Andy's Mercedes, the two

His and Hers chauffeur-driven limousines, the other five family cars, and one of the two Palm Beach condos.)

Nancy's lawyer had immediately appealed the ruling across the board. The higher court, called the appellate division, restored Gabel's original June grants of $1,500 maintenance and $350 child support.

In late September 1983, Nancy submitted an anti-Myerson visitation motion asking the court to prevent the children from visiting their father when his girlfriend was present. Justice Gabel denied the motion.

One of the family's most valuable baubles was a particularly elegant $195,000 painting by Cy Twombly, bought for the new dining room. Executed in monochrome gray and white, the painting is Twombly's version of a chalkboard handwriting exercise, similar to but considered much finer than some of the Twomblys owned by the Whitney Museum of American Art. Andy's lawyer told the court that the painting was the property of Nanco, and he asked permission to sell it to improve Nanco's cash flow.

On the day this motion was scheduled to be argued, October 18, the SMALL WORLD article was published. Justice Gabel's primary legal assistant, Howard Leventhal, and her legal secretary, Brenda Shrobe, both knew how strict she was on matters of integrity, and both assumed that SMALL WORLD would cause her to recuse herself. In a prior case, for example, she had recused herself simply because both attorneys were among the scores of persons to whom she had sent Sukhreet's résumé. Another time, she had chewed out a grateful teenager who sent her flowers after she ruled in his parents' custody fight.

In court, Justice Gabel cited the article and asked if "anyone" wanted her to recuse herself. Raoul Felder said no; both sides were confident of the court's integrity and impartiality. Felder later let it be known that since he did not know how much of SMALL WORLD was in fact correct and how much a product of Myerson's imagination, he chose not to object. Later Justice Gabel told Leventhal, "They both said how fair they thought I'd been, and how honored they would be if I continued to preside . . . and that they thought I was straight as an arrow. They were very supportive."

Some lawyers say that questions like Gabel's to Felder are a common judicial maneuver. The judge puts the burden of whether to recuse herself onto the lawyers, who rarely ask it. If a judge really thinks she should recuse herself, the thinking goes, she does it. She doesn't need to ask the lawyers.

One lawyer in a matrimonial case in front of Gabel recalls being asked the same question by her. He said yes, he thought she should recuse herself, not because of partiality, but because his client was complaining she had taken five months to decide some simple alimony motions. Justice Gabel was deeply hurt, she told him later, and asked, "How could you do this to me?"

"She wasn't angry, just hurt," said the lawyer, an old friend and political colleague. "I don't really think Horty is capable of anger. She would regard anger as sinful."

At the end of the SMALL WORLD day, Justice Gabel okayed Capasso's sale of the Cy Twombly painting, providing he posted a $100,000 bond. But Nancy had exclusive occupancy of the Fifth Avenue apartment, and she refused to relinquish the work of art. Andy then tried to punish Nancy by asking the court to find her in contempt. Nancy cross-moved for a money judgment of $2,900 for alimony arrears.

In January 1984, Justice Gabel held Nancy in contempt. Once again Felder appealed to the appellate division, which again reversed Justice Gabel's decision and directed that the Twombly not be sold before trial.

In February, Justice Gabel granted Nancy reimbursement for monies she had laid out for the children's tutoring fees. It was Gabel's only pro-Nancy decision since her initial $1,850-a-week award for alimony and child support in June, and later she reversed it.

In March Felder's appeal was successful, and the appellate division made the $1,850 award retroactive to the date it had been cut off. Nancy waited in vain for the money to come in.

Early in May, Justice Gabel granted Andy's motion to reargue the tutoring fees, and denied Nancy expenses.

Later in May, Nancy applied to the court for $85,570 in arrears in support money due her from Andy. This motion took an entire year to be decided, and the final amount awarded, by a different judge, was for some reason not $85,000 but $65,000.

Still later, Andy moved to have Nancy pay the school tuition and the summer-camp fees. He said his mounting troubles at Nanco had left him financially strapped.

At this, Nancy and Felder stepped up their efforts to determine Andy's true cash position. They knew by then that the previous fall Andy had bought a Park Avenue apartment for $1.6 million, and had paid all cash. Presumably, this would one day become the city residence of the embattled lovebirds. Felder filed a set of financial questions and asked that Andy be compelled by the court to answer them, and he sought to subpoena Nanco records and other business accounts.

On June 24, 1984, Hortense Gabel was rotated out from the motion part to the trial part; her two-year ordeal on the "Russian front" was over. Several pretrial motions in *Capasso* v. *Capasso* were still undecided. But four days earlier, on June 20, she had vacated Nancy's interrogatories and quashed her third-party subpoenas for Andy's financial records, which is lawful language for telling a petitioner to forget it.

For some time Nancy had been convinced that Justice Gabel would never give her a fair shake. She pressured her lawyer to complain. Felder refused, and wrote his client what she later termed a "cover-your-ass letter" that said, "Judges are like shoemakers . . . interchangeable . . ." Nancy, by now understandably perhaps somewhat paranoid, felt that Felder was not about to insult and infuriate an honored judge just to please the latest hysterical about-to-be-ex-wife to come along in his thriving matrimonial practice.

Eventually, against the advice of all lawyers, Nancy would write to Justice Gabel directly in December 1984, appealing to her to disqualify herself.

> Since the inception of this case, your decisions have endangered my ability and that of my two small children to subsist pending the ultimate trial of this matter . . .
>
> As a result of your prior decisions, my husband was given the use of four out of our five residences . . .
>
> You took away from me and my children every single car that we ever had at our disposal, totally depriving us of our means of transportation . . . [to school; for weekend trips; for marketing] . . .

You denied my application for medical and dental expenses for myself and the children . . .

That we are surviving this ordeal at all is due entirely to the Appellate Division's reversal of your decisions.

Because we have heard of your fine reputation for protecting women in my circumstances, your decisions in my case are inconsistent with your rulings in other cases and are inexplicable. I am sure you can see this.

In sum, the only appropriate action you can now take is to remove yourself from my case. For the record plainly presents, at the least, an appearance of impropriety.

Although Nancy received no reply from the court, her letter was considered of sufficient eloquence to be reprinted in full in a neighborhood newsletter and later in *Harper's* magazine.

One day Nancy spotted Justice Gabel on a Fifth Avenue bus, and in another inappropriate move, appealed personally and respectfully that she remove herself from the case, again of course to no avail.

Nancy was sick at heart about her treatment by the court, and she had lost faith in Felder. In midsummer 1984 she replaced him with Herman Tarnow, also a matrimonial specialist, but one whose formative years at the bar had been spent in the more rough-and-tumble precincts of criminal-defense practice. Tarnow was tough, stubby, dogged, and appeared willing to get as mean as necessary to accomplish his objective.

Nancy was broke. Until she collected from Andy, she would not be able to pay Felder's fees, and all that she was able to scrape together as a retainer for Tarnow was $5,000 plus a note.

The motions phase of the case was nearly over, and Tarnow began preparing to go to trial. In 1981 New York had modernized its archaic divorce statutes in several ways, the most important of which was to adopt a doctrine of equitable distribution of the marital property without regard to fault. No longer would the divorce court serve as an arena for moral blamesmanship. Pejorative terms like *alimony* were replaced with the more neutral-sounding *maintenance*. As Howard Leventhal has expressed it, "Under the equitable distribution law, the breakup of a marriage is no longer viewed as it had heretofore been, as a question of morality versus immorality.

But rather it is viewed as the breakup of an economic partnership, and the purpose of the law is not to punish the wrongdoer or reward the virtuous spouse, but rather to see that the marital assets are fairly distributed between the spouses."

The new system requires each side to make full disclosure of its financial position, and in a bitterly fought contest this can take some time. In *Capasso* v. *Capasso*, the preparatory period lasted thirty months, from January 1983 until July 1985.

Tarnow's first task was to find out how much his new client's husband was really, actually, currently worth. Andy considered this nobody's business but his own, and he was disinclined to cooperate one whit more than the law required. Complicating Tarnow's problem was the possibility by this point that Capasso himself was not entirely sure what he was worth.

Andy was a man besieged. In addition to his wife and her lawyers, state authorities were becoming curious about Nanco's business practices. Later the feds would join in. These investigations, in turn, tended to cause subcontractors to slow down their work and debtors to hedge and dawdle on their payments, creating Nanco's alleged cash-flow problem.

Capasso's chief debtor was the City of New York. But the greatest pressure on him at this point was coming not from his adversaries but his friends: his very good business friends, the Aetna Insurance Company and the European American Bank, and his girlfriend Bess, eager for renovations to begin on the Park Avenue apartment that he had bought late in 1983.

Capasso's marital skirmishings and his relations with Aetna and EAB had grown ever more tightly intertwined. In July 1981, he had switched Nanco's bond reliance from a small firm to the big Aetna Insurance Company.* The middleman, bond broker Richard Ferrucci, was Andy's buddy. Such bonds are a safety measure required by the city to minimize its risk. Should a contractor get

···

* Aetna Insurance Company was originally a subsidiary of Connecticut General Life Insurance Company. In 1982, when Connecticut General and INA Corporation merged to form CIGNA, Aetna was incorporated into CIGNA's property casualty group. Save for purposes of old lawsuits, Aetna Insurance Company no longer exists.

into trouble, the bonding agent steps in to pay off the subcontractors and get the job done. The contractor, Nanco in this case, pays Aetna a premium on each bond.

The bonds sound like a kind of business catastrophe insurance, something like health insurance, but there is a crucial difference. When Blue Cross pays the hospital bills, one does not incur a debt to Blue Cross. When Aetna stepped in to pay Nanco's bills to subcontractors and finish up uncompleted jobs, Nanco incurred a debt to Aetna.

When Nanco switched its business to Aetna, the insurance company required Nancy to co-sign her husband's indemnity (bonding) agreement, both individually and as secretary for Nanco Equipment, one of Nanco's spinoff companies. This meant on the face of it that Nancy, like Andy, was co-responsible and equally liable for Nanco's debts.

Aetna routinely requires wives to co-sign bonding agreements made by their husbands. There are several reasons. For instance, if the property is held jointly, and the husband dies, and the wife gets title, a creditor then cannot enforce a lien against the wife, the new titleholder, unless she is also liable. Furthermore, since the wife still holds half the property, the creditor cannot evict her.

As Nanco's bonding agent, Aetna kept track of Capasso's finances and approved bonds for each individual project. The insurance company's confidence in its ambitious, industrious new customer was demonstrated on April 12, 1983, when Capasso met with his friend Ferrucci and two officers of Aetna. The meeting accomplished two things for Andy, each of which would prove crucial to Nanco over the next three years. Aetna agreed to bond the biggest job in Nanco's history, the Owl's Head contract. Aetna also gave Andy its tacit permission to tinker with the Nanco books in order to deceive Nancy and her lawyer about his true financial status.

In April, Capasso estimated a final profit on Owl's Head of $6–8 million. At the April 1983 meeting, Nanco's latest informal balance sheet showed an anticipated net after-tax profit for July–December 1982 of $396,000. But, Capasso told the Aetna men, he did not intend to prepare a formal end-of-year financial statement for 1982 because of his pending divorce settlement. A formal statement would have handed Nancy and Tarnow just what they needed to know before going to trial.

For the next three years, Nanco struggled through the Owl's Head job, and Andy battled Nancy in the courts. In this period, to accommodate Capasso, Aetna would continue to base its evaluations on Andy's informal in-house accounting, rather than on impartial CPA audits.

Figures for fiscal year 1983 are unaccountably unavailable but, on October 12, 1984, Aetna bond officer Neil Donovan wrote, "Assuming the 'in-house' figures are accurate, 1984 was a good year for Nanco." The company claimed to have generated net after-tax profits of $417,000 on revenues of $25,367,000 in its 1984 fiscal year ending June 30. But Donovan's hedge—"assuming the 'in-house' figures are accurate"—made clear that Aetna had only Andy's word for his success.

In 1984, rather than bypass a year-end financial statement entirely, as he had in 1982, and possibly in 1983, Capasso asked Aetna to let him show a "break-even" year on his books, thus concealing the $417,000 profit from Nancy and Tarnow.

Aetna was agreeable. "Basically we told Andy we could live with a lot of things as long as he keeps us informed and up to date," Donovan wrote. In plainer English: "We don't care if or how you screw Nancy, even though she is a co-signer of our bonds. Just so you keep us posted."

Andy's objective of a paper "break-even" year could be accomplished by reducing the estimated profit on Owl's Head, although he indicated to the Aetna men that he remained confident he would meet his original final profit estimate of 6\frac{1}{2}$-$8 million.

By 1984, Andy's reports to Aetna showed a cash shortage that Andy said was partly caused by $1 million overdue from the city on two long-completed jobs, repaving Ocean Parkway in Brooklyn and Merrick Boulevard in Queens. This money was being held up while the New York State Department of Transportation disputed whether Nanco had met the minority-business-enterprise requirements.

The minority-business statute required a public contractor to give 15 percent of the work to businesses owned by minority groups or women, and the minority-owned and female-owned enterprises had to be on an approved list on file with the Department of Transportation. New York said that Nanco had dealt with the requirements illegally in one instance by setting up its own dummy minority-owned firm, and in another instance by listing as a subcontractor a female-owned firm that did not actually do the work. In July 1986, Nanco would be indicted on charges of fraud and falsifying records dealing with these jobs. The case was expected to go to trial early in 1990. When the city used the state indictment as a reason not to pay its $1 million bill, the default marked the beginning of Nanco's downhill slide.

Capasso's lawyer Jay Goldberg later said that when Giuliani started poking into the BessMess and Owl's Head, looking for something to embarrass Koch, the state "got jealous. They're vultures," and sought to find something to investigate as well. The lawyer added that the state statute is unconstitutional, "because it is affirmative-action doctrine without affirmative-action mechanisms in place." Similar statutes had been thrown out in Georgia and other states, he said.

Capasso's story is that he had had a quarrel with a black subcontractor, "and the next thing he knew, a black state senator and a black guy from the Department of Transportation showed up and tried to shake him down for several hundreds of thousands of dollars."

Capasso wrote to the state and city commissioners of investigation, complaining about the shakedown. Neither the city nor state responded, Goldberg said. But Nanco subsequently got hit with the fraudulent-minority-business-enterprise indictment.

Upon reading a newspaper account of Capasso's indictment, Herbert Rickman advised Mayor Koch not to attend Bess and Andy's Fourth of July beach party. Koch went anyhow, but Rickman did not. Instead he called on Rudolph Giuliani and said that "for appearance's sake" he had terminated his relationship with both Capasso and Myerson, and he offered the prosecution his help. Whether Rickman knew that he would be expected to "help" prosecute his friend Justice Gabel, as well as his friends Andy and Bess, is unknown.

At this point, reflecting back on his 1983 visits to Bess and Andy's

Westhampton Beach setup, Rickman said to a friend, "I saw a Potemkin village there. I felt that already the pact with the devil was on. It seemed like Andy was saying to her, 'Bess, make me kosher. Make me legit.' "

The holdup on the Ocean Parkway and Merrick Boulevard money, in addition to costs associated with Owl's Head, dried up Nanco's cash flow, and the company was relying on $2 million in bank credit from EAB. Donovan concluded one memo by saying that Aetna was "distressed" at the cash-flow problem.

"We should make sure we touch base with the banker periodically, to watch the extent of borrowings and make sure they start to trend downward in a month or two. We should also push, push, push for quarterly WOH ["work-on-hand" progress assessments] and request an 'in-house' F/S [financial statement] at six months."

Evidently Nanco also had a paper-flow problem, and was sluggish about producing the information Aetna wanted.

However, Donovan added, "Assuming that information is received and is favorable, the writer is agreeable to extending $25,000,000 of bond credit (excluding Owl's Head)." That is to say, Aetna would cover Nanco up to $25 million for other work, in addition to the Owl's Head bond. At a later date, Aetna formally approved Donovan's recommended additional bonding in principle, while continuing to demand individual approval of each new job.

Andy told Aetna that he intended to make his future bids through a newly created company, Capasso Contracting, that would not be up for grabs in the divorce settlement. Aetna wanted Nanco to indemnify Capasso Contracting, so that Aetna could go after Nanco assets to recover from any losses on bonds issued to Capasso Contracting. But Andy said Nanco could not indemnify Capasso Contracting, because then Nancy could go after Capasso Contracting's assets. At this same meeting, therefore, Aetna agreed to accept Andy's signature as a personal indemnitor for Capasso Contracting, with his promise that Nanco would indemnify the new company once the divorce was settled. This meant that Aetna was willing to accept Andy's signature as an individual, not as an officer of Nanco. So Andy's personal assets, not Nanco's, were at risk.

Donovan wrote, "By bidding work in Capasso [Contracting],

Andy is hoping to lead his wife's attorneys into believing that he is running down Nanco, and building up Capasso, thus forcing them into a faster settlement."*

The Capasso divorce was finally granted on December 18, 1985. As of January 6, 1986, Aetna was covering Nanco for $25 million in outstanding work on Owl's Head, and another $20 million in other jobs. While Aetna's plan had been to cover Nanco for a maximum of $25 million in addition to Owl's Head, a January 6 memo discusses bonding Capasso for a new $25 million job that would raise the total value of the bonds other than Owl's Head to $45 million.

However, Andy had by then told Aetna that $4 million of the anticipated $6–$8 million profits on Owl's Head had yet to materialize. "Hence we are pretty much going along as an article of faith in Andy and hope that these good profit numbers will be reflected in both the 6/30/86 and 6/30/87 fiscal year-end results," the memo admits.

It was a touching revelation that even insurance men have hearts, and observers would watch with interest to see whether Aetna's "faith" was justified. One reason for optimism was that Dun & Bradstreet was about to award Nanco its highest rating.

Aetna viewed Nanco as having a healthy net worth, even though its working capital was low. Three days later, on January 9, 1986, Nanco indemnified Capasso Contracting.

ON THAT SAME Thursday, January 9, late in the evening, Donald Manes made his first suicide attempt. In the wee hours of Friday morning, well before Koch's news conference, Andy Capasso and Stanley Friedman were seen prowling the hospital corridors. It was not clear whether either of them actually got into Manes's room.

The possibility that the mysterious stabbing was in fact a suicide attempt occurred immediately to Rudy Giuliani. His men had been working undercover for months to nail Manes firmly to the center of the fast-developing Parking Violations Bureau corruption

························

* Two other Capasso-owned companies were Nanco Equipment, formed before Capasso tied up with Aetna, and Big City Contracting.

scandal. Friday morning Giuliani decided to go public and begin arresting other suspects. The first one, phony sex therapist and political hack Geoffrey Lindenauer, was pulled in the following Tuesday. By the end of June 1987, eighteen top-echelon Koch men and Democratic party bigwigs had been forced out of office, and seven were already behind bars.

17

CAPASSO

V. CAPASSO

V. AETNA II

START TO FINISH, THE CAPASSO DIVORCE TOOK four and a half years to decide. By midsummer 1984, the cast of characters had changed somewhat. Tarnow had replaced Felder, and Justice Stanley S. Ostrow had replaced Gabel as the motions judge. The pretrial phase was supposedly over. But legal wrangling over unpaid fees would continue throughout the discovery phase, which was about to begin under Herman Tarnow's aggressive leadership. Nancy, for example, had been trying for months to get Andy to pay the $10,000 summer-camp fees, part of the children's expenses he had promised to take care of in his famed "voluntary pledge" of May 1983. Finally she had filed a motion to compel payment. Andy replied to the court that he was "absolutely financially incapable of paying for my children's camp at this time."

Nancy fumed. "This time" referred to the same time that Andy's men were renovating the Park Avenue apartment, the one he had bought for $1.6

million in cash. Nancy sold a Dubuffet painting for $56,000 and paid the camp fees herself.

In the early spring of 1985, Herman Tarnow was midway along in his efforts to discover how much money Andy actually had. The important issue after that was custody. Andy was seeking to deny his wife custody of the children.

"When you're handling a custody case, it's very important to paint a picture of reality. I like to think of myself as a mosaic-maker," Tarnow said, and Bess Myerson was by then integral to Andy's mosaic. "So I said to Nancy, 'Get yourself a little tape recorder. Because you report to me that Andy is behaving hysterically, you are entitled to do this.' "

Capasso had already installed an elaborate bugging system throughout the Westhampton Beach house. Nancy bought a $40 tape recorder at Radio Shack and attached it to the condo phone. The couple was set for a long, hot summer.

The concept of equitable distribution entitles an attorney to find out a couple's normal scale of living before the trouble began. Experience had taught Tarnow that it takes about a year for an artful husband to bury assets and cover his fiscal tracks. "So when I do a divorce case, we go back and look at how things were two years before the storm."

Tarnow approaches a case as if it were an IRS fraud audit, and he employs a pair of IRS-trained accountants with the sensitivity of bloodhounds and the thoroughness of aardvarks. He sent them to Nanco's Long Island City offices with orders to go through thirty months of canceled checks. "I want you to look front and back, and anything that looks funny—pull."

It became apparent that something funny *was* going on. Certain cash was unaccounted for. Tarnow's men were turning up checks written by Nanco that had not been deposited, as a business normally does when it receives a check, but cashed. The funny checks totaled about $200,000, and many were cashed at the Long Island City branch of EAB.

Soon Tarnow had more. "I even got the confidential loan file, the one they keep at the main office, not the branch bank. I got it because I told the lady, 'You can avoid a subpoena if you send me the stuff.' And she did! Through a combination of luck and of my tenacity, I now had the bulk of financial information about the assets of Nanco."

Tarnow's accountants had worked in Nanco's offices, always under the eye of a Nanco employee. Once the fiscal harvest was in, the venue changed, and Tarnow grilled Capasso in Sam Fredman's office. One day Tarnow was taking Capasso's daylong deposition when Andy, normally cool, slowly grew monosyllabic, then sarcastic, and then overtly hostile. Tarnow said later, "Every question I ask him, I get the most evasive series of answers I've ever heard!" Coming from Tarnow, this is quite a compliment.

"All I cared about was: How much was he worth?" But when Andy dodged and turned nasty, "it became apparent we had touched a raw nerve. Therefore we assumed Andy had some cash that we hadn't found. I started probing. . . ."

That day or the next, it was blazing hot and Nancy was out at the little Westhampton Beach condo removing her clothes and belongings as per court order, even though Andy and Bess—ensconced as they were amid the splendors of the big estate—had no intention of moving in. She was steaming mad at Bess, who she believed was behind this latest deprivation and humiliation. The phone rang; it was Andy, telephoning from the city. Nancy switched on the tape recorder as he launched into a rambling, hour-long conversation, sometimes almost pleasant, sometimes near incoherent, in which it became evident he greatly feared Nancy and Tarnow might know more about his business affairs than they had so far let on. "Your lawyer is onto something," he said. "You know something that can put me in . . . jail . . . Do you intend to go to the prosecutors, to the IRS . . . ? What will it take for you to settle this case?"

"Make me an offer I can't refuse," said Nancy in homage to *The Godfather*.

"Where is your head with turning canary and putting me in jail for four hundred, five hundred years!"

When Tarnow heard the tape, he thought the case was over. No divorce lawyer wants to go to trial. He wants to settle and get on to the next case. That moment seemed suddenly at hand. Although he did not have all the pieces of the puzzle, he knew Andy did. For several years Capasso had been doing illegal things with Nanco money—filing false health claims, evading taxes, using Nanco funds to remodel private residences—and now he knew that Tarnow's accountants were onto him.

"At that point," says Tarnow, "I could have said, 'Pay or die.' "

But Tarnow is as much a gentleman as Capasso is, so instead he arranged a breakfast meeting at the Hotel Carlyle with Andy and his lawyer. He opened with "I am here to settle," adding, "I've heard the tape."

Tarnow was prepared to settle for the apartment, plus the condo. Surprisingly, incomprehensibly, Capasso would not yield an inch. He still offered Nancy $2 million, take it or leave it.

"You know," said Tarnow later, "I like Andy. He's a very, very nice fellow. But he is one tough guy."

Tough, yes, but hardly stupid. Why wouldn't he settle? One possibility is that Fredman had by now advised his client of something Tarnow already was well aware of: Proving criminality was not at all in Nancy or Tarnow's interest. It would only prolong negotiations and eat up money in lawyer's fees. Very well. If Tarnow was bluffing, Capasso would bluff back.

Another man would have given Nancy what she asked for just to get rid of her. But not Andy. Instead he chose a course that inevitably would land him either in divorce court or in prison, or both. No deal, he said.

At that point, alas, Tarnow's luck ran out. The case was assigned for trial to Manhattan supreme-court judge Andrew Tyler, a Harlem pol and former district attorney who had a colorful, not unblemished background. In 1977 he had been convicted of three counts of perjury for lying to a grand jury, the first conviction ever of a sitting Manhattan judge. He had also been indicted for improperly granting bail to a defendant, though the charge was dismissed before trial. After a long legal battle, Tyler's conviction was overturned, at least in part through the good offices of his close friend Stanley Friedman, whose office decor included a sign that said CRIME DOESN'T PAY—AS WELL AS POLITICS.

The Bronx boss had also taken care of other allegations, including bribe taking, mob ties, and alcoholism, and finally, on December 20, 1978, the grateful Tyler had been exonerated, received two years of back pay, and was once more back on the bench trying cases.

Under Judge Tyler's relaxed gavel, *Capasso* v. *Capasso* dragged out from July to October 1985, and his decision came late December. The judge assumed the bench at about 11:00 A.M., broke for lunch at 12:30, worked for perhaps an hour and a half in the afternoon, and frequently appeared to doze off. Over nearly four months, Tyler devoted twenty-one days to this case.

A few days before Christmas, Tarnow was in Dunhill's doing his Christmas shopping when his office beeped him and said the Tyler decision had arrived.

"Just give me the bottom line," the lawyer said.

"Zilch."

Judge Tyler had grossly undervalued the Nanco real estate in Long Island City at $268,000, though documents Tarnow had placed in evidence had shown it to be worth in excess of $4 million. The court also found that Nancy Capasso had contributed almost nothing to the matrimonial assets. This finding ignored the fact that she had made many direct contributions to the business; she had kept certain books, and had been personally involved in bidding for contracts. As the appellate division later ruled, Tyler's ruling also ignored the fundamental concept of equitable distribution: that a spouse's contribution to the marital assets as a full-time wife and homemaker must be given a significant value.

Tyler awarded Nancy $2 million of Capasso's $15 million net worth, one third of what she had asked. For her interest in 990 Fifth Avenue she was awarded $1.5 million and ordered to vacate the apartment. The other $500,000 would come from various other small assets. He ruled that Andy no longer had to make any maintenance or child-support payments. He had earlier agreed that Bess Myerson did not have to testify.

Justice Tyler had also ignored the manner in which such findings must be made. In an equitable-distribution case, it is the express obligation of a trial judge to set forth the factors the court considers and the reasons for its decision. The statute requires that this be done by the judge; it cannot be done for him by the attorneys. Yet Justice Tyler signed Sam Fredman's forty-two-page "Proposed Findings of Fact and Conclusions of Law" verbatim, without changing so much as a comma. This "wholesale, verbatim adoption of the husband's requests for findings" was found to be an error of law by the appellate division.

Tarnow had to file immediately for a stay. Tyler's order required Nancy to vacate the Fifth Avenue apartment and turn over the valuable Twombly painting forthwith. Lawyer and furious client were up until 5:00 A.M. drafting the necessary papers. But a stay merely put things on hold. The critical matter was to obtain a reversal of Tyler's decision on appeal. It was clear that Nancy now required a specialist in appeals.

Raoul Felder's diminutive wife, Myrna, had been a featured Broadway dancer. When she became pregnant, she quit show biz for law school. In time she had two children, acquired a law degree, and gained a reputation as one of the finest appellate lawyers in the city. Nancy Capasso now asked Myrna Felder to represent her. Within a couple of months Felder had filed the appeal in the appellate division. The five appeals judges were properly exercised, and strongly rebuked Judge Tyler. They sent the opinion back down to him with instructions to revise it. The judge simply ignored them. He did nothing.

Felder then filed a writ of mandamus, requiring Judge Tyler to act, whereupon he issued a new decision that changed the Fredman wording but tracked exactly each and every provision of his original decision. In time the appellate division threw out Tyler's work and, on July 2, 1987, substituted its own findings.

That decision, which was final, awarded Nancy properties valued at $5.53 million, and additional assets worth another million or so, more than triple what Tyler had given her. She got the Westhampton Beach estate, the little beach condo, another piece of beach property worth nearly $900,000, half the proceeds from the sale of the Twombly painting, and $3 million from the sale of the duplex at 990 Fifth Avenue. The date of the decision was July 2, 1987.

But it was a Pyrrhic victory at best. Just before the prison gates had clanged shut less than a month before, Andy and his lawyers had put into play one last brilliant idea. Andy had "confessed judgment" against himself, a procedure that made Capasso effectively "judgment proof," and said that his bonding company and his banker, Aetna and the European American Bank, shared a first claim on all his assets. He gave them liens and mortgages on all his properties, commercial and residential, for a total amount of $18 million.

Confessing judgment is something like declaring bankruptcy, but it saves on legal fees and cuts the baloney. A bankruptcy proceeding would have divided Andy's assets among all his creditors, Nancy included. This way, Andy gave everything just to the two creditors he wanted to pay off. Confessing judgment also required much less financial disclosure than a bankruptcy proceeding, which would have laid bare Capasso's entire fiscal skeleton.

Thus disburdened, his fiscal modesty still inviolate, Andy Capasso was able to enter Allenwood Federal Penitentiary on Monday morning, June 15, 1987, an apparently penniless but relatively happy man. He had ensured that, whatever might happen next, Aetna and EAB had a secure first claim on every single thing he owned, and Nancy Capasso would not get one dime. Again, he had accomplished two things at once: He had outsmarted and punished his wife, while at the same time strengthening his position with Aetna, and possibly preserving certain properties for himself (Aetna did not require that 563 Park Avenue be sold).

The confession of judgment meant that Aetna and EAB were legally empowered to put liens on properties subsequently awarded to Nancy. Lest there be any doubt, nine days after the appellate division's July 2 decision, Aetna filed a $15 million lawsuit against Nancy for defaulting on the Nanco bond. In her answer and counterclaim, Nancy sued Andy for the money to reimburse her for anything she might have to pay to Aetna and EAB, and to recover her legal fees in the Aetna suit. Nancy was forced to agree with Aetna and EAB that monies from the sale of properties awarded to her would be locked away in escrow until the litigation was resolved.

Since June 1987, Nancy has been represented by yet another lawyer, Steven Hyman, forty-eight, as tough and accomplished in his own field as Myrna Felder and, like her, willing to work for perforce deferred compensation. Hyman relishes single-handed assaults on major corporate Goliaths, and he and his partner Paul Levinson have put in several years trying to prove that the whole confession-of-judgment scam was in fact a conspiracy among Andy, Aetna, and EAB to defraud Nancy Capasso of her rightful claims. By 1989 the end was not yet in sight, but prospects were not quite as bleak as one might think.

Nanco was eventually done in by Andy's legal entanglements. The first bad year had been 1986, when the company began to have cash-flow problems because the city was stalling on payments, and suppliers were getting sluggish as word spread of Capasso's mounting, compounding troubles with his wife's lawyers, his bonding company, and his banker, as well as with various state and federal law-enforcement authorities. By the autumn of 1986, Nanco found itself unable to start $28 million worth of projects, and its Dun & Bradstreet listing had fallen to "unrated with condition unbalanced."

Things got so bad that Andy was able to forestall one set of problems by invoking another one. For example, when Aetna began to express concern over Nanco's suddenly evaporating profits—a net loss, before income tax credits, of $301,000 for fiscal year 1986, as compared to a net profit of $118,000, after taxes, the preceding year—Andy told Aetna that the loss resulted from "several hundred thousand dollars in legal fees, plus $200,000 a year for the last four years in alimony payments drawn from the company," rather than from any default or slowdown on Nanco's part.

Aetna seems to have bought the whole thing. Their confidence in Capasso was in some respects extraordinary. "I think one has to look at where the problem is in this case," a December 1986 internal company memo begins. "First off, the work that Nanco/Capasso does have is getting done and is profitable. The problems are a combination of Andy's going through a divorce of which all his personal assets have been tied up over the last 3½ years. During the same time he has been performing on a $57,000,000 job [Owl's Head] that didn't go as well as expected . . . When we stopped providing bonds to Nanco/Capasso back in mid-1986, coupled with the indictments [on minority-business-enterprise charges in July], newspaper articles, and other rumors, the sub-contractors and suppliers became tougher to deal with since they were concerned whether the companies would remain in business. Andy pointed out that they have tried to dispel these rumors by 'plowing' through the work they have."

What's more, Nanco was "maxed out" at EAB, having borrowed $2.75 million in the previous twelve to fifteen months.

As if all this were not enough, Andy was having a few problems with Bess. The least of it was that in December 1986 she had been called before the grand jury investigating the possible Myerson-

Gabel-Capasso conspiracy, and taken the Fifth. Additionally, after she had invited a recently divorced woman, Betty Beinan, to join her therapy group with Dr. Rubin, a group that Andy himself attended on occasion, Andy and Beinan had begun dating on the sly. Bess had somehow found out, possibly via Nancy, who had been strolling down Madison Avenue one day and seen her $90,000 diamond bracelet, the one Andy had said he couldn't find, twinkling on Betty Beinan's wrist.

All in all, Capasso might not have been too terribly sorry to have been sent away to prison a couple of months later, and especially, being sent there as a pauper, with all of his property in hock to Aetna and EAB. He had strengthened his position with Aetna and EAB for future bonding once he had served his time. Bess came to visit him regularly, as so indeed did Betty Beinan, and perhaps others. Jay Goldberg told people the prison was having to build higher walls to keep the women out.

The big penitentiary in Allenwood, Pennsylvania, is known as the country club of the federal system. Some even call it "the spa." Andy Capasso's condition improved from the moment he checked in. He at once began to eat less, drink less, exercise more, and keep regular hours. In addition, his financial position enjoyed a major change for the better. Nanco's relationships to Aetna and EAB were now so complex that Aetna put Andy on its payroll for the years of his Allenwood residency as a $60,000-a-year "consultant."

On June 12, the Friday Andy had confessed judgment, Aetna had set dates by which time the Capasso beach properties that it held liens on had to be sold, but it didn't require that Park Avenue be sold. Hyman was trying to find out why not. There had never been any litigation on whether Park Avenue should be considered part of the marital property. By the time Andy went to prison, Bess was living in it, and, Hyman said, "that really sticks in Nancy's craw."

When word of the appellate division's decision reached Myrna Felder on July 2, 1987, she had taken immediate steps to restrain "Carl A. Capasso, his agents, or anyone acting on his behalf" from removing any of the furnishings from the house before it could be turned over to Nancy. Eventually an injunction was obtained.

But the ever-vigilant *Post* had stationed a photographer in a tree across the street and, on October 13, readers saw a front-page picture of a grim-looking Bess Myerson lugging a pair of andirons out of the house. It looked to Nancy and Myrna as if the injunction were being ignored, but it took several more weeks of legal maneuvering before they could gain access to the house. When they did, they were astonished. "The place was stripped!" both women said later.

Eventually Capasso was found in contempt of court for permitting the property to be looted, though it was clear he himself was not the culprit, as he was in prison at the time. The missing property was never officially valued (although Nancy testified that it was worth $65,000), and Andy or Bess presumably still has it.

The house and remaining contents were sold in December 1987 for $2.6 million, which went into escrow.

On May 27, 1988, Bess was in the papers again, this time arrested for shoplifting. She had been caught taking $44.07 worth of lipsticks, sunglasses, and nail polish from a little discount store in Williamsport, Pennsylvania. She had visited the store right after seeing Andy in prison, and the front-page pictures and stories were very sad.

Lawyer Goldberg had been working diligently behind the scenes to ease the pain of the parted lovers. After Andy, a model prisoner, had served one year of his sentence, his lawyer filed a motion to have his original four-year sentence reduced to three, stressing the hardship his children were suffering at having an absent, idle, non-working father. At the same time, Goldberg quietly asked that the status of Andy's $500,000 fine be changed from "committed" to "uncommitted." A "committed" fine means that the wrongdoer does not get out of prison until it is paid. An "uncommitted" fine has no such restrictions.

Because of his good behavior in prison, Capasso was required to serve less than two years of his three-year sentence before being sent to a halfway house. By June 1989 he was a free man. The fine so far remains unpaid. Until it is, one may continue to marvel at Capasso's ability to stiff not only his wife and children but the government of the United States.

IN THE FOUR months between Bess Myerson's arrest for shoplifting and the commencement of the BessMess trial, she remained totally out of the newspapers except when she pleaded guilty to the shop-lifting charge, and paid her $100 fine and $48.50 in court costs.

Trial had been set for early October, pretrial hearings for September. For the duration, Andy was moved up from Allenwood to MCC (Metropolitan Correctional Center), the shiny new federal pen clamped onto the backside of the worn granite courthouse in Manhattan like a potato beetle on a spud.

On the eve of the trial, September 9, Nancy's lawyer Steve Hyman filed a civil RICO suit against Andy, Bess, Hortense Gabel, the City of New York, and former DCA assistant commissioner Richard Bruno, accusing them of being a "racketeering enterprise" and guilty of "gross negligence" in policing municipal corruption. (In a grotesque distortion of culpability and honor, poor Bruno had been pressured into resigning his post when *The Village Voice* published the Tyler Report. His sin: lying to the press, and to Mayor Koch, to make the hiring of Sukhreet Gabel appear more incidental and orthodox than it had been. That his boss the commissioner had ordered him to lie did not seem to count. Indeed, Bess had then ordered Sukhreet to go to Bruno's office and "thank him for getting you off the hook." And, feeling wretched, she had done so.)

One count of Nancy's suit sought damages of $3 million under the RICO claim, plus attorneys' fees. She asked for another $2 million in actual and punitive damages for violation of her civil rights. Had the three defendants been convicted, her suit might have had a fair chance of success. When they were acquitted, the suit was quietly dropped.

The story of the embattled Capassos, their lawyers, the construction companies, the bonding company, and the bank would of course keep going long after the trial verdict, whichever way it went. One could not possibly predict the story's end, nor its outcome. But on balance it seemed likely that Andy, once out of jail, would rise to the top again. Obviously he was a capable, adroit businessman with the ability to handle huge construction jobs, and such people and companies are rare. Nanco was a big company, and Aetna had taken a big risk, but Andy's prospects were as bright as they were because mighty Aetna had consistently said Nanco was a good, well-run company.

Wives and other creditors notoriously have had a hard time collecting anything from people in the construction business. It has always been very hard to trace income and profits. Such companies are famous for starting up other companies. They can always show they are losing money. They have huge payrolls and expenses. They can always claim that the city, or the state, has stepped up its demands. Finally, some construction companies, like Nanco, are run by very wily and imaginative men. It is almost certain that Andy Capasso was unfamiliar with the works of Nikolai Gogol. Yet his scheme to generate money by filing phony damage claims for nonexistent accident victims seemed to have sprung directly from *Dead Souls*, wherein the rogue Chichikov buys up title to serfs who have died, and then generates money by borrowing against "his" dead souls.

As for Nancy, Aetna had sought to hold her fully liable for the whole amount, even though she had nothing to do with, and was not around for, the later deals and companies. Similarly, once Andy had confessed judgment for $10.6 million, EAB claimed against Nancy for $10.6 million, taking the position that since she was a guarantor of Nanco's and Andy's debts, she was liable for those debts.

But when the discovery period in the Aetna suit ended, Nancy would claim that the evidence obtained substantiated her position that Aetna's actions with Andy constituted a breach of their good faith. In addition, she would claim that Aetna's and Andy's actions in forming other companies such as Capasso Contracting, and diverting monies and business opportunities from Nanco, had so altered the very nature of Nanco that she was no longer bound by the original agreement of indemnity. Hyman and Levinson were defending the EAB suit in a similar manner.

So, Nancy, too, would probably come out all right, if the lawyers didn't eat up every bit of the money.

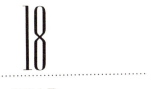

STAR

WITNESS

WHEN LAST WE SAW SUKHREET GABEL, IT WAS JUNE 1984, she had just escaped the insult and ignominy of her job at DCA, and was embarking on a new one at more than twice the salary. She was deputy executive director of the New York City Commission on Human Rights, the agency's number three position.

Alas, things did not go well at Human Rights. Dr. Marcella Maxwell said she saw at once that Sukhreet was not going to be able to handle the job. She "could not relate to others, could not focus on her responsibilities, did not understand what was going on at the agency, and lacked good judgment."

Sukhreet was also in the middle of a stormy romance, and both her private life and her office life were beginning a precipitate downhill plunge. Within weeks, Dr. Maxwell was on the phone to Judge Gabel. Sukhreet wasn't working out; she would have to be replaced.

Hortense pleaded with her old friend Marcella. If

Sukhreet was fired again, so soon after her humiliation at DCA, it would be too much. She might not be able to bear it, and the one thing her mother dreaded most in the world would happen: Her daughter would commit suicide.

Dr. Maxwell was a mother too. She said all right, she would let matters continue a while longer, and would not fire Sukhreet but instead permit her to resign.

Sukhreet remained at Human Rights for a couple of more increasingly unhappy months. Her personal life was crashing around her. After moving to New York, Sukhreet had had lovers but few serious relationships. John Levenson, a management consultant, had been different. Soon after they met they were living together and engaged to be married. A few weeks after Sukhreet was dropped by Dr. Maxwell, Levenson told her he could not bear to be around someone who was always so blue, forever moping about being a total failure. So saying, he moved to California, and Sukhreet fell apart.

The two metaphoric radios began playing again, crackling with static, booming the sound of her failures through the wall as she lay alone on her pink platform bed, sobbing and unable to get up.

By December Sukhreet was in a profound depression. Her condition continued to deteriorate, and in the late spring of 1985, electroconvulsive therapy was advised. Psychiatrists have used shock therapy since the 1930s to treat the more severe types of depression. The procedure involves attaching electrodes to the temples and sending enough current through the brain to cause a massive convulsion. At one time, the therapy was not dissimilar to Dr. Frankenstein's technique for bringing his creature to life, and nobody knew how it worked, just that it did. But the old techniques have been much refined. Muscle relaxants are first administered, and a very small amount of current is used, thus reducing the seizure as much as possible.

A series of treatments is given every other day, or three times a week, and the immediate effect is a lifting of the crippling depression. An inevitable side effect is that the shocks wipe out some memory of events for some months before and after the treatment. Then comes a period of patchy amnesia and partial memory that can last two or three years. Eventually, normal memory function usually returns.

Electroconvulsive therapy is almost always administered in a hospital, but a few doctors perform it as an office procedure. In the early summer of 1985, Sukhreet Gabel was given fifteen electric-shock treatments over a monthlong period as an outpatient in the office of a Manhattan psychiatrist.

Her mood began to brighten almost immediately, and within a few months she felt back to normal except for odd patches of amnesia that continued to surprise and trouble her. They affected her memory "selectively," she said, "rather like a Swiss cheese with holes in it. Big holes and little holes, up to a time period between six and eight months before the treatment began."

The smallest hole in the Swiss cheese had to do with events surrounding her hiring by Dr. Maxwell. When her fiancé took off, the holes got bigger. Sukhreet had no memory of the treatments themselves, and she had difficulty enumerating and dating them. She would tell the grand jury that she received nine shocks in fourteen days, and the petit jury at trial that she had "about fifteen" shocks. She gave conflicting dates.

One year after her therapy, the BessMess investigations began. The first one, directed at the allegations against Justice Gabel only, was conducted by the Commission on Judicial Conduct in July 1986. Toward the end of May, Justice Gabel was again hospitalized. She had suffered a slight stroke, as well as more eye problems, her lawyer Philip Schaeffer told the press, and the "ministroke" had left her with "a memory lapse and inability to recall certain events."

Howard Leventhal, her law secretary, blamed her illness on a combination of harassment by the press and worry over Sukhreet. Yet a few weeks later, on June 23, the beloved judge, who would be seventy-four in December, was pronounced well enough to be recertified by New York State for her third two-year term.

The following month, the CJC began its inquiry. Justice Gabel told the commissioners about her occasional memory lapses since her minor stroke, but assured them that on most things her memory was clear. She said she was certain that her first awareness that Myerson was involved with Capasso came from a September 14,

1983, *Post* photograph of Bess and Andy chatting on the steps of City Hall.

The CJC investigation provided Sukhreet with her first experience in giving testimony under oath, an activity she would repeat at least forty-four times before various investigative authorities prior to her nine-day public appearance as star prosecution witness at the Myerson/Gabel/Capasso trial.

Although a grand-jury witness testifies without counsel present, it is customary to have a lawyer stationed just outside the hearing room, and to consult frequently, lest the prosecutor stray into pastures where he has no right to graze.

Mr. Schaeffer or an associate accompanied Sukhreet on each of her grand-jury appearances. They gave her stock advice: Listen carefully. Answer truthfully but as briefly as possible. "Yes," "no," or "I don't recall" is usually sufficient. If you can't remember, say so. Don't guess. Come out and consult your lawyer every twenty minutes or so.

For the first nine months of sworn testimony before the CJC and the grand jury, which began taking testimony in February 1987, Sukhreet was represented *pro bono* by Philip Schaeffer. He also represented her mother at the CJC inquiry and before the Tyler Commission. Michael Feldberg, a Harvard Law School–trained specialist in criminal-defense work, represented Justice Gabel before the grand jury, and would be her attorney at trial.

Although a grand-jury witness is not permitted to have her lawyer with her, the government's lawyer is present. He is the prosecutor, the person asking the questions. That individual in this case was David Lawrence, thirty-two, a slender, bearded graduate of Brandeis University who was an Orthodox Jew. In high school in the 1960s Lawrence had been an antiwar activist. After law school, he had worked awhile for a prestigious commercial firm. Then his idealism resurfaced, and he decided he would rather accept less money for more work as an assistant U.S. attorney on the Giuliani team.

David Lawrence worked out at the same health club as Herman Tarnow, which is how he first heard of the events surrounding the hiring of Sukhreet Gabel by Bess Myerson. He persuaded his boss

Giuliani to let him investigate further, and subpoenaed the sealed Capasso divorce records, which included the never-used tape of Capasso asking if his wife was trying to "send him to jail for four hundred, five hundred years."

Sukhreet's patchy memory brought on by the shock therapy worried her. At times she remembered the answer to a question some hours or days after it had been asked, and wondered if she shouldn't go back and fill in the blanks, so to speak. Everybody's memory works the same way, of course. But Sukhreet's therapy had made her especially sensitive and anxious about her performance. The lawyers advised her that her present recollection under oath was all that was required.

Sukhreet was growing uneasy about Schaeffer. It seemed to her that his real client, or the one he really cared about, was her mother.

THE THIRD INVESTIGATION, by the Tyler Commission, was somewhat different from the other two. Tyler had been asked to prepare a confidential report for Mayor Koch only. His assignment was to find out for the mayor if his commissioner was guilty of trying to bribe a judge. Tyler concluded that she was, and his report said so. He was able to use much harsher language than David Lawrence and his team of prosecutors could use at trial, bound as they were by the rules of evidence.

Dr. Marcella Maxwell told Tyler that after Justice Gabel wrote letters recommending her as the new director of the Commission on Human Rights, her friend Hortense "simultaneously began suggesting that if she were appointed to the position, she would need someone she could trust and that she should hire Ms. Gabel." Tyler's report added, "A job for Ms. Gabel . . . was sewn up one weekend morning at Justice Gabel's apartment." Gabel asked Dr. Maxwell to telephone Bess Myerson and "clear the hiring" of Ms. Gabel, and "with the agreement of Ms. Myerson, Ms. Gabel shifted agencies."

Justice Gabel had told Tyler it was her "firm testimony" that she had never suggested Dr. Maxwell hire her daughter. Sukhreet took a position midway between her mother and her ex-boss. As Tyler put it to Koch, Sukhreet "was more candid" than her mother, and told him she got the job "to some extent [due to] my mother's good offices."

At a press conference at Halloran House after Sukhreet's testimony to Tyler, Schaeffer told reporters in essence, "She's unreliable. Don't believe a word she says."

When Sukhreet Gabel read the contents of the Tyler Report in *The Village Voice* on Wednesday evening, June 10, 1987, she fully understood for the first time the scenario being developed by the government against her mother and Bess, and her own role in it. She began to steam. Particularly galling was the report's assertion that she "had a long history of emotional disturbances and had, in her father's words, 'limited talents.' "

The report also said Bess Myerson "had an intense, almost surrogate mother, relationship with Sukhreet," and quoted Hortense Gabel as telling Tyler her daughter had "a crush" on Myerson.

On Thursday, in *The New York Times*, Sukhreet accused her mother of "hubris." But this was just the beginning. Friday every metropolitan newspaper was abloom with news stories and poisonous editorial comment on Myerson, Koch, and the whole mess. Sukhreet brooded and stewed over the long weekend. Monday, June 15, at just about the time that Andy Capasso was being numbered in to Allenwood Federal Penitentiary, Sukhreet Gabel was talking privately, under oath, to David Lawrence in the U.S. attorney's office in downtown Manhattan.

That morning Sukhreet had phoned Lawrence and said she had not told him the full truth on May 4, her third appearance before the grand jury. He then suggested she come to his office and make a deposition ancillary to her prior testimony. She arrived alone. When the government offered to provide counsel since no lawyer was with her, she refused. She preferred to handle this herself, and she would waive the immunity to prosecution that she had previously been granted as a cooperating government witness.

She gave another ancillary deposition June 29, after telling the government that she and Schaeffer had mutually agreed to split. She didn't want and didn't need a new lawyer. What she wanted and most desperately needed was "to get to the bottom of all this." Had they all really betrayed her? Her mother by fixing up a phony job? Her father by having been in on the "fix," and then by having had the disloyalty to tell the Tyler Commission his daughter had "limited talents" and "emotional problems"? And what of Bess, the glamorous woman who had befriended her, and praised her, and wined and dined and hired her? Was that, too, a fraud?

Sukhreet's emotions were mixed, and complex, but she was sure of one thing: She intended to find out the truth, no matter how terrible the price, and total truth on all sides would be her means of finding out. She would offer her cooperation to both prosecution and defense, and tell absolutely everybody the truth about everything, let the chips fall where they may.

Courts and lawyers do not do well with such people. To the legal mind, someone like Sukhreet seems less a pilgrim for truth than a loose cannon. Here was Sukhreet talking about Bess in one of her early forty-four confessions: "I saw our friendship on two levels: one as a woman-to-woman friendship where age and status attainment meant nothing. We were friends because we had a lot in common. On the other hand, I saw it as a mentor/protégé relationship . . .

"I would say that I still, in some ways, consider Bess Myerson a mentor. I have learned an awful lot from her . . . I identified with her . . . her beauty and celebrity, more closely with her intelligence. She is not very well educated, but she's very bright. I enjoyed her shrewdness and her street smarts, which is something I don't have . . .

"She took the trouble to make an effort to understand what was going on in my personal life and to help me and advise me . . . As my boss/mentor she would say, for example, 'Don't overspeak. Don't state your case too heavily. Just say "yes" or "no" and shut up.' "

By the time the case came to trial, this advice seemed to have fallen through one of Sukhreet's memory holes. She would prove to be arguably the most loquacious government witness since Joe Valachi. But trial was still more than a year away. Meanwhile, what was she to make of Bess once the Tyler Report was out? Had all the fairy godmotherly attentions been just a setup, a cynical ploy to influence her poor mother to make favorable rulings in the Capasso divorce?

Yes, her "poor mother." Sukhreet didn't always think favorably or compassionately about her mother. But she knew her mother's weak points better than anyone. She knew how tired and frail she sometimes seemed of late, and she loathed the idea of Bess Myerson kicking Hortense around, manipulating her for Bess's own purposes.

The government was meticulous about advising Sukhreet of her rights. Her first private conversation with Mr. Lawrence began:

Q. Do you understand that in coming forward today, and in prior meetings, that you are doing so without the benefit of immunity?

A. Yes, I do understand that.

Q. And that anything you say can be used against you in a subsequent legal proceeding?

A. I understand that.

Q. That your statements that you give could be used in possible perjury or obstruction-of-justice or false-declaration prosecutions—

A. I understand that.

Q. —against you; do you understand that?

A. Yes.

Q. You have the right at this proceeding, Ms. Gabel, not to answer any questions that we may put to you, and to invoke your Fifth Amendment privilege. Do you understand that?

A. Yes, I do.

She seemed to understand everything except one thing: that what she was doing could well send her mother to prison.

What Sukhreet had originally neglected to tell the grand jury was that she had tried to protect her mother. After describing how she had learned from Andy's housekeeper that her mother was the judge in the Capasso divorce, she had deliberately omitted mention of the first part of her phone conversation with her father. She did not say that her father had spoken of her mother in the conversation, saying, "Your mother knows what's going on. Let her handle it. You stick to your business of just finding a job."

Sukhreet told the prosecutors about four or five other occasions, in her testimony to the CJC, the grand jury, and the Tyler Commission, in which—after having said she could not remember—two or three days later she *did remember* the correct answer, and at once called her lawyers and asked: "Is there some way we can put this in the record?"

They would tell her: Don't bother; it's not relevant. It's not significant. It will only prolong things. You are only required to give your best recollection at the time.

At one point she had been summoned to the office of Milton Gould, senior partner of her mother's trial lawyer, Michael Feldberg. Feldberg and Philip Schaeffer were both present. "In your own words, just tell me your story," Gould said. She told it, deliberately leaving out the part about her father saying her mother knew all about it, to test whether Schaeffer would interrupt to correct her. He did not. Instead, he told her afterward, "You did the right thing." To have included the part she had omitted, he said, "would only prolong the whole thing a year or a year and a half."

Feeling betrayed and abandoned by her mother, her father, her wonderful new "friend" and employer Bess, then by her boyfriend, and now by her lawyer, Sukhreet Gabel was a soul up for grabs. She turned for help to the government of the United States, as personified by David Lawrence and his aides.

Recognizing her value as a prosecution witness, the U.S. attorneys and their investigators were kind to her. They listened to her. And listened. Sukhreet told Lawrence that Phil Schaeffer had described Capasso to her as "one of those legitimate businessmen who is a front man for the Mafia." She told Lawrence that Bess Myerson had told her Capasso had personally paid off her $1 million debt from her Senate campaign. When she ran this information by Phil, saying, "This could bring down the mayor!" Phil had "looked nervous," she said. It had been somewhere around this time that Phil told the reporters not to believe what Sukhreet said, and made her look like "a crazy person, or a liar."

Sukhreet gave the prosecutors complete financial information on her parents: how much they had in their checking account, how much in savings, how much in municipal bonds; what they paid for rent; what Judge Gabel's pension was.

At one point, Sukhreet's attorneys made a motion to Judge Morris Lasker to quash any further appearances by Sukhreet before the grand jury. Sukhreet's resentment increased when she was told by the prosecutors that Jane Connolly, Schaeffer's assistant, had wept while presenting this motion, and had described her client as an unfortunate, emotionally disturbed woman who was being subjected to prosecutorial abuse. Reading *The Village Voice* had made Sukhreet's burgeoning anger explode into full-blown fury.

Rarely has a government witness had so much, and such various, pretrial preparation as Sukhreet Gabel. By the time she called David Lawrence and volunteered her assistance, she had testified twice to the CJC, three times before the grand jury, and once to the Tyler Commission. Thereafter she would be summoned three more times to the prosecutor's office for lengthy ancillary depositions to her grand-jury testimony. Additionally, she would be interrogated by the government five more times under oath, in a room especially set aside for her depositions in a different government building from the regular U.S. attorney's offices, and would there give the government attorneys 231 more pages of testimony.

In August she would bring to the prosecutors five shopping bags of her mother's papers taken from her personal files. No, she would say later, she did not take them without her mother's permission. She had been helping her mother, who could no longer read, to sort through the papers. They had been stored in the bathroom since her mother had brought them home from her judicial chambers after retiring from the bench. Late in the evening Sukhreet had said she was tired, and would take the papers home to her own apartment around the corner and continue the sorting job in the morning.

"Oh yes," she had added, "I may want to show some of these papers to the lawyers." She did not specify which lawyers.

"That's fine, dear," said her mother.

In October, Sukhreet told the prosecutors all about lawyer Schaeffer's personal relationship to her parents. He had been her mother's campaign manager. His wife and the judge had been especially close friends. After his wife's death, Horty had made a clumsy attempt at matchmaking between her daughter and the newly widowed lawyer.

She described Schaeffer as belligerent toward the prosecution, and said he badgered her in the corridor outside the grand-jury hearing room. He had berated David Lawrence as being "slime," the "worst of the worst. . . . David is a shark . . . you can't trust him . . . these are bad people." He told Sukhreet that one of his clients was a psychiatrist who had several assistant U.S. attorneys as patients. They all complained to the doctor that they could not sleep at night because they felt so dirty about what they did at work.

Sukhreet frequently telephoned the prosecutors. Whoever answered the call made handwritten notes. These notes were turned over to the defense as "discovery material" on the eve of trial. One notation said that one week before Christmas, 1987, she had called the government to apologize for her tantrum in a previous call. She was worried about leaks, and said, "One is Mom . . . who is gunning for me!"

She reported in another call that the previous night her mother's lawyer Feldberg had said he wanted to get together for dinner, and then didn't want to see her again until trial. She said she had told Feldberg she believed her mother was guilty, but thought that her mother's "lack of mental capacity contributed to this greatly."

The handwritten notes continued thus:

Defense Possibility:
    Problems on the bench—
        protected by fellow State Judges
        Did not appear before litigants—to protect herself
        Hidden story is in Medical Records
        call Expert Witnesses

Reading through these forty-four repeated, uncounseled phone conversations and depositions in government offices, in agents' handwriting and in notarized transcripts, one can literally watch Sukhreet Gabel, the accomplished linguist, learning a new language. One can see her gradually becoming fluent in not five but six languages, the sixth being the language of the brainwashed, the imprisoned, the enslaved, and all adepts at giving their interrogators the answers they want to hear.

In her 115-page deposition on St. Patrick's Day, 1988, she

seemed to relish Lawrence's questions as if, after six years of rejection, failure, and depression, she was grateful that somebody was speaking to her as a human being in her own right. At last she was being regarded as herself, an individual, not just as the judge's daughter.

Q. Would you talk a little bit about how you were treated at the Department of Cultural Affairs?

A. Perhaps the best way to characterize it is that I was the unwanted child. The child that arrived when no one was expecting it . . . and nobody quite knew what to do with it, and nobody quite wanted it, and nobody quite loved it, and everyone wished it would simply go away.

    And yet, here was that crying infant, as they saw, cared for and diapered and babysat for and generally kept out of mischief. It was a general mess.

Then, toward the close of the marathon grilling:

Q. Has the government at any time suggested any answer to you?

A. No.

Q. . . . In fact, the government has told you that . . . we are just fact-finders. Is that correct?

A. I have been assured of that and I have no reason to believe that is not the case.

Q. And that all we want to hear is that which you can remember accurately?

A. . . . I would characterize the government's behavior, if I may, as being sportsmanlike, solicitous . . .

Q. When you say that, why don't you explain what you mean?

A. In that realizing the delicacy of my position, and that my mother has been indicted in this matter, and the fact that in addition, many of these areas are of great emotional weight for myself, the government has been very solicitous of the trauma that I am going through, and the efforts that I'm making to give a value-free presentation. Not only truthful, but value-free.

Without question, she was trying. But "value-free" did not exist. It was a phantom, a construct used by the government to mold her into their instrument to destroy Mom, and Bess. . . .

Reading further through the huge stack of materials, one can sense the government beginning to stagger under the riches of her endless bounty. "The Boys," as she had nicknamed the prosecutors, had lately been canceling meetings with her, rendering her very angry indeed. She had become like the Grand Duchess of Blab, and she would not be dammed up. If she did not continue to flow, she would cease to exist.

This poor, hunted, hounded creature, driven to distraction, had at last found sanctuary in the truth. That was why she was available to both sides—all sides. Why she was able to lecture her interrogators on the true meaning of the term *witness*. She had become holy, a not-so-mad saint, and in the process, become funny, become a teacher, become human. Her story read like a blend of *Darkness at Noon*, *Saint Joan*, *Candide*, and *Saturday Night Live*.

In her June 17, 1987, grand-jury testimony, page 48, one could see it beginning. The prosecutor was again asking if she felt she was being treated fairly by the government.

> A. Once you determined that I was basically trying with you to get to the truth, feeling that I was a member of the team whose job it was to establish what the facts were . . . you in effect relaxed with me . . . after that I experienced no stress at all. . . .
> Q. So after the first appearance before the Grand Jury you became far more comfortable. . . .

Yes. Until now she'd had no team. She had been totally abandoned.

We have become accustomed in this century to accounts of forced, false confessions and how they are made to come about. "Brainwashing" is the common term for the procedure, which is also sometimes known as "thought reform" or "coercive persuasion." They all mean the same thing.

The classic description of the process is the one given in 1948 by Jozsef Cardinal Mindszenty, the Hungarian prelate who, five weeks after his capture by the Communists, confessed to being a criminal and an American spy.

> My physical strength perceptibly declined. I began worrying about my health and my life . . . My heart flagged; a sense of being utterly abandoned and defenseless weighed upon me.

My powers of resistance gradually faded. Apathy and indifference grew. More and more the boundaries between true and false, reality and unreality, seemed blurred . . . I became insecure in my judgment. Day and night my alleged 'sins' had been hammered into me, and now I myself began to think that somehow I might very well be guilty. Again and again that same theme was repeated in innumerable variations . . . I was left with only one certainty, that there was no longer any way out . . . My shaken nervous system weakened the resistance of my mind, clouded my memory, undermined my self-confidence, unhinged my will—in short undid all the capacities that are most human in man . . .

After the second week of detention . . . I could feel my resistance ebbing. I was no longer able to argue cogently; I no longer rejected coarse lies and distortions. Now and then I resignedly said things like, 'There's no need to say anything more about it; maybe it happened the way others maintain.' . . . Without knowing what had happened to me, I had become a different person.*

Sukhreet Gabel was Mindszenty spelled backward. The star government witness in the Myerson trial was manipulated by public prosecutors and private demons, not to falsely confess but to elaborately, extensively accuse. And whereas the cardinal's strength ebbed, that of the star witness appeared daily to have increased. Where his apathy grew, hers faded. His memory gradually clouded, and hers slowly grew clear. Whereas his sense of reality blurred, hers appeared to be coming into focus, perhaps for the first time in years.

Gabel was questioned by government prosecutors perhaps forty-five or fifty times before taking the witness stand. It is characteristic of the brainwashed subject that each time he is interrogated, he remembers a bit more. In Sukhreet's case, this tendency was complicated by two other factors. One was her electric-shock treatments and the patchy, partial residual amnesia that was still lifting, and shifting. The other was an unusually vigorous capacity for fantasy. This accounted both for her creativity and, at times, for a seeming difficulty in distinguishing fantasy from reality. She imagined things so vividly, in color and 3-D, that they seemed real to her. Her "experience" as a trained nurse, an operating-room nurse,

·····································

* Jozsef Mindszenty, *Memoirs* (New York: Macmillan, 1974), pp. 110–14.

a psychiatric nurse, is one example. In reality, she had attended nursing school for one year, then dropped out.

Sukhreet Gabel's need for self-affirmation found more than one outlet. She began to appear on every TV show, in every gossip column, on every local news broadcast and panel show. She was available to every reporter, and every goon. Her number was in the telephone book. When she was at home, she answered every call: reporters, lunatics, lost souls, heavy breathers, she didn't care. When she was out, her answering machine flirted that if you left "an interesting message," she would return your call, and she did. She regarded her conversations with the vox populi as training for her coming performance as the star witness in the big trial. She appeared on countless TV shows, often in outré costumes and outrageous hairdos and makeup. She became the Apple's latest media freak. By the time the trial began, her moony face and breathy voice were as well known to New Yorkers as Myerson was.

But always there was something droll about her, or amusing. She was knowingly ridiculous, mocking her own preposterous situation.

Newsman on courthouse steps, after a pretrial hearing: "What did Bess Myerson say to you in court?"

"She told me that I looked very pretty—which I consider a great compliment, coming from Miss America." This is being said by a pop-eyed, overweight woman wearing Mother Superior–style white robes and a red fright wig.

"Does she actually know what a fool people take her for?" people asked. Her humiliations daily deepened. On the Morton Downey show, the host said, "As a woman, you are the dreck of the universe." The audience roared approval. She smiled.

Men in particular hated her. Men who loved their mothers, men who had been mama's boys, and men who had grown up to be good sons despised her. Mocking her mother, she was in some way mocking *them*. They could not see her as madcap, as surreal, as a jest—her own—not a fool.

As a pop celebrity, Sukhreet's timing was unfortunate. Her fifteen minutes of fame seemed to have occurred in the wrong time and place. Had she flourished in Paris in the 1920s, she would have been seen as a flower of Dada, surrealism's darling. Her wit, eccentricity, and ample *joie de vivre* would surely have made her the toast of Gay Paree. In the 1930s in London, or Philadelphia, she might have been a Noël Coward or Philip Barry heroine, a madcap-heiress type down on her luck. But in the sour Apple 1980s, in humorless, stale, decaying, exhausted, rachitic, nervous, heartless New York, she was an affront. She had violated the last taboo. You could watch people fornicating on television; you could become junk-bond king of the world; you had the permission of the Supreme Court to execute the mentally retarded. But you still couldn't testify against your own mother. Even in Gomorrah-on-the-Hudson, that was still a sacrilege.

19

ON TRIAL

On OCTOBER 4, 1988, THE BESSMESS FINALLY WENT
to trial. Outside the courthouse, a media circus
played nonstop, a Roman carnival of cameras and
microphones and shoving spectators, through
which each day Bess and the Gabels made their way
with confident smiles pasted firmly in place. Inside
the big old high-ceilinged courtroom, the atmosphere was somber, the pace stately. The high point
was Sukhreet Gabel's nine days on the witness
stand. The other government witnesses were clerks
and servants and a few city officials, including Ed
Koch. The mayor's day of testimony contributed
absolutely nothing in the way of evidence against
Bess. This plus the fact that Koch looked so excruciatingly uncomfortable on the witness stand,
frowning, fidgeting, and occasionally writhing, led
the writer Murray Kempton to observe that the
mayor had been called not as a witness but as an
exhibit.

The case took eleven long weeks to try, eleven

weeks of lawyers talking. None of the defendants took the stand. None offered any defense save a few character witnesses for Justice Gabel—former Mayor Wagner, Robert A. Caro, and Robert Weaver, former secretary of housing and urban development—and a brief explanation from Bess's attorney that she certainly didn't need Andy's money; she was a millionaire many times over in her own right. Other than that, they relied on the fact that a defendant is considered innocent until proven guilty, and that the jury would conclude that the government had failed to prove its case.

So it was a defense that, save for opening and closing arguments, consisted entirely of cross-examination, the best sort of lawyering to watch. Particularly adroit were defense lawyer Goldberg's interrogations of the first two government witnesses, a professor of marital law, and Gabel's assistant Howard Leventhal. Both men were there to make clear to the jury the intricate evolution of Justice Gabel's three different orders on maintenance and support. Goldberg's questions managed to make the whole business at once infernally complex yet seemingly reasonable. He alternated simple statements—alimony is deductible for the husband and taxable to the wife—with cascades of razzle-dazzle numbers scrawled on blackboards and charts, so that sooner or later most listeners got lost, or turned off.

Strangely, the government failed to put on any substantial redirect of either witness. Thus artful confusion spewed by the defense was left to hang like a brown cloud over the central part of the government's case, the allegation that Justice Gabel had manipulated the alimony.

The crucial decisions in most trials take place out of the presence of the jury. In this instance, a critical one took place just before the trial began. Twice before, the government had sought secretly to drop Hortense Gabel from the case on the ground that her ailments rendered her incapable of fully assisting in her own defense. Implied was some question as to her mental competency. The truth was that the little blind judge was proving such a sympathetic figure in the press that the prosecutors thought they would improve their chances by getting rid of her. They also may have had second thoughts about the palatability of seeing a daughter testifying against her mother. Sukhreet might be a much more effective witness against Bess, and perhaps Andy, if she were not seen to be savaging her pathetic mom. On the other hand, a medical severance for Justice Gabel might create an awkward precedent regarding Giuliani's next big celebrity prosecution, his tax case against the Helmsleys. Harry Helmsley was at least as decrepit as Hortense Gabel.

But Justice Gabel solved the prosecutors' problem. She refused to accept a medical severance each time it was offered. "I find myself deeply offended," she said. She didn't want charity or mercy; she wanted her good name cleared.

During jury selection, the prosecutors detected further underground wellsprings of compassion for the judge. As a result, they made a last-ditch effort to drop her at a confidential hearing held in the judge's chambers on the eve of trial, after jury selection was complete. Present were Hortense and Milton Gabel and the lawyers for both sides.

The defense did not want to lose Horty. She was the best thing they had going. It would not be easy to persuade a jury to convict an old blind lady for loving her daughter not wisely but too well. And if the jurors decided the judge was not a part of the conspiracy, it would be much more difficult for them to find Bess and Andy guilty of conspiring to bribe her, although still within the realm of legal possibility. If both Horty and Bess were acquitted, Andy was sure to walk.

There were other problems for the defense. With Feldberg gone, who would tell the jury all the reasons why Gabel wasn't guilty, which would then make the guilt of the other two so much harder to prove? Said Goldberg, "This has never ever happened to me before. It's a very, very low blow. Our trial preparation is now all wrong; we have to restrategize. They will still try the case as though Gabel was corrupt, but now there will be no one there to do Feldberg's job. It's very, very crafty. A shocking move."

Hortense Gabel saved the day by rising to her feet and declaring for the third time, in a suddenly very firm voice, that she wished to go ahead. A medical severance was neither acceptable to her nor necessary. Nor was merely dropping the charges. She wanted nothing less than total acquittal. Some observers thought her stubbornness showed heartlessness. A truly loving mother who understood what was in store for her daughter would have done anything to spare her the coming ordeal. Such a mother would not have put her own pride and need for exculpation ahead of all other considerations. Sukhreet Gabel had no idea of the savagery in store for her when cross-examination by the three defense lawyers began. Horty presumably did.

But Sukhreet knew her mother better than any of these lawyers. "My mother is a creature of the system," she said later, "so she needs to be vindicated by the system."

As for Sukhreet, she still believed the trial would "get to the bottom" and reveal the "truth." She never understood what her mother and the lawyers had always known: Trials are not about truth; trials are about winning. And using a daughter as chief witness against her mother guaranteed a cruel spectacle, no matter which side won.

The BessMess defendants were lucky in the judge they drew. Judge John F. Keenan, a better-looking, more genial José Ferrer in steel-rimmed glasses, was without pretense, and made one feel on sight that one could get a fair shake in his courtroom. Judge Keenan and Goldberg had been prosecutors together under Frank Hogan thirty-four years before, and they had maintained an amiable relationship. Hence Keenan had offered to recuse himself should the government wish it, but was told that would be unnecessary. The original BessMess judge had been Kevin Thomas Duffy. When Giuliani objected that the Duffys were personal friends of the Gabels, Duffy had firmly denied the allegation and recused himself anyway. Keenan's name came up next, by which time the government was anxious to get on with the case.

Jay Goldberg, who had been Andy's lawyer before he and Bess got in trouble, was chief defense counsel. To represent Bess, Goldberg had selected Fred Hafetz, forty-two, a quiet, bookish man with substantial experience in criminal trials, both as a state and federal prosecutor and as a defense lawyer.* But Bess was not pleased. She wanted Goldberg; let Andy take Hafetz. The senior lawyer was at length able to persuade her that her own flamboyance

·····························

* After his defense of Myerson, Hafetz was chosen by his brethren to be vice president of the newly formed New York Council of Defense Lawyers.

would be enhanced and set off better by a more sedate personage than himself. Hortense Gabel's lawyer, Michael S. Feldberg, thirty-seven, former assistant U.S. attorney under Giuliani and now a partner in Shea & Gould, had a serious but boyish quality that contrasted nicely with his seventy-five-year-old client.

The overall defense strategy was to say that the greedy machinations of a vindictive ex-wife were the only reason that these three honorable people were on trial. Goldberg intended to retry the Capasso divorce. His strategy was to put on a minimal defense, just enough to get what is known as a "Scotch verdict," one in which the jury does not say *not guilty*, it says *not proven*.

The government strategy was to strengthen a difficult circumstantial-evidence case by using Sukhreet Gabel to show not the crime but the motive. This was a daughter a loving mother might indeed be desperate to help.

After the first day, devoted to opening statements, the trial quickly settled into a routine. Most mornings little Hortense Gabel arrived first, bundled in floppy, 1960-ish clothing, and led down the aisle by her lawyer, like Lucky being driven by Pozzo in *Waiting for Godot*. Following was a lean, erect old man with a full head of gray hair. Dr. Milton Gabel, eighty-one, sat just behind his wife on a folding chair.

Andy Capasso usually appeared next, escorted by federal marshals. He wore an expensive blue suit and short prison haircut, and looked like a man whose former beer belly had now diminished to short-beer size. His face was open and at ease.

Myerson usually entered last, coming down the middle aisle, a tall and still strikingly beautiful woman. She had dieted down to near-skeletal thinness, and her unflattering sports clothes hung limply on her hipless flanks. En route to her seat she always paused to greet the Gabels. Milton stood up and she cradled his head in her hands and kissed him all over his face. Then she bent and hugged Hortense, stroking her hands and cheeks. Bess and Andy murmured greetings, and sat chatting quietly, like old friends, until it was time for their lawyers to go to work.

The seating arrangement in multidefendant trials is carefully plotted for maximum psychological influence on the jurors. Capasso sat farthest away from the jury box, and was practically invisible behind three lawyers, three or four assistants, and the other two defendants seated at the long defense table. Myerson sat dead center. On the other end was the frail little judge, practically in the jurors' laps and directly in front of the witness box so that eye-to-eye confrontation with her daughter was assured.

When the marshals opened the courtroom on the fifth morning of trial, a pink rose in a water glass was on Justice Gabel's desk. A fresh new rose would be there each day for the next eight days.

The press, in their tightly packed benches, were already snickering. "D'ja hear Sukhreet is working for her Ph.D. at Creedmore?" Creedmore is a state psychiatric hospital.

The jury of six men and six women filed in, and David Lawrence was on his feet. "The government calls Sukhreet Gabel." A composed, smiling, plump woman with milky skin and long, silken hennaed hair entered the witness box. She folded her perfectly manicured hands like a soprano about to give a recital. Her appearance suggested a beautifully groomed Pekingese. Walt Disney once made a feature-length movie in which all the characters were dogs— a dog heroine, dog villain, dog comics, dog cops, and dog robbers. Sukhreet Gabel was a Disney dog heroine: liquid-eyed, silken-voiced, impeccably ladylike, beautifully combed, and perfectly groomed.

Sukhreet Gabel said that after receiving immunity, signed by Rudolph Giuliani himself, she had testified on numerous occasions to several investigative groups. On June 15, 1987, she said, she had called David Lawrence and told him she had more information that she had just remembered, "which might be useful for getting at the truth."

In pursuit of that truth, Gabel went on, she subsequently met with representatives of the government dozens more times. Each session began with a formal reminder of her rights, and each time she waived them. The FBI had asked her permission to attach a tape recorder to her phone "for conversations with Mr. Schaeffer."

"Tape anyone else?" asked David Lawrence.

"My mother. Twice." The courtroom gasped. Once while she was looking for Mr. Schaeffer, once "inadvertently."

Peering down quizzically from his bench, Judge Keenan inquired, "You mean you recorded your mother by mistake?" Yes. She had not known the record button was on.

Asked about her health, she said it was "excellent." Jurors were attentive; they seemed compassionate and understanding as she described her medical history, her marital and educational background, her return from Chicago to New York, and her mother's letter-writing campaign.

By March 1983, Sukhreet had been actively job-hunting for twelve months, she said, and told her mother that "I was despondent, despairing, and depressed. She felt a lot of sorrow and pity for me. I was broke. My small nest egg was gone." She began to receive small gifts of money from her parents.

She described her drive to Chicago: "I drove that car in hopes I would meet with an unfortunate accident." The jurors looked uncomfortable.

She described meeting Myerson at her parents' dinner party. At the defense table, Myerson's face was expressionless, a hooded mask. The prosecutor led his witness through her story of weekends in the Hamptons.

As soon as Sukhreet got home after the second weekend, she said, she called her parents. Milton answered. "Hi, Dad. I was out for the weekend at Bess Myerson's place, with Andy Capasso."

Judge Keenan again interrupted. Was this not the very next day, after you had just seen your father? Wouldn't he *know* where you'd spent the weekend?

"I refreshed his recollection," said Sukhreet in purest lawyer-speak.

David Lawrence elicited a timetable of that summer's crucial events from the time Bess met Sukhreet to the time Justice Gabel reduced the *pendente lite* award.

Michael Feldberg argued vigorously. "A message slip, a dinner party, a visit to Mattituck, a Chinese dinner—none of this indicates *any* presence of a conspiracy!"

If the government's star witness had no more damning testimony than this, what was everybody doing here? Judge Keenan had said once, and would say again before it ended, that he didn't want his courtroom turned into the setting for a soap opera. But it seemed at this point that Bess Myerson might only have been conspiring with herself, and that Rudolph Giuliani could really have overreached himself. These people were not engaged in criminal acts. They were engaged in human acts, family acts, normal homo sapiens behavior.

Heretofore, after court, Judge Gabel and her husband had been happy to banter with reporters as they slowly made their way down the courthouse steps and into the subway home. Today was different. Their wrinkled old faces were closed and locked; they did not seem to hear the questions; they did not speak. It appeared they might be understanding for the first time how badly chewed up their daughter would be in the days ahead.

The third fresh rose was at Judge Gabel's place, and the morning headlines blared, HOW SUKHY TURNED IN HER MOM and TRIAL AIRS DIRTY LAUNDRY. Sukhreet told the jury that one day at DCA she found a message on her desk; a Richard Johnson had called her from the *New York Post*. When she told her boss about it, Myerson's mistrust of the press was such that she instructed Sukhreet "not to return the call by myself," but to go to lunch, and then call back after arranging for Myerson to be listening in on one extension and her deputy Bruno on the other.

Sukhreet thought this was idiotic. The reporter surely would know that others were listening in and attempting to dictate her responses. So "I came back five minutes early, and called him from my desk."

But first Sukhreet had called her mother, seeking counsel on what to say to the *Post* reporter. Judge Gabel said she too had had a call from him, and advised her daughter, "Tell the truth. Answer his questions. Be polite."

However, Sukhreet did not take her mother's advice. She lied to the reporter and denied she saw Myerson socially after hours. Why? Because "I was aware of Bess's negative, hostile attitude to the press. I was also aware of my new status in the office. I just did not want to discuss what I considered my private affairs in such a public forum."

Since Sukhreet's recent medical history included events that affected her memory, it was important that the jury learn the facts from the government before cross-examination began. Lawrence gently led her through her story. Severe mental depression is treated in two ways, with drugs or electricity, and she had experienced both. She received the second type of treatment in the spring of 1985, and as a result, "my short-term memory is impaired. . . . I never laid down the raw material of memory—my brain was so traumatized." Jurors looked grave. Right after the treatment, she suffered "fifty percent amnesia. It wasn't that I couldn't remember things; it was that I never learned. Because of the stimulation my brain received, no memory traces were laid down. Before treatment, my memory was masked by the overwhelming sadness I felt."

Lawrence abruptly switched subjects. Sukhreet needed to find a new apartment. Perhaps Sol Goldman, her mother's kindly, long-time landlord could help. "I'd rather not approach him. I don't know him all that well," Hortense had told her daughter. "But I'll call a friend of mine who is a judge who knows a lawyer who is a good friend of Sol Goldman." This was a nice incidental confirmation of Sukhreet's recognition that "my mother is above all things a creature of the system."

"The system" had a relatively small number of players, all of whom more or less knew one another. The lawyer herein referred to was Raoul Felder, Nancy Capasso's original divorce counsel.

Of the three defendants, Hortense Gabel had the greatest number of personal courtroom supporters. In addition to Dr. Gabel, one or more close women friends were daily among the spectators. They escorted the judge back and forth to the ladies' room, and provided companionship during recesses and lunch breaks. Edward Wittstein, a cousin and stage designer, usually occupied an aisle seat, making notes for a play he intended to write.

On school holidays, Capasso's devoted sixteen-year-old son, Michael, came down to sit behind his father and chat with him at recess.

Nancy Capasso was careful to maintain a low profile throughout the trial. Despite her urgent interest in the goings-on, her good sense told her to stay well away from the courtroom, and content herself with the abundant media coverage. Nancy knew many in the press corps. They liked her, and she could always telephone a reporter for fill-in details.

For more than half of the trial, Myerson came to and left the courthouse entirely alone. Like the Gabels, she traveled by subway. She distrusted taxi drivers, she said, because they would talk indiscreetly to reporters, whereas she drew strength from the crush of workaday subway riders, "my people." Neither her sisters nor her daughter turned up. Bess said she had asked them to stay away, to "spare them." During the final third of the trial, Sandy Stern, Bess's eerie, larger-than-life look-alike-contest winner and current big sister/best friend, was in daily attendance. (After the verdict, Bess would go off alone with her friend Sandy and her publisher, Esther Margolis, to celebrate at home with vodka and day-old chicken retrieved from the refrigerator.)

MYERSON'S LAWYER, FRED HAFETZ, was first to cross-examine. He strode to the lectern with a fat, liver-colored folder of documents. His first job was to convince the jury that Sukhreet Gabel had been a competent assistant well worth hiring. Thus the jury learned that Sukhreet, the ex-wife of a Dutch diplomat, was fluent in Dutch, French, Spanish, and Italian, and could make herself understood in Arabic, Japanese, and Russian. Hortense Gabel was leaning forward, listening hard, newly alert.

The lawyer read letters of recommendation from her NYU professors to the new ones in Chicago, describing the witness as "a truly brilliant woman . . . exceptionally lucid . . . among the top five percent of my students . . . highly original mind . . . extrovert with quick wit . . . exceptionally imaginative, mature and resourceful . . . one of the most unusual students I've ever encountered." Her faculty adviser found her "competent, articulate, well-organized, and I highly recommend her for employment."

"Do you know how many times you've testified under oath?"

"Five or ten."

"It wouldn't be fifteen, would it?" A rough, new note had appeared in the lawyer's voice.

You say, said Hafetz, that once you came back to New York, you and your mother developed "a plan," and your mother contacted one hundred and fifty to two hundred people. You say you saw over half of them, seventy-five to one hundred. "But that hasn't

always been your testimony, has it? You told Mr. Tembeckjian*
under oath . . . twenty-five to thirty people. Miss Gabel, which is
it? Or is it a third category?"

"Closer to the first."

"So your memory has gotten better as time progresses, right?"
Correct.

Now a hard punch: "You received fifteen electroshock treatments
to your head . . . after you left DCA," over a period of one month?

Yes, in 1986.

Didn't you testify this morning that it was 1985?

"I thought it was 1987 . . . I get all confused when it comes to
those years."

"Are you telling this jury you don't remember *the year* that you
got these fifteen electroshocks to your brain? . . . Does your memory get better as you sit with the prosecutors, is that it? . . . Didn't
you say the electric-shock treatments make your memory rather
like a Swiss cheese, with holes in it?"

Judge Keenan was nodding unhappily. He did not appear to like
the new turn of events. Heretofore Hafetz had seemed a rather
quiet, studious man with a nice precision of language, warning the
jury at one point "not to confuse the belaboring of the obvious and
indisputable with evidence of the credible."

On the attack, he had become a pit bull. "So you had made three
appearances under oath concerning the Capasso matrimonial case
and your employment at DCA by the time you testified at Thirty
Rockefeller Center† in March '87, am I right?"

"That is correct."

"And after having been questioned three times, under oath, in
three proceedings, before you appeared at Rockefeller Center to be
questioned, you *still didn't know*, in late March 1987, what year you
worked at DCA? Is that correct, Miss Gabel?"

"I said: 'To the best of my recollection.' "

"Is that an answer you rehearsed with the prosecutors?"

....

* Robert Tembeckjian was counsel to the Commission on Judicial Conduct, and he had been
her first interrogator back in July 1986. He was not identified at trial because it would have
unfairly prejudiced the jury to know that there had been prior investigations, and that Justice
Gabel had resigned from the bench as a result.
† The Tyler investigation.

No.

"*Did* you rehearse with the prosecutors?"

"I am not certain that I understand the nature of the question."

"*Did you* rehearse your testimony in preparation for cross-examination with the prosecutors? Yes or no?"

He picked up a news clipping. "Did you tell a reporter from the *New York Post* yesterday, quote, that you were well rehearsed by the government attorneys. . . ?"

She demurred.

"*Yes or no*, Miss Gabel!"

"I don't remember."

"You don't remember *yesterday*! . . . But your memory is pretty good on 1983, right? A lot better than yesterday. Am I right? Yes or no?"

"My memory for some events that took place in 1983 is better than that memory for some events which took place yesterday."

"And as to other events, it is Swiss cheese?"

Poor Hortense and Milton. Their faces were hidden from the spectators, but any parent could feel them cringing.

"How many times did you meet with the prosecutors in the week before you took the stand? Just twelve days ago. In 1988? Surely you can remember that!"

About ten times. Maybe thirty to forty hours. And the week before that? Twenty or thirty hours. And the week before that? Maybe four times. So you had a total of fourteen meetings with the prosecutors in the two weeks before you took the stand, and before that, twenty-five or thirty meetings? So it's approximately forty-five meetings, right? Yes.

At Twenty-six Federal Plaza, right? Not at One Saint Andrews Place, right? So they set up a special office just to meet with Sukhreet Gabel, right? Did you like that?

"Frankly, no."

"Did it make you feel important? *Did* it?"

"I had company when I was there."

"I see. Did it play up to your ego a little bit?"

"Unwelcome company."

"*Did it play up to your ego?*"

"Mice don't play up to my ego."

"*Who* doesn't?"

"Mice. M-I-C-E. Mice."

Moderate laughter. Score one round to Sukhreet Gabel.

Have you described yourself as a member of the prosecution team? No.

"When you took the papers from your mother's apartment to the prosecutor's office, May eleventh, 1988, did you tell [a TV reporter] 'I took, as I saw it, a terrible risk in so openly declaring my allegiance to the prosecution?' "

"I do not remember making that statement."

Did she remember telling Marcia Kramer of the *News*, at the time of the indictment, October 1987, "There is the thrill of having worked so hard to testify, and to have something come of it"?

Raising his voice: "And it was after the filing of that public criminal charge against your own mother . . ." that you gave that statement in which you spoke about *the thrill* . . .

"Mr. Hafetz, I'm *proud* of that statement . . ."

Very loud now: "*Did you, or did you not* . . . make that statement after the public criminal charge filed against your own mother. Yes or no!"

Broad, moonbeam smile. "Yes."

It was a classic demonstration of the most trenchant, ugliest aspects of the adversary system at work.

At recess, Hortense Gabel was on her feet even before the last juror had filed out, making straight for the witness box. Sukhreet stepped down and gently retied the bow at the throat of her mother's blouse. She appeared fond and tender. Hortense summoned Milton. He kissed his daughter's forehead.

After recess, Hafetz said, "You've testified to things under oath that you really weren't sure of, haven't you?" His point was to demonstrate that her oath had no meaning to this witness. "Your thirty or forty meetings with the 'Boys,' as you called them, helped your recollections, didn't they?"

"That was some help. Meeting with Mr. Feldberg helped. Meeting with *you* helped." Then she scored a telling point. Yes, her memory had varied under oath. But variation is the *truth* of memory. Most people lie, and say their memory does not vary.

She scored another point for truth when Hafetz asked, "On

October twelfth, page eleven ninety-seven, you told this jury that in Foo Chow's 'Ms. Myerson said I should come to work for her,' and also go to law school . . . But you told the grand jury, March seventeenth, page thirty-nine, line seven: 'That's not what I think of as a job offer.' Now, one and a half years later, didn't you tell *this* jury there *was* a possibility of a job discussed? Yes or no?"

"Mr. Hafetz, yes or no is not an appropriate answer to that question. . . . If I said it, it was my mistake at the time."

A few moments later: "Are you telling us that as you move farther away from an event, sometimes your memory improves . . . as you search it, and are asked the same question three or four or five times, your memory *improves*? Is that right? You start to invent . . . you paint a scenario . . . isn't that what you said?"

"It is the terror of anyone who has to testify under oath that that in fact may be the case."

"Who are you afraid of? Your mother?"

"It's not a question of being afraid of anyone. It's a question of making sure. Knowing that your words are being written down, that there is a roomful of people, including a judge and a jury, listening to those words. You want to be absolutely sure those are the best words, the most correct recollection that you can possibly muster."

"And is the terror of testifying under oath what led you to call the prosecution team on approximately half a dozen occasions so you could voluntarily come in and have your testimony taken under oath?"

"Yes. It *is* terror when you say something under oath, and you realize twenty-four hours later . . . Hey! I made a mistake. Or: I remembered *more*. It was not the whole truth. There's more to it."

At lunch hour, the courthouse elevator was crowded with hungry lawyers, some of whom had slipped into the rear of the courtroom to catch Hafetz's performance. "This whole courthouse hates Sukhreet Gabel," said one. "I call her the 'Slug,' " said another. A third, a balding man with ratlike teeth, said with authority, "I've crossed every kind of stool pigeon. She is the worst."

But those who saw Sukhreet Gabel as a "snitch" suffered from lawyers' tunnel vision. The adversary system is inadequate to deal with matters of mood and nuance. Hafetz was like a man trying to dissect a butterfly with a meat cleaver. Furthermore, if he piled it on too strongly, he risked alienating the women jurors, for this was an unmistakable, classic mother-daughter confrontation. And all the while, Hafetz's gaunt client watched the witness with the narrowed, slit-eyed gaze of an Apache warrior.

He tried to depict Gabel as a job snob, someone who felt far superior to the task she was assigned and was speaking now as a disgruntled ex-employee. "Am I correct, Ms. Gabel, that . . . the position that Bess Myerson offered you was basically a gofer with brains?" Yes.

"And is it correct . . . that you—with your degrees, and your nine years of graduate education at the University of Chicago, and your Oxford training, and your Johns Hopkins certificate, and your editing on books, and your teaching of three graduate courses at the University of Chicago, and your sterling reviews from the Chicago State University students—felt that you deserved a more *exalted* position than that of a nineteen-thousand-dollar gofer with brains . . . am I correct? That bothered you, right?"

When she sought to explain, he cut her off with a bark: "Yes or no, Ms. Gabel? . . . Did you feel yourself equal in ability with Bourscheidt and Rubenstein and Bruno and the other top management staff?"

She tried again to explain.

"Yes or no!"

"Equal in *ability*? Yes."

"You say your memory improves as you get further away in time . . . You studied logic, didn't you, Ms. Gabel?"

"That's entirely logical, Mr. Hafetz."

"The electric-shock treatments have something to do with that?"

"No, I don't believe it had anything to do with that."

"It doesn't have anything to do with that. I see."

"The question [of memory] is one of repetition," she explained, and of devoting time to "thinking hard and concentratedly about a particular issue. . . . If I think about something, if I am questioned about it, if I know that I am responsible for remembering those things, then details do come back into focus. Things which one believes one has forgotten in fact one realizes that one remembers."

She was right, of course. Proust had got it all from one madeleine. But that was poetic logic and had no place in the courtroom.

"Your best recollection is not very good, is it, Ms. Gabel? You're not one hundred percent certain of *any* of your answers since last Wednesday."

"As far as humanly possible, I am."

"Am I correct that when you use the phrase 'to the best of my recollection,' that denotes *less* certainty?"

"I take my oath to tell the truth very seriously . . ."

Yes or no! Yes or no!

Cornered now like a dog, she said, "I don't know."

"*Did you* record your own mother . . . with a tape recorder supplied by courtesy of the United States government? . . . Yes or no, ma'am? Yes or no!"

"Everybody take it easy," said Keenan. "Your voice is getting a little high, Mr. Hafetz."

The lawyer apologized. The witness said yes, she did.

"That wasn't hard, was it, Ms. Gabel? You understood that question, didn't you?"

"It wasn't painless." The wide smile was beginning again, spreading across the moon face like ripples crossing a pond.

"Excuse me?"

"It wasn't painless."

"Is it humorous? Worth a smile when you go about recording your mother? Do you find something funny in that? *Do* you, Ms. Gabel?"

After you purposely taped your mother, didn't you turn over the tape to the government? Yes. And you taped her another time, didn't you? And you did that one inadvertently, right? Yes. "However, notwithstanding the fact that it was inadvertent, you nonetheless still turned that tape of *your own mother*"—he was shouting now—"and father over to the prosecution, did you not?"

Hafetz produced a small black tape player and placed it on her mother's table alongside that day's pink rose. Sukhreet Gabel had never looked so composed, her lips full, her expression serene, head slightly tilted, as she did in the stage wait while the tape player was being set up.

The judge warned the jurors it would be hard to hear. To make it easier, Hafetz removed the player from Judge Gabel's table and placed it directly on the jury rail. To make sure his client could hear, Feldberg asked the court's permission for her to come closer, and he led the old lady up to the jury rail, which she grasped with both freckled hands. The jurors leaned forward. Judge Keenan was on his feet, leaning down over his own bench to hear better. The scene had composed itself like a Giotto Pietà, every eye and ear in the courtroom straining toward the little black box.

"Hello, darling," the scratchy tape began.

"Mother, we should all get together, you and Daddy and I. Discuss this. Figure out what went on. What really happened. I'd like to have a family conference. Just the three Gabels. Let's do some brainstorming . . . I need some help. It's not for Rudy Giuliani; it's for me. I'm operating in the dark . . ."

"All right, honey," said Hortense, sounding exhausted. "Anything you want."

"It's like *Rashomon*, Mother. We now have three different versions of the same mess. . . ."

Hortense was patient but monosyllabic, and entirely noncommittal. Though blind, she seemed to see only too clearly what was going on. "Sure, honey . . . Okay, honey. . . . All right . . . Will do . . . Right . . . We'll see you tonight . . . You know, I think you're so *wonderful*. . . ."

In the witness box Sukhreet looked innocent and luminous, suffused with a pearly light like Saint Joan. Bess Myerson had stood up to hear better, both hands pressed like an open book over her nose and mouth. She was crying. Capasso stood up too, and whispered something in her ear.

More Sukhreet: "I think we should try . . . the three of us, to cooperate, try to reconstruct the events. And then to figure out what the hell is going on today in terms of Myerson's strategy and a lot of other things. Because obviously we are her enemies at this time, and she is a very rich, very manipulative lady . . ."

"Sure, honey . . . Sure . . . Okay, honey . . . We'll try. . . ."

Judge Gabel seemed not to want to try to remember, but to forget.

The three Gabels were something like the Three Bears, and Baby Bear could be very dangerous. This was the inadvertent tape, she would later explain. She did not know how or when she had pushed the record button. She had returned the machine to the government thinking the tape was blank.

The tape ended. Had all the jurors been able to hear? Judge Keenan asked for a show of hands. Most had not. He promised to play the tape again when court resumed. Meanwhile transcripts would be made. The jurors were dismissed and left the box. The lawyers gathered at the bench with Keenan to discuss how to improve the tape quality.

Hortense Gabel was suddenly alone, still holding on to the jury rail. She began creeping forward like an old, blind worm toward the witness box. When she reached the far end of the rail—as close to the box where her daughter still sat as she could get—she straightened up and clasped her hands behind her back. She was perhaps five feet tall, wearing a navy-blue dress and what looked like a blond wig slightly askew. Was there ever a more powerful, tender image of unrequited love than what one could read in that mother's straight, mute back?

20

WHEN SHE

WAS GOOD

THE NEXT WEEK THE TRIAL WAS IN RECESS SO THAT Judge Keenan could deal with the Imelda Marcos case and other responsibilities. But the press found ways to keep the story on the front page. Said the *Post*, ANGUISH OF SUKHREET'S DAD. "I cannot understand . . . why she's doing this to her mother and me." The Gabels had had no idea their daughter had taped her mother. "Sukhreet is brilliant," he said. "But she's always been odd. I guess it's sort of a mental thing. . . . Before all this happened," she didn't see her parents for six months at a time, though they lived only a block apart. "We'd only see her if she wanted something.

"We don't know why she did what she did, why she went to the prosecutor," said Dr. Gabel. Still, "she's our daughter. We raised her . . . we're supporting her." It was the hurt, pathetic rage of an old man, and in its self-pity one could see that Sukhreet was her father's daughter. The only Gabel with the dignity to shut up, seemingly, was Hortense.

Sukhreet had spent the entire free week appearing on TV. She answered questions, gave advice, had a beauty make-over, let herself be insulted, and sang in a couple of underbooked nightclubs. In her campy nightclub "debut" at El Morocco, she had a bad cold but gurgled her way through songs from Gilbert and Sullivan's satirical operettas on the bar, *Iolanthe* and *Trial by Jury*. She amused everybody, and looked as if she were having fun herself.

A week later, back in the courtroom, she was already in place in the witness box, dressed in a coat of fluorescent yellow, when the public doors were opened. A new rose was at her mother's place. Myerson wore a stern black Chanel-type outfit appropriate to her tightly controlled demeanor and rigid diet—nothing to eat all day but three large containers of black coffee accompanied by three cigarettes. At lunch she went to the cafeteria and brought back coffee for Andy, who, since he was in custody, was not permitted to leave the courtroom.

Judge Keenan had summoned the attorneys up to the bench. There a huddle of more or less middle-aged men, all of whom had committed their lives to the adversary system, were trying to deal rationally with what is arguably the most complex and ferocious bond within the human family, the one that exists between mother and daughter.

The most devastating cross-examination related to the memo Sukhreet had written at the suggestion of Philip Schaeffer the morning after Bess came to see her. Fred Hafetz handed the witness a few handwritten pages on yellow legal foolscap, and then recalled her prior testimony in this trial. You told us Ms. Myerson told you: *I'm very worried. There is a lot of trouble.*

Is that statement in your "detailed memorandum"? No.

Also: *You know that Andy's been before the grand jury.* "I ask you," Hafetz sneered, "in the detailed memo you made of this alleged walk around the block, is there any mention of that?" No.

You can make a lot of trouble. That's not there either. No.

We have got to get our stories straight. Is *that* in the detailed memorandum? No.

Hafetz read several more alleged statements: *I want you to contact me before you talk to your lawyer or anybody else. This is a very dangerous situation, and you contact me first. You've got to keep your mouth shut.*

We've got to think, so we can have the same story. Keep in close touch. I don't want you using your own name when you call the office. Use Ms. Grant.

Not one was in the memo to Schaeffer.

"Yet when you sent the memo to Schaeffer, you said you had not left out anything substantive!" Turning away from the witness stand in disgust, Hafetz said quietly, "No further questions."

Judge Gabel's lawyer was next to cross-examine. Michael Feldberg looked young, slight, and nonthreatening. His task was delicate and he spoke quietly. Sukhreet had suffered a bad battering at Hafetz's hands. In simple kindness to his client, Feldberg wanted to do something toward rehabilitating her daughter. But he did not want to do too much.

What were the three simple words that had constituted Hortense Gabel's advice to her daughter since day one of this case? he began.

"Tell the truth."

"You know, one thing this jury is going to have to decide is whether your mother had something called *criminal intent*." And on the tape you made inadvertently, you said to your mother, "You know, the truth is going to exonerate you." Please tell the jury what *exonerate* means.

"It means it would get my mother off the hook. It would prove she was not guilty of the charges."

Did you also say in that conversation, "I don't think you are guilty of a damned thing?" Yes. "Your mother has never tried to prevent you from speaking to the government?" Never. "To the press?" Never. "Your mother has had just that one admonition— tell the truth. . . . Your parents support you to this day. Your mother has not cut you off financially. . . ."

After again mentioning the high points of his client's long and honorable career, just as he had done in his opening statement, Feldberg turned to the difficult subject of Ms. Gabel's unreliable memory. The day ended as, one by one, he listed twenty-one other instances of memory lapses in her direct examination. As it built, it became a kind of catechism of amnesia, a bubbling fondue of Swiss cheese.

At the start of the trial, the overall strategy for Capasso had been to put on a minimal defense. The evidence against him was negligible, and Jay Goldberg, his lawyer, contented himself with a brief, dry review of Sukhreet's few mentions of Capasso in restaurants and at the beach house. That disposed of, it appeared he would rest. But Goldberg's lie-low trial strategy was at odds with his own bravura nature, and the next morning, instead of resting, he went for the jugular.

After staying up all that night studying his trial notebook, he had told his wife, "You know what I think? I think she's full of crap. I think she's not crazy at all. I think she's narcissistic. That's a personality disorder. I think she never looked for those jobs at all. That's why her father nagged her—because she wasn't out pounding the pavements like she said; she was like a tub of lard. She's so narcissistic, she believes she should only get a job as a CEO. She believes *she* should be the commissioner, and Bess should have the desk by the bathroom. I am going to do a dance on her head."

He began softly. Ms. Gabel, you testified that in June 1986 Bess Myerson told you, "You know Andy's been before the grand jury, don't you?" Long pause. "You know, Miss Gabel, that that's untrue. . . . See, what you are doing, years after the event, you're adding something that never occurred."

"No. That's not correct."

Now you have in the course of these proceedings given your mother roses . . . and blown her a kiss . . . but these acts don't reflect your true feelings, do they? Didn't you tell the prosecutors that you harbored deep resentment toward your mother?

Probably.

He showed her a handwritten document on yellow legal paper and asked, "Did you ever inform the government that your mother had viewed you as mad—M-A-D?" Yes, mad as in mad/crazy. And no, she did not like it. And yes, her mother had often urged that she see a psychiatrist. And no, her father did not view her as crazy. He viewed her as lazy.

Sukhreet had with her on the stand a copy of *DSM III*, the standard physician's diagnostic manual of mental disorders. Noticing it, Judge Keenan asked, "What did you do, diagnose yourself?"

"No. As a former nurse, as one who worked in psychiatric wards, as one who has undergone considerable diagnosis and treatment for affective disorders, specifically major depression and unipolar depression, I am somewhat familiar with the nature of my own disease."

She had the book with her now, she said, because yesterday she'd noticed a copy on Mr. Goldberg's table, and she wanted to be prepared.

But she was scarcely prepared for Goldberg's attack.

The book contains the term *narcissism*, right? And she is familiar with the word? And it means someone who has grandiose visions of himself, "and is preoccupied with their own brilliance, isn't that so?" And isn't a narcissist someone who engages in exhibitionism? Yes.

"Weren't you on television yesterday?" Don't you cut the stories about yourself out of the newspapers when you get home from court?

"Going on with your lay understanding of the narcissist," he sneered, "this person who has a preoccupation with their own ideas of brilliance, and self-importance, is also someone who has periods of rage—isn't that so?"

Had she ever heard that an individual who comes out of a depression is very vulnerable to suggestion? No.

Goldberg turned to the people she called the "Boys." "Investigator Tony Lombardi, you said earlier that you love him, right?"

"I adore him." At the prosecution table, treasury agent Lombardi blushed.

And your nickname for David Lawrence is "Tight Ass," right? Yes.

Did she ever hear of the interrogation technique known as the good guy/bad guy approach? Yes.

Goldberg suggested that Lombardi was playing the sweet and loving good guy, and Lawrence the nasty tight ass, or "the ferret," as she also called him. He reminded the jury that she was always alone with the prosecutors, with no one to advise her, and she was on medication prescribed by her psychiatrist. "And there would be times when David Lawrence would be sort of hostile to you, but then Mr. Lombardi would be there to like soften it for you? Yes or no?"

"Sometimes the roles were reversed."

"And sometimes the good guy became the bad guy, and the bad

guy became the good guy. Is that a correct statement?" Yes. "Did it ever dawn on you that this was a technique designed to mold you into a government witness? Did you ever think of that, yes or no? *Yes or no!*"

"I reject the suggestion."

But you had nobody to advise you if you were being used, right? You had to make that decision yourself, right?

I had no money to get a lawyer. And I also chose not to get a lawyer. She made no effort to hide her contempt for his profession.

In any of her forty-five sessions with the government's men, did any one of them *ever* tell you what they were looking for?

"No!" The answer was spat out.

So you had no one to talk to, no boyfriend, and no lawyer, and you've told us you hated your parents, and you had a love/hate relationship with Myerson—"and then you found in the U.S. attorney's office someone you adored. Is that a fair statement?"

"Same as I adore you, Mr. Goldberg."

"That love I can do without, okay?"

The questions turned uglier. Didn't there come a time when you knew your mother was going to be brought into court, not as a judge this time, but for arraignment? And that was a very, very sad day for her, right? And at that time your mother had no idea you had taken her documents in satchels down to the U.S. Attorney's office, right? And that you had secretly tape-recorded your mother and father's conversation?

At that time, "I didn't know it either."

Did you tell your mother about it? No. But if her mother had asked her about it, she would have told her.

Sneering: "But if she didn't happen to ask you that question— Did you ever take satchels of my papers to the U.S. attorney's office?—you didn't feel you had any obligation to tell her. Right? *Is that what you are saying?*"

Yes.

When your mother had to come down here to be arraigned, and plead not guilty like a criminal—that was a point of public humiliation for her such as she had never experienced in her long and honorable life, right? And she didn't take it very well, did she?

"I thought she took it with remarkable grace."

"With remarkable grace. I see. And this was the day you told Marcia Kramer that you experienced 'a certain thrill' that all your work had finally paid off?"

He showed her the article and brought out that at the time of the arraignment, Justice Gabel had just suffered another small stroke and been hospitalized, and that her eighty-year-old father also had been in failing health. And this is the time she speaks about as a *thrill*!

Sukhreet succeeded in reading the full quote into the record: "There is the thrill of having worked so hard to testify in the grand jury and to have something come of it. Still, there is a very tragic feeling to have people you love indicted."

Did the U.S. attorney tell you you had to come to the arraignment? No. But you did, didn't you? And you sat in the front row, in a green flowing cape! And "you, the loving daughter," escorted her up the courthouse steps, and you held her arm, and you said, "Mother," as you walked up the stairs to her public humiliation; with all the press there and the cameras rolling, you said, "Mother, act like a madonna," right?

Sukhreet said no, she used the proper name, Madonna. But Goldberg had made his point. He had depicted the witness as a combination Judas Iscariot and Madame Defarge, pushing her way into the front row to enjoy the spectacle of not only her mother but her fairy godmother Bess Myerson being arraigned on criminal charges.

He turned it up still another notch: Does she know of any parallel in world history where children betrayed their parents? Does anything in the 1930s come to mind? No.

He reminded her of her earlier admission that her mother thought her crazy, and her father thought her lazy. "So that day was the culmination of your long-standing, deep-seated *hatred* of both your mother and your father. . . ." No.

You told Fred Hafetz and Mike Feldberg you resented the way your parents had treated you, and their lack of appreciation of your special qualities as a child . . . you resented your mother's fame. . . . Goldberg still held the handwritten document.

"Would it be possible to describe the provenance of this document for the benefit of my mother?"

"Object! Not responsive!" Goldberg barked.

"Not responsive. Strike it," said the judge.

The document was from a private interview she had given to Feldberg to help him understand his client and her family. Feldberg had promised to keep it confidential, and now Goldberg was waving it under her nose. She recognized that most of Goldberg's cross had been based on these confidential materials she had given to Feldberg. So she was the victim of lawyers' tricks on both sides.

A couple of more cheap shots, and it would be over. She had mentioned she was thinking of writing a book. "Have you thought of a title, such as *Daughter Dearest*?"

She admitted she lived on a monthly $1,775 check from her parents. Of that, $800 was for rent, the rest for food, student loans, and medical expenses. But "you took that money . . . that your mother had given you, and you stole it, isn't that so?" Weren't eviction proceedings once started against her for nonpayment of rent?

Yes, but . . .

"But you took that money and you used it for some other purpose, isn't that so?"

"I bought drugs!" The reference was to her expensive psychiatric medications. Prozac cost $1.55 per pill.

Goldberg pressed on. The money came from her mother's pension and her father's savings, right?

He was interrupted by Hortense Gabel, asking him to make it very clear to the court and jury and the media that her daughter bought medicinal, not recreational drugs.

Unlike Bess Myerson, who had a mother who would never say she did anything right, Sukhreet Gabel had a mother who would never say she did anything wrong.

On redirect, David Lawrence brought out that "Mr. Feldberg had assured me that he was not sharing my confidences with his fellow defense attorneys at my express request."

What about her feelings toward Bess Myerson, which she characterized as "a mixture of love and hate." Would she explain?

"There was a little girl . . ." she began. But this time Hafetz shouted an objection, and the court sustained.

Lawrence tried again, but Keenan cut him off. Love and hate "are fairly self-defining words."

Not the way the witness used them, said Lawrence, so Judge Keenan, impatient with so much folderol, asked Sukhreet directly, "What do you mean when you say you love Ms. Myerson?"

"I revere Ms. Myerson. I admire Ms. Myerson for her beauty, for her talent, her hard work, and the genuine kindness she has often shown me."

". . . and when you say you hate Ms. Myerson?"

"I often find Ms. Myerson manipulative, intrusive, rude, and thoughtless in her behavior toward me and others."

Your father? "I enjoy my father for who he is, for what he does, and for what he stands for. I enjoy him as a human being, and as a friend. I also love him because he is a wonderful human being with human qualities which I admire. He genuinely cares for other people. He goes out of his way to help other people. He virtually always has a cheerful demeanor.

"There are times when I strongly disagree with my father's attitudes, and with the ways that he chooses to express them. I become very annoyed when I am nagged, for example, about things that I cannot control, or cannot change readily . . . such as the fact that I have not been able to find a job."

And her mother? "My mother is a very special, very complex woman. I think that the quality I revere and love most about my mother is her essential fairness. [She] is a liberal in the truest, best sense . . . the fact that she practices what she preaches causes me to have great love, respect, and affection for my mother. There are times when I disagree with my mother's views. . . . There are times when I resent my mother's overweening interference in my life. There are times when I have less than a great deal of patience [with her]."

"Do you have mixed emotions concerning your mother's professional success?" Keenan asked.

"No."

"Next question."

Lawrence asked about her feelings toward Capasso. She didn't know him well, she said, but "I found him a very pleasant man."

Lawrence rehabilitated his witness on the matter of the eviction notice; checks had crossed in the mail. "Ms. Gabel, do you wish any of the defendants any harm?"

Her "no" answer brought on Myerson's first smile in a week. Normally her face was masklike, under iron control. Bess would confess later that being on trial had felt like being on a torture rack. Some mornings she couldn't get out of bed; she felt suicidal. She would talk to herself aloud: "One step at a time. Go inside now . . . brush your teeth . . ." She described her feelings in the very words Sukhreet had used to describe her feelings at DCA: *Helpless. Abandoned. Like a crying baby.*

Bess had turned to her religion. She had joined a self-help group of women Orthodox Jews. She lit candles on Friday nights to celebrate the Sabbath. She spoke directly with God in her prayers. It worked. Finally "I was off the torture rack. . . . All my stories have happy endings. Success is the best revenge. I've always had it, and I'll have it again."

The government's star witness had now been on the stand for nine court days. People were getting sick of her, no one more so than Judge Keenan, who confided to friends backstage that, except for homicides, this was the most unsavory case he ever had to preside over. Before letting her go, David Lawrence again brought up the shopping bags of documents, to show what honorable men the prosecutors had been.

They had asked Sukhreet to compose a memorandum, had they not, stating how she obtained the documents and what she did with them? They had brought in a court reporter to take down her statement. They had told her, The fact that you brought them here does not mean you have to give them to the government. She had been put alone into a separate room and given an opportunity to read through them, had she not? "You got an opportunity to reflect on what you'd done?"

But if Mr. Goldberg was correct, and Sukhreet Gabel was a quintessential narcissist, she would be incapable of seeing what she had done. She would gaze into Narcissus's pool and see only herself.

Once her testimony was over, Sukhreet in theory was free to join the other spectators in the courtroom. Her mother wanted her there, but another defendant—Myerson—objected, so she left. Compromises are necessary in a multidefendant defense, but Goldberg felt that banning Sukhreet was a serious strategic mistake. He would have preferred the jurors to see her every single day throughout the coming seven weeks of trial, while lesser witnesses fleshed out the government's case.

The BessMess went to the jury on December 19, and it took four days to decide. The jurors had difficulty understanding Judge Keenan's instructions on how to apply the law, and several were troubled by a vague feeling that Myerson "did something," and perhaps Gabel as well, but they weren't sure what. Two or three times a day they returned to the courtroom to hear parts of Keenan's instructions or bits of testimony reread to them.

On the fourth day, December 22, they were exhausted and close to agreement on acquittal, but one juror was holding out for guilty. That morning Goldberg had one of his inspirations. He slipped into a courthouse phone booth and called Sukhreet and told her there was no longer any reason she need stay out of the courtroom.

The next time the jurors came in for a readback, they saw the star witness sitting in the back row. This small reminder was all it took. A few hours later, the BessMess case ended in total triumph for the defense, as Myerson, Gabel, and Capasso were acquitted of all charges.

Bess cried and flung her arms around Andy. "I'm grateful for the American judicial system," she said, and thanked the jury.

"Outstanding," said Andy.

Hortense Gabel said, "I'm proud of her. She stood by me . . . she told the truth."

Goldberg said, "Had it not been Bess Myerson, Giuliani would not have brought the case. It was an attempt to turn the federal court into a divorce court."

Mayor Koch said, "I'm glad for her as a personal friend."

Nancy Capasso said nothing, and when her lawyer was asked what she had actually received, he said, "Try zero. Nothing. Nancy's been awarded a lot of money, is being sued for much more, and has received nothing. This isn't what I would call a positive situation."

Said Sukhreet, "My mother is the only one who has treated me fairly in this whole mess."

SOME CASES ARE ill suited to courtrooms. The BessMess was one. The questions it raised are daily dealt with by wise psychiatrists and village rabbis, but they grind the gears of the adversary system. The law deals best with facts, and the BessMess was essentially a tangle of emotions.

The "Scotch verdict" strategy worked; the lawyers got everybody off. Still, the feeling persisted among the jurors, they later told reporters, that Bess and perhaps Horty had indeed "done something," though not something criminal. After the ordeal of indictment and public trial, even total acquittal cannot put Humpty Dumpty together again, and these people's lives had been permanently altered, and devalued.

Amazingly, the very day after the verdict, Justice Gabel gave voice to precisely the same feeling as the jurors. Myerson "might have been" trying to influence her rulings in the Capasso divorce by giving her daughter a job, she told a reporter. "It's possible." The reason she had not alerted the authorities, she said, "was that I was naïve enough to think that everybody I knew thought I was as honest as I am."

The biggest question was: Why had Bess and Andy tried it? It had been from the start a terrible idea. The stakes were too small, the hazards too great. What difference could a few hundred thousand dollars more or less make to a multimillionaire bent on dumping a wife of fifteen years to go off with the great love of his life, a woman worth $10 million or $20 million in her own right? The downside risk, should they be exposed, was overwhelming.

Whose idea was it? At first the terrible idea seemed to have been born of Bess, an accomplished manipulator wishing to show off her power to the man who loved her partly for her power, and to give him a gift beyond price.

At first it seemed unlikely that a strong man would be capable of such petty vindictiveness. An explosion in the heart can happen to almost anybody. But this was no crime of passion. It was the product of perfectly matched, twinned obsessions: He wanted to punish Nancy; she wanted to deprive Nancy of (his) money. The result was a sustained act of vengeance, carefully plotted and mutually reinforced by the triumphant new lovers, with some help from the dumped wife thrashing around in her own pain and fury—in short, a common constellation in the postmatrimonial firmament.

The Capasso divorce saga shows what a fiery forum the courts can become when such people are involved. Alas, as divorce rates rise, so does the inability of parting spouses to reach reasonable compromises. Today in New York State about one in five divorces must be fought out in court. Criminal and family courts are increasingly overworked as the amount of matrimonial litigation expands and greed marches on.

Bess and Andy's vindictive behavior toward Nancy must be seen as an act of sheer irrationality, given their own wealth. Bess could have had her man *and* a pile of money. But it would have meant giving up something deeply neurotic in her. Instead she got the man everybody wanted, then ultimately destroyed her own good fortune.

The case raised other questions. Chief among them: Had Justice Gabel ever understood what was going on? Sukhreet said, "I think my mother didn't catch on fast enough. Bess and Andy did form a conspiracy, but Mother didn't see it until it was too late to extricate herself. Thereafter she became a victim of extortion by Bess and Andy, and paralyzed by her fears that I would kill myself." Perhaps.

Sukhreet's question about Justice Gabel was the same one asked at Watergate: What did she know, and when did she know it? She had gotten the case in January 1983, and made her first ruling in February. But when did she know that Bess Myerson was the Other Woman? Gabel had been forced at trial to admit that she knew of the Myerson/Capasso relationship by September 14, 1983, because by then there was proof. A *Post* photograph of that date showing Bess and Andy chatting on the steps of City Hall was attached, as an exhibit, to one of Nancy's motions.

But it seemed to many that Gabel must have known of the Myerson-Capasso connection long before that. Her mother was a "creature of the system," Sukhreet had correctly observed. By the time Justice Gabel got the case in January, just about everybody in

New York knew of the Capasso-Myerson affair. It had gone on quite openly for three years. Certainly everybody in the system knew.

But if she did not know it then, how could she have missed the *Post* story on March 7, IRATE WIFE EVICTS BESS MYERSON'S ESCORT? And the one on March 11, NO WEDDING BELLS, SAYS BESS'S BEAU? Both stories resulted from, and mentioned, Gabel's own first order in *Capasso* v. *Capasso*, the one granting Nancy and her children exclusive occupancy of the family apartment. Gabel had told pre-trial investigators that she was a regular reader of the *Post*, and kept a personal clipping file. Her two law assistants and her secretary also read the newspapers attentively.

Finally, even if she and her staff had missed both March stories in the *Post*, there had been Rickman's testimony that at Koch's May 25 Gracie Mansion reception for Bess, Horty had asked him, "Is what's-his-name here?"

"I said, 'You mean Andy Capasso?' She said, 'Yes.' "

Sukhreet also knew of the relationship; she spent two August weekends at the love nest. All she didn't know, until Shirley Harrod told her, was that her mother was the judge in the divorce case. So her wonderful job was only a sleazy bribe, and she had been sold out by everybody involved. For Milton Gabel must have been in on it too. Otherwise, when his daughter told him on the phone of Shirley Harrod's news, he would have been astounded and upset, not conciliatory.

In retrospect, it appeared that Sukhreet was at first willing to go along with the charade, despite her pain and anguish. These feelings turned to fury when she read her father's disparaging words in the Tyler Report. There they were on page 5 of the seventy-five page document: "SUMMARY OF CONCLUSIONS: . . . Although Sukhreet Gabel was well-educated, we learned she also had a long history of emotional disturbances and had, in her father's words, 'limited talents.' "

THE BESSMESS CASE had been a tough call for everybody involved, starting with the jurors. In a circumstantial-evidence case, the law says that if there is an interpretation of the facts consistent with innocence, then you may not find defendants guilty. One can see, then, why the jury acquitted the defendants of conspiracy.

Yet, if there was no conspiracy, there was at least a flirtation with the administration of justice on the part of a city official and a judge. This is the "something wrong" that the jurors sensed, even though they were unable to put a legal—or rather, illegal—label on it.

One reason for their difficulty was Judge Keenan's instruction that Justice Gabel had "had an obligation to continue" if she could, as well as an obligation to recuse herself if she could not. Hence, although one may conclude that her conduct was highly questionable, one must also say that she had a high order of obligation, that it was a tough call for her.

The case was a reminder that prosecutorial discretion is unlimited. As Justice Sol Wachtler, New York's senior administrative judge, had so famously said, a prosecutor can indict a ham sandwich. But that indictment must be strong enough to withstand a defense motion to dismiss it.

The case also raised questions of simple prosecutorial good judgment. How could the government have erred so egregiously in relying on Sukhreet Gabel as chief witness? How could the prosecutors have been so totally insensitive to the deep taboo against a child turning on its parents, a taboo that has existed since the dawn of human society? The Book of Exodus tells us, "He that smiteth his father, or his mother, shall be surely put to death . . . And he that curseth his father, or his mother, shall surely be put to death."

In Greek myth, the taboo is central to the story of the murder of King Agamemnon, victorious leader of the Greeks in the Trojan War, by his faithless wife, Clytemnestra, and her lover Aegisthus. In consequence the daughter, Electra, demands that her brother, Orestes, avenge their father's death. Thomas Bulfinch, the great nineteenth-century authority on mythology, comments, "This revolting act, the slaughter of a mother by her son, though alleviated by the guilt of the victim and the express commands of the gods, did not fail to awaken in the breasts of the ancients the same abhorrence that it does in ours."

It is only in our century's totalitarian societies that the taboo vanishes, and the abhorrence ceases to exist—there and, apparently, in the true-believer prosecutorial mind-set. For the BessMess prosecutors seemed blind to the public revulsion their trial strategy was certain to cause. Or perhaps they felt that Sukhreet was necessary to show *motive*, and revulsion be damned. She embodied the depth of the problem she presented to her loving parents. Her presence could help jurors understand that this mother could have been so desperate to help this daughter that she might have allowed herself to be bribed, or murkier still, *appear to be* bribed.

It was a tough call for the government as to whether to bring this case. It is hard to make out such a case under the circumstantial-evidence rule.

David Lawrence and his team of prosecutors perhaps could have won if they had tried the case with greater knowledge and understanding of the fine points of New York matrimonial law. But they were feds, trained to a different drum.

Suppose, for example, after Goldberg's artful flimflam minimizing the differences among Gabel's successively smaller monetary awards, that the government had recalled the expert in matrimonial law to the stand so that he could have provided the jury with a true, complete, and accurate understanding of Justice Gabel's rulings, and their major consequences to both parties in the dispute? That was one of the great what-ifs in the case.

There were others. What if the chauffeurs' testimony had come in? The chauffeurs had told the grand jury and the Tyler Commission that they had seen Myerson bring large amounts of cash from Nanco to a Manhattan stock brokerage; that they had overheard Bess boast to Andy that she could "get to anybody" in New York; that they had overheard Andy threaten Nancy that he could "fix any judge in this town." (The testimony was not used because of various prosecution/defense trade-offs.)

What if Bess Myerson had not been a public figure? Or what if the commissioner of cultural affairs had been a man, not a woman, a man who had found a doxy who made him happy?

What if Rudolph Giuliani had not been contemplating running for public office? Would the public still have been asked to pay for this eleven-week, multimillion-dollar legal circus? By the time the case went to trial, it was known along the back alleys of the Apple's legal community that some members of the team of government lawyers assigned to the case had been less than enthusiastic about going ahead, especially with Justice Gabel as a co-defendant. But their boss had pulled rank and forced them to continue.

Knowing that circumstantial cases are tough to win, and this one tougher than most, how unlike Rudolph Giuliani to needlessly expose himself. The loss caused him major embarrassment. Had he won, it would not have been his greatest victory. (His convictions of so many high-level officials of the Koch administration were of far greater consequence.) But losing made it without question his greatest defeat. Why did he bother? One possibility: If Giuliani was contemplating challenging Koch for mayor, nailing Bess was a bravura opening move. Huge headlines were assured, and the Tyler Report had given him the hammer. Report in hand—a document saying that illegal acts had been committed by a city official and by a state judge—Giuliani was in a position to say he had no choice but to prosecute. The Tyler Report, made public June 10, 1987, may have helped convert a possible ham sandwich into reasonable cause to believe that a crime had been committed by the time Giuliani announced the grand-jury indictment on October 7.

So the case had been a succession of tough calls, and even before the case came to trial, its chief defendant had made herself the toughest person in the courtroom. Somewhere along the way, probably quite early on, Myerson's self-toughening had warped her character. She was not a beauty queen who had "transcended her tawdry throne," as somebody wrote. Her conduct *was* tawdry. But, as Jean Harris has pointed out, Bess was first and foremost a fighter: "She's tough. . . . She's learned you have to grab, to hang on, to get what you want in life." Andy Capasso turned her on. Faced with the prospect of losing him, she was ready to burn down the world.

Nancy Capasso also was tough. She fought toe-to-toe. It takes a lot of courage to attack a judge. Nancy Capasso had a rare order of fortitude to say, to insist, This is not a fair hearing that I'm getting.

Unfortunately Nancy was not represented in court. No high-priced, award-winning lawyer was present to rise to defend her good name when the chief lawyer laid down his winning strategy— his master "Goldberg maneuver"—and told the jury: This case is the fault of a greedy, bitter woman bent on vengeance and determined to sink the ship on which the lovebirds are sailing off into the sunset.

No one was there to say, Hold it, buddy. Nancy Capasso was not the manipulator; she was the victim. Bess got off, and she may have gotten Andy as well.

Nancy got a $5.53 million settlement, lawsuits totaling $25.6 million, and a promissory note. Of the four women, she was the second-biggest loser. The first was Horty. In retrospect, it was clearly wrong for Justice Gabel to have handled the Capasso case. She should have recused herself. Did she know it? Or was she blinded by her concern for her daughter's future? Or so debilitated by age and infirmity that she was unaware?

She must have known it. Her comment to Leventhal about the Capasso lawyers bespoke consciousness of guilt: "They both said how fair they thought I'd been, and how honored they would be if I continued to preside . . . and that they thought I was straight as an arrow" really suggested the opposite. The lady did protest too much. It seemed to show what lawyers call "guilty mind."

Hortense Gabel had faced the toughest choice. In Keenan's charge, he told the jurors that it is a judge's obligation not to have an interest in the case. Hence Justice Gabel had excruciating options: her concern for her daughter versus a judicial obligation to get out. For very human reasons, Gabel did not do what she should have done.

Sukhreet Gabel was not tough. She was a wise fool. She was also the only noncynical figure in the case. The others—defendants, lawyers, prosecutors, and judge—knew only too well what they were doing in that courtroom. But Sukhreet Gabel was Prince Myshkin; and Sukhreet Gabel was the only one who played the game entirely straight, the only one who took the whole criminal justice system literally. So of course she got laughed at.

True, Sukhreet Gabel sometimes did not tell the literal truth, as in her testimony about nursing school, or in her improbable, gradually improving recollection of the famous walk with Bess around the block.

But one must distinguish between lying and fantasy. The liar is fully aware of what she is doing. The fantasist is not. Her fantasy gradually takes on the feeling of reality. Such persons do not fare well in courtrooms. The law concerns itself with the true and the false, and sorting out which is which. But sometimes a statement is both true *and* false. "I love my daughter," for example, or "I hate my mother."

At such moments the law stumbles. That's why Keenan took over from the lawyers and asked Sukhreet: What do you mean when you say you love your mother? love your father? Her replies had resounded with the kind of truth one rarely hears in courtrooms, or in churches. One hears it only in the heart.

21

AFTER THE JURORS HAD RENDERED THEIR VER-
dict, what became of our four ladies so royally betrayed by love?

Officially, Bess moved back to her old apartment
on Seventy-first Street. This was a consequence of
Andy's release from prison in June 1989. He returned to the Park Avenue apartment, now refur-
bished and worth $4 million. He was seen driving
around the Apple making telephone calls from his
limousine or his Mercedes-Benz. He turned up
nightly at Regine's or another of the city's posh
nightspots, awash in champagne and wreathed in
the smoke of fine cigars. He was always with a small
group of friends that did not include Bess.

This did not necessarily indicate that love had
lost its magic; it merely showed the lovers still attentive to their lawyer-puppeteers. The week he
came home, Andy's attorneys filed court papers
seeking an end to his $350-a-week child-support
payments, pleading poverty. He claimed a gross

weekly income of $1,153, leaving him only $425 after paying current and back taxes. Nancy's lawyers wondered aloud where he found the estimated $4,000 monthly maintenance on the Park Avenue apartment, and what had happened to his $96,000 annual income—$60,000 salary from Aetna and $36,000 from a mortgage he somehow owned? Nancy herself said nothing.

Then, after nine years of total silence, Andy talked. His mouthpiece was Myerson's longtime good friend Cindy Adams, a gossip writer for the *Post* who specialized in intimate glimpses of the impossibly rich, people like Imelda Marcos and Doris Duke.

"I never wanted to reduce myself to my ex-wife's level," Capasso began, and lowered himself several stories beneath it in the course of a single interview. He accused Nancy of telling the press the same thing that his lawyers had in fact already told the court: that "I don't want to support my children." In fact, she had said nothing, nor did she comment publicly on this outburst.

"That's something I cannot tolerate," Andy fulminated to Cindy. He complained that he should no longer have to pay any child support because the kids preferred to live with him. If this were so, it would not be surprising. Andrea and Michael were now fifteen and seventeen, and had sorely missed their father during his two-year imprisonment.

Capasso added that Nancy "rarely works . . . [but] picks up restaurant checks like crazy." He again accused her of "turning me in," and sounded like a man willing to do anything, say anything, and pay anything, to destroy his ex-wife. He had sounded off despite a gag order on both parties in the unseemly dispute, and if he achieved nothing else, his remarks served as a reminder that when parents who are engaged in marital warfare seek to manipulate the children to their own advantage, the children are utterly helpless, and nobody wins.

Bess herself remained silent in the press. Privately she quoted Mike Tyson's comments on his own tumultuous year: " 'What I *would've* done . . . Woulda, shoulda, coulda—that's all in the past.' I'm putting everything behind me too. I'm sixty, right? So I'm gonna live till a hundred and twenty, and never, ever look back."

As for Bess and Andy's future together, the battered lovebirds were sometimes seen together, and were also spotted apart and with others. What did it mean? That whatever their ultimate fate as a couple, for the time being their legal advisers had reasserted control over their pounding, wayward, aging hearts. But there was more. Cindy Adams said Bess and Andy had told her that each "would always be there for" the other. Maybe so. They had walked through the fire together, and neither one had betrayed the other. After the ashes of passion have cooled, does any greater turn-on exist, especially for a stand-up guy? So for once, at the very least, Bess had not lost her man.

Save for his unfortunate interview, Andy was untarnished by his time in the pen. He was guilty; he admitted it; he paid. His children still adored him. He was very good at his business, so Aetna still believed in him, and he was almost certain to become rich again. He would never find another woman like Bess Myerson, so perhaps he would stick with her. Surely these lovers had earned, and deserved, each other.

Bess Myerson may have been right when she said all her stories have happy endings. Acquitted of all charges after a grueling eleven-week trial, Bess had shown herself tougher than ever, and she still looked great. Impossibly lean and tall and tanned, planed smooth by time and by the surgeon's art, and burnished to brazen luster, she had become like a sharp stick hardened in the fires of her own life.

As for Nancy Capasso, she was the only one of the four women who appeared to have come through it all with honor and soul intact. She was still supporting herself selling real estate, still trying to wring money from her ex-husband, and nowhere near free of her financial imbroglio with Aetna and EAB. But it looked as if one day she could be. Andy notwithstanding, four of her five children still loved her very much. (Her second child, Steven, twenty-seven, married and living in California, had legally changed his name from Herbert to Capasso during the divorce battles, and proclaimed himself firmly on his stepfather's side.)

There was a new man in Nancy's life, a kindly, attractive Jewish man, a widower and an old friend, and they seemed easy and content with one another.

Hortense Gabel was surely the biggest loser. Despite acquittal, the ordeal had clearly diminished the only capital she had: her perfect integrity and reputation.

After the media spotlight shut off, Sukhreet continued trying to merchandise Sukhreet, and she acquired an agent to help her. Soon there were greeting cards and T-shirts, and she was writing an album of original songs and contributing a monthly column to a downtown newspaper.

After the verdict, Sukhreet had become predictably bitter about "the Boys." She was angered by their ingratitude, their rudeness, their sudden lack of interest in her. When she reached her "adored" Tony Lombardi on his beeper on Christmas Day, "Tony accused me of losing the case for them!" Sukhreet subsequently made repeated fruitless calls to David Lawrence seeking return of documents and childhood photographs she had loaned him, as well as books on pharmacopoeia and on mental depression.

As to her role as star witness, Sukhreet continued to maintain that she "always felt that I testified as a material witness, a 'fact' witness, not as a witness for the prosecution *or* defense. But why should anybody *be* a government witness?" she now ruefully asked. "I gave the prosecutors everything. I gave them two years of my life.

"You know what I've learned from all this about the criminal justice system? A defendant has rights; a witness has none. With a witness, everything is fair game. A witness cannot be exonerated, or have the charges dropped, as a criminal defendant can. Nobody says, This witness is innocent until proven guilty. *Nobody* presumes innocence on the part of a witness!

"I'm the enormous flaw in the system. I'm a party without any standing. I'm just a poor, unhappy shade forever wandering along the corridors of justice."

Perhaps. But Sukhreet was also the game's only winner. She had gotten what she always wanted—attention—more than in her wildest dreams. She had revenged herself against her mother on the world stage, and not been punished. Indeed, after the media spotlight shut off, the center of the senior Gabels' life was still their daughter. A few months after Horty's acquittal, on Mother's Day, she and Milton sat at a ringside table for Sukhreet's nightclub debut in the back room of a bar called King Tut's Wah Wah Hut. They beamed and applauded good-naturedly when Sukhreet offered a bluesy rendition of "Sometimes I Feel Like a Motherless Child."

Career aside, the center of Sukhreet's life was still her mother and father. She said of them: "I've never forgiven them for what they said about me to the Tyler Commission. They've never forgiven me for what I did. But they've forgiven me functionally. They need me. My mother is blind and my father is now receiving radiation for cancer, and is so ill he can hardly walk."

So at the end of their lives, Baby Bear would be taking care of her parents. In that sense, Mama and Papa Bear would have gotten what they really wanted, a daughter who was home and available to them, whose life still revolved around them. Sukhreet was a kind of perpetually resentful adolescent who never escaped, and was never able to force them to reject her, though God knows she tried. But life had made her grow up, too, because she was the caretaker now. Soon she would be alone, with only the internal Mom and Dad to haunt her, and the assurance of Horty's pension to support her for life.

SO NOW PERHAPS it is time to look back where we began, the mists of Mount Olympus, where amid the gods at play we noted the four who prefigure the women in this story: Venus, Minerva, Juno, and Eris, goddesses of love, wisdom, wifehood, and discord.

The casting was close to perfect. The part of Venus, goddess not just of beauty but of sensual love, was for Bess a natural fit. The ancients depicted Venus always alone, sufficient unto herself. To incarnate beauty and love was enough; she was expected to give nothing more. That seemed to be about right for Bess.

Minerva, incarnation of wisdom, was also a goddess of just war. It was believed that she sprang full-grown from the brow of Jupiter, dressed in battle array and sounding her famous war cry. Like Minerva, Hortense Gabel seems never to have been a child, and to have arrived on the scene already embattled in the just war for civil rights and decent housing for the poor.

Nancy, as Juno, incarnated perfect wifehood, for which one may substitute the term *fidelity*.

Sukhreet, as Eris, caused plenty of discord. But she was also this fable's symbol of naked truth, almost always a guarantee of discord.

Of the four main parts, Nancy's was surely the hardest to play.

It may be more difficult today to be a good wife than ever before in human history. The modern women's movement—so various, so beautiful, so new—has sown so much confusion among both sexes nonetheless that one suspects Eris herself of having had a hand in it.

Nancy, the alleged villainess of the piece, turned out to have been quite the reverse. She began brave, gutsy, full of humor, of appetite, of life. She never sold out, and ended up a lot poorer but otherwise essentially undamaged.

Along the way she revealed herself as a romantic first and last. Most women are that. Most get over it, which is one definition of middle age. She was also a hip, urban Everywoman. Then, when Andy met Bess, Nancy came into her own as an avatar of faithful, abandoned wifehood. When it was over, she looked like the dumped wife of all time. Betrayed wives the world over should build a statue in her honor. She came through the ordeal without resorting to drink or pills or self-pity or psychotherapy or preying on her children. Indeed, as she felt herself hitting bottom, she used the pain to quit smoking. She concealed her anguish, concealed it for quite some time even from herself, then fought back as best she could. It was not easy. For she was an abandoned woman in a man's world, and that is still a stacked deck. What's more, she was up against not one but three very practiced rascally rogues, not just raging Bess and amoral Andy, but Andy's ever-resourceful Leporello, Jay Goldberg. To hold one's own against these three was truly remarkable.

Nancy was also a reminder of how wondrously different women are from men, and how little we still know about that difference, though after three or four thousand years of patriarchy, our ignorance is not too surprising.

Certainly women love differently than men do. The fact is so obvious that most of the time we don't see it. Then when it is pointed out, we see it everywhere. What happened at the start of the tale when Nancy discovered Andy in bed with the airline stewardess? She decided if she wanted him she'd better marry him. The discovery pushed her into matrimony after six years of wise indecision. Would Andy have reacted that way if he had found Nancy in bed with the pilot?

When, much later, Nancy found Andy with Bess, and found him again, and again, she behaved in much the same way. It was a very wifely way. She did not want to see. She could not see what the whole town saw. She preferred to think that *she* was crazy. Hence the gaslighting.

For further evidence that women love differently, look at Bess. What happened after Koch betrayed her? She hung on for dear life, despite the rejection. If she couldn't be in his cabinet, she'd settle for being his companion at a movie or a Chinese restaurant. If she could not be at the banquet table, then she would be under the table, watching for any crumbs that fell. Would any man do that? Ed Costikyan? Arnold Grant?

Look what happened when, beaten down, battered, flat on her back, she met Andy Capasso. He must have touched some still-young part of her, and the rest was instinct. Some part of her primitive brain stem seemed to take over. Once she'd found Andy, *nothing* could make her give him up. She became like a badger hound with her nose in a burrow, teeth clamped on. Pull hard enough and you may pull her in half, but you will never get her to loosen her gripping jaws.

Look at Bess when her political payoff finally arrived, too little and five years late. Not commissioner for economic development, the powerful post she wanted so much that she, the moochmeister, was willing to take it on for $1 a year. Instead, Cultural Affairs. She grabbed. The offer was shopworn from having been pawed over and rejected by so many other candidates. She didn't care. She ordered new ball gowns and embraced the culture scene with great energy and open arms.

Two years in office, she threw herself a sixty-first birthday party and presented herself to the leading luminaries of New York as, first, a gorgeous grandmother, holding aloft two-and-a-half-year-old Samantha. Then, in her birthday speech, she made light of her own rejection and later laughingly admitted to Beth Fallon of the *News* that her wonderful job should rightfully have gone to her deputy Randy Bourscheidt.

"But, for whatever reason, Ed Koch *owed* me," the self-made survivor told her audience, and reaped the expected guffaws. "And he had no place to put me. So here I am." Applause. Then more

of her brand of personal politicking. "We are the landlords for some
of the world's great institutions. I *own* the Metropolitan Museum of
Art. I *own* Snug Harbor. Beverly Sills? She's my tenant!" It's a
joke, one triumphantly successful Jewish girl to another, and across
the room Bess's friend, the former Bubbles Silverman, the retired
diva who turned down the Cultural Affairs offer and was now
president of the New York City Opera, smiled.

All this public merriment was taking place at a precious time in
Myerson's life. The date was July 18, 1985, nearly two years after
SMALL WORLD, and still the sun shone, the seas were calm. The fine
weather would last another six months, right up to the Romanesque
occasion on January 1, 1986, when Bess Myerson presided at Ed
Koch's third inauguration as mayor of the City of New York. Eight
days later, the blood-drenched Donald Manes was found in his
automobile, and the sky fell down. By the end of the year, the
self-proclaimed Queen of the Jews was in front of a grand jury
pleading the Fifth Amendment rather than fink on her boyfriend.

Watch Bess over these years as she begins messing up her precariously recovered career, her image, her life, and perhaps even
her love, by hiring the judge's daughter, and you see that Bess
internally *is* a mess; you see that emotionally she is all chopped up,
and that this neurotic disturbance is the seedbed of what became
known as the BessMess.

We watch as she insists on giving the man she loves a gift he
doesn't need. *Why is she doing this? What's in it for her?* Is it only the
thrill of feeling, and being able to say to Andy (as Bella never said
to her): Look how much I gave you! Isn't she saying the same thing
to Sukhreet, the daughter figure who is a cartoonlike travesty of
Olive Oyl?

We watch as Bess deludes herself that she is binding Andy to her
ever more tightly by doing this. Men like Andy are not bound by
anything. Not at this age. That only comes much later, if it does at
all, when they are old and weak and feeling the need of a good
woman to look after them, as once their mothers did.

We watch in awe as she messes up and, being Bess, gets caught
out in her manipulative scheme. We watch as she not only hires the
judge's lonely daughter, but first cruelly seduces her. We watch as
she forces poor Bruno to carpenter up an alibi letter to Koch. At the

bottom of this two-page string of perjuries and half-truths, how does Bess sign off? She closes with a phrase that no Bruno, nor any other man, would write: "As always, I look to you for wisdom and advice."

In our time, only the females say things like this. One heard the same tone of voice a few years ago on the steps of the nation's Capitol when Sandra Day O'Connor, just confirmed by the Senate as first woman on the Supreme Court, appeared before the TV cameras to say she was "absolutely overwhelmed with the expression of support from the Senate. My hope is that ten years from now, after I've been across the street at work for a while, they'll all be glad they gave me that wonderful vote." Would any male justice say something so sappy? *Make senators glad.* Who the hell are senators, compared to the court's nine mighty justices?

The inappropriate little-girl voice popping out on so august an occasion was caused by the dread old Disease to Please, still epidemic among women today. All the women in this story are infected with it—all but Sukhreet. That she is *not* infected is a severe abnormality, and a main element in her singularity. It is why so many people don't like, and even can't stand her. It's what Jay Goldberg sensed, and played on, to swing the holdout juror.

This disease is congenital; all women have it. Perhaps nature long ago arranged it so. Perhaps it springs from woman's primary need to keep the human race alive. To do this she must first, no matter what, please the demanding, helpless, irrational creature to whom she has just given birth.

A kinder term for the disease might be *self-sacrifice.* This too seems to be an essentially female quality, and seems it even when one considers the millions of modern husbands slowly immolating themselves on the altar of family. Probably it is female first because of the mother's primary tie to the children.

Nancy is not the only, nor even the best example of self-sacrifice in our story. That honor must go to the judge. Throughout the entire ordeal, Hortense Gabel held steadfast to her most important image of herself, to herself—not the spotless public servant, but the good and adoring mother.

Although Bess Myerson is a very different woman from Hortense Gabel, self-sacrifice is also at the core of her nature. In her, it never took the form of altruism. Bess rarely if ever sacrificed herself for others. Rather, her sacrifices were all to her own inner demons, to voices only she could hear, loudest amongst them the shrieks of icy, pitiless Bella. But Bella Myerson was implacable, and no sacrifice could ever be enough.

In the end, Bess's mother, who took the attitude that her daughter could never do one thing right, was not so different from Sukhreet's mother, who took the attitude that her daughter could not do anything wrong. In the end, the mother who could never be pleased and the mother who could never be displeased were the same mother. In the end, one can see Bess and Horty and Nancy and Sukhreet linked together like paper dolls, all of them cut and strung from an ancient Yiddish folktale told throughout the *shtetls* of nineteenth-century Russia and Eastern Europe, and known today to the millions of these people's descendants everywhere. Interestingly, the story did not originate among Jews. Folklorists have traced it back to Giovanni Boccaccio, the masterly fourteenth-century storyteller, a nice reminder that the entwinements, as well as conflicts, between Jews and Italians reach back farther in history than one might have thought.

ONCE UPON A time there was a young woman who longed for fame, and wanted attention and love from the king. The king told her she could have all these things if she did one thing. She would have to slay her mother and bring the king her mother's heart while it was still beating. The young woman went to her mother, slew her, and cut out her still-beating heart. She then ran as fast as she could toward the castle, clutching her mother's heart in her hands. As she ran, she stumbled and fell, and her mother's still-beating heart cried out, "Have you hurt yourself, my beloved child?"

INDEX

....

ABOUT

THE

AUTHOR

SHANA ALEXANDER is a lifetime reporter and com-
mentator on the American scene. She lives near
New York City, where she was born and raised.
When She Was Bad is her eighth book.